D1355733

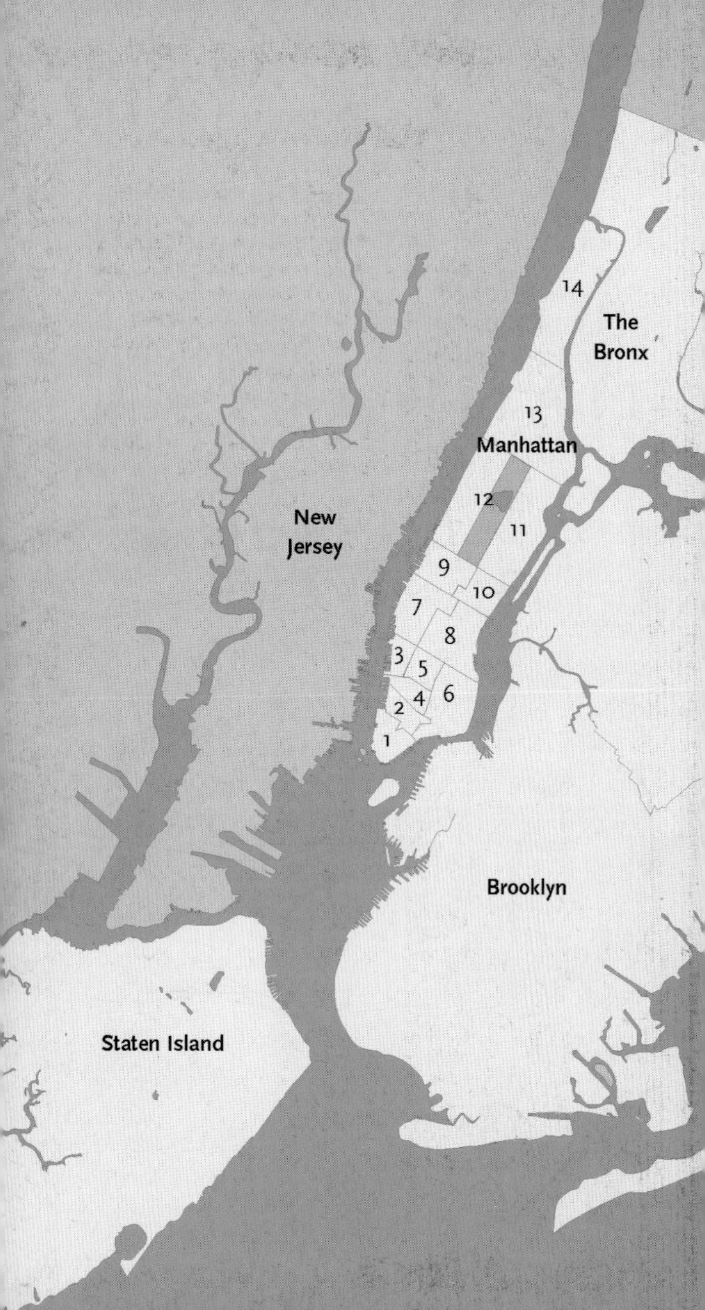
14
The Bronx
13
Manhattan
12
11
New Jersey
9
10
7
8
3
5
6
4
2
1
Brooklyn
Staten Island

MANHATTAN

Granta Publications
12 Addison Avenue
London W11 4QR

First published in Great Britain by Granta Books 2012

First published in the United States of America by
Fang Duff Kahn Publishers, New York
www.citysecrets.com

A CIP catalogue record for this book is available from the British Library.

1 3 5 7 9 10 8 6 4 2

ISBN: 978 0 9835400 7 6

Printed in China through Asia Pacific Offset

Distributed in the U.K. by TBS Ltd.

TABLE OF CONTENTS

"One belongs to New York instantly, one belongs to it as much in five minutes as in five years."

—Thomas Wolfe

PREFACE

E. B. White wrote that New Yorkers have "the sense of belonging to something unique, cosmopolitan, mighty and unparalleled." Although much has changed since he wrote these words over fifty years ago, the heart of the message remains as true now as it was then.

Whether entering this great city for the first time or the hundredth time, it is difficult not to be awed by the possibility of New York. From afar, there is the exhilaration and grandeur of the great metropolis, yet within, there is the comfort and familiarity of one's own neighborhood. The city is made up of hundreds of small villages connected by streets and avenues, parks and playgrounds, bridges and tunnels. For many, no neighborhood is more important or interesting than their own. New Yorkers take great pride in knowing their particular corner of the city and, as this book demonstrates, in telling others about it. This willingness to share personal "secrets" does not surprise me, for I have found New Yorkers to be generous and gracious people. I know of no other city that so quickly accepts anyone choosing to be a part of it—perhaps because it is a city that rarely forgets that it was built by and for immigrants. New York can be inconvenient, preoccupied with commerce and success, at times overwhelming... yet we New Yorkers cannot imagine living anywhere else. This sense of belonging was never more evident than in the days and months following the tragedy of September 11th, 2001. On that day, New York became everyone's city. This book is a reminder that the city exists as a continuum of the people who live here and the places they inhabit. What follows are the personal insights of our extraordinary contributors—a love letter to New York.

ROBERT KAHN
New York City

HOW TO USE THIS BOOK

This is a highly subjective guidebook that reflects the personal tastes and insights of its contributors. We asked architects, painters, writers, and other cultural figures to recommend an overlooked or under-appreciated site or artwork, or, alternatively, one that is well-known but about which they could offer fresh insights, personal observations, or specialized information. Respondents were also invited to describe strolls, neighborhoods, events, shops, and all manner of idiosyncratic and traditional ways of spending time in Manhattan.

These recommendations have been organized into fourteen chapters. Each chapter has an accompanying map, keyed to the text by numbers. Two icons appear throughout the book to reference restaurants and shops.

The editors are delighted with the high number of unusual and delightful recommendations included here. At the same time, we acknowledge that Manhattan provides an endless number of rich experiences. It is our hope that you will be inspired by the enthusiasm of our contributors to explore even further and discover secrets of your own.

USEFUL WEBSITES

Central Park (www.centralparknyc.org) The official website for Central Park. Includes maps, schedule of events, as well as information about bike rentals, guided tours, sites, the zoo, sports programs, the history of the park, etc.

Lincoln Center for the Performing Arts (www.lincolncenter.org) The official Lincoln Center website provides up-to-date information about the New York City Ballet, Metropolitan Opera, New York Philharmonic, and Lincoln Center theater.

Go City Kids (www.gocitykids.com) All sorts of information about children's activities, kid-friendly restaurants, events, etc.

New York Magazine (www.nymag.com/visitorsguide) Restaurant reviews, recommendations for shopping, sightseeing, hotels, etc. Organized by topic and neighborhood.

Manhattan User's Guide (www.manhattanusersguide.com) Up-to-date information about food, shopping, art, cultural events, etc.

Context Travel (www.contexttravel.com) A network of scholars and specialists who design and lead in-depth walking seminars for small groups of intellectually curious travelers.

Nosh Walks (www.noshwalks.com) Walking tours in ethnic neighborhoods primarily to the markets, bakeries, and eateries.

NYC The Official Guide (www.nycgo.com) Offers information about events, restaurants, tickets, restaurants, etc.

Hop Stop (www.hopstop.com) For directions by subway or bus in the five boroughs.

Metropolitan Transportation Authority (www. tripplanner.mta.info, www.mta.info) Maps, schedules, directions via public transportation, and train schedules.

1
Nelson A Rockefeller Park
Chambers St
Warren St
River Terrace
Park Pl West
Murray St
North End Av
Battery Park City
West St
Greenwich St
West Broadway
Reade St
Chambers St
Warren St
Murray St
Park Pl
Barclay St
Vesey St
City Hall
City Hall Park
Park Row
Spruce St
Beekman St
Ann St
Fulton St
Nassau St
Dutch St
Dey St
World Trade Center Site
World Financial Center
North Cove Yacht Harbor
Church St
Cortlandt St
Maiden Ln
John St
Platt St
Liberty St
William St
Cedar St
Washington St
Thames St
Pine St
Albany St
Carlisle St
Rector Pl
Rector St
Trinity Pl
Broadway
Wall St
Exchange Pl
Financial District
Edgar St
New St
Broad St
W Thames St
Ward St
Esplanade
Third Pl
Second Pl
Morris St
South Cove
Battery Pl
First Pl
Bowling Green
Beaver St
Marketfield St
S William St
Stone St
Whitehall St
Bridge St
Pearl St
Water St
State St
South St
Robert F Wagner Jr Park
Battery Park
Pier A
Staten Island Ferry Terminal
Brooklyn Battery Tunnel
Hudson River
Ellis Island Ferry
Liberty Island Ferry
New York Harbor
Staten Island Ferry
Ellis Island
Liberty Island
1 2 3 4 5 6 7 8 9 10 11 12 13 14 15 16 17 18 19 20 21 22 23 24

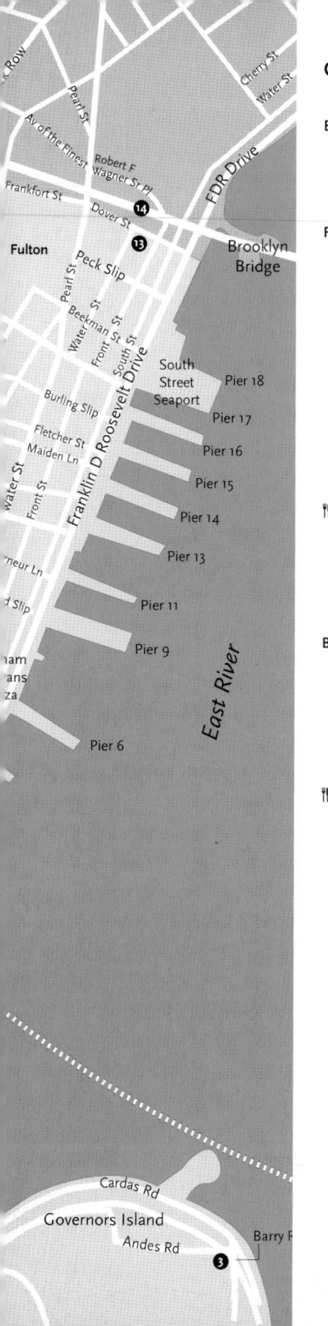

CHAPTER 1

ELLIS ISLAND & STATUE OF LIBERTY

1 Ellis Island
2 Statue of Liberty
3 Admiral's House (p. 281)

FINANCIAL DISTRICT & VICINITY

4 Staten Island Ferry
5 Wall Street Bull
6 Battery Park
7 Museum of the American Indian
8 Bank of New York
9 Wall Street Wall
10 Trinity Church
11 George Washington Statue
12 Marine Midland Bank (see p. 199)
13 Bridge Cafe
14 Brooklyn Bridge
15 AT&T Building
16 Woolworth Building
17 New York Telephone Co.

BATTERY PARK CITY

18 "The Real World"
19 "Inscribed Writings"
20 North Cove Yacht Harbor
21 Museum of Jewish Heritage
22 Robert F. Wagner Jr. Park
23 Gigino (see p. 36)
24 The Skyscraper Museum

Ellis Island, Statue of Liberty, Financial District & Battery Park City

ELLIS ISLAND & STATUE OF LIBERTY

1.1 Ellis Island National Monument and Ellis Island Immigration Museum

1900, Boring & Tilton; 1991, restoration by Beyer Blinder Belle and Notter Finegold & Alexander

Ellis Island information: ☎ 212 363 3200; www.nps.gov
Ferry: ☎ 877 523 9848; www.statuecruises.com

Not exactly a "city secret" this, but a visit to Ellis Island is so rewarding that it should not be missed by anyone curious about the history of New York or, indeed, the United States. About a hundred million Americans, roughly forty percent of the population, are related to someone who entered the country through Ellis Island. The museum presents the history of this extraordinary story, good and bad, in an intelligent, moving, and entertaining way.

You enter through the Baggage Hall. Suitcases and bundles stacked onto original baggage carts set the scene. You climb the stairs that, had you been an immigrant, would (unbeknownst to you) have been your first medical test. Any sign of distress and your coat would have been marked with a chalk code to alert the doctors to investigate further. America wanted immigrants, but she wanted them healthy.

At the top of the stairs is the impressive Registration Room with its vaulted tiled ceiling. The museum designers have been clever here: the room is restored, but left more or less empty, save some of the original inspectors's desks and some benches the immigrants would have waited on.

Looking down on this space from the balcony, one imagines today's tourists almost in the role of extras; as they shuffle around, it's easy to imagine them as immigrants waiting their turn to be registered.

The historical information is presented upstairs in a series of small former inspection rooms. Here you can hear audio recordings of Ellis Island immigrants.

Not only is a visit to Ellis Island informative, it is also a great day out. The view back to the island of Manhattan is alone worth the trip.

CHARLES MARSDEN-SMEDLEY
Museum and exhibition designer

1.2 Statue of Liberty National Monument

1871–1886, Frédéric Auguste Bartholdi, sculptor; Alexandre Gustave Eiffel, engineer; Richard Morris Hunt, architect of the base
Liberty Island information: 212 363 3200; www.nps.gov

Although it is often thought of as a tourist trap, the Statue of Liberty is also a magnificent monument to dichotomy in architecture. It is at once both metal and masonry, frame and load bearing, literal and abstract. As a representation of old and new, the lady has better folds and warped surfaces than anything in current architectural fashion, and is in contrast to the finely composed base by Richard Morris Hunt. The star fortress below is just an added attraction. With contributions by Hunt, Eiffel, and Bartholdi, "base-middle-top" has never been played better and there is no finer example of "firmness, commodity and delight."—Vitruvius

ROBERT LIVESEY
Architect

Yes, you'll be on a boat with a thousand tourists, surrounded by seagulls that won't leave you alone. Yes, it's kind of corny. Still, I'm always surprisingly moved by the entire experience.

ERIC STOLTZ
Actor

FINANCIAL DISTRICT & VICINITY

1.4 Staten Island Ferry

South Street at foot of Whitehall Street
718 815 2628; www.siferry.com
Ferry runs 24 hours.

> *We were very tired, we were very merry—*
> *We had gone back and forth all night on the ferry.*
> —Edna St. Vincent Millay

The best free ride in the world, a round trip on the Staten Island Ferry offers unparalleled views of the Statue of Liberty, Governors Island, Ellis Island, the New York Harbor, and the downtown skyline. The ferry connects lower Manhattan with St. George in Staten Island for seventy-thousand commuters and tourists twenty-four hours a day: during rush hour at fifteen-minute intervals, at thirty-minute intervals most of the day, and hourly late at night. It was the sole lifeline to Staten Island until 1964, when the Verrazano-Narrows Bridge opened. For decades the fare was just a nickel; now it's free. Peter Minuit Park, named to honor the man and the twenty-four-dollar deal that enabled the Dutch to buy (steal) Manhattan from the Indians, fronts the Staten Island Ferry Terminal. The terminal was designed by Walker & Morris in 1907, but a series of subsequent additions and renovations has all but obliterated the original structure. Imagine that it once looked exactly like its magnificent neighbor, the landmarked Battery Maritime Building. Board the ferry after work with your sweetheart and uncork a bottle of champagne. On the way over, watch the sun set behind the Statue of Liberty. On the way back, you'll see the downtown skyline and a thousand twinkling lights.

FREDERIC SCHWARTZ
Architect

Floating the Apple
Check website for locations.
212 564 5412; www.floatingtheapple.org

This organization rows in beautiful old-time rowboats, not little chunky modern things, but twenty-five feet long, the kind of boats that raced out to bring passengers in from the latest sailboat over from Europe in 1820.
PETE SEEGER
Songwriter

Melville's Manhattan

Herman Melville may have written *Moby Dick* while looking at a mountain out his window in the Berkshires, but he was born and lived most of his life in New York City. Melville liked islands (England, Tahiti) and never got too far from "the insular city of Manhattoes." His best friend Ishmael wonders why people, island people in particular, are so attracted to water, and why it is that on a Sunday you will find countless citizens congregating at the Battery simply staring at the water. This water-gazing is as true now as it was in 1851, when Melville wrote *Moby Dick*, or back in 1819 when he was born only yards away from the Battery, on Pearl Street, so named because of the glistening oyster shells strewn upon it. People are water-gazers, and the Battery is still the place to stroll along the breezy promenade, lean against the rail, and watch people looking beyond the Statue of Liberty (in full view) for the opening to New York's bay (just out of view) and the rolling Atlantic beyond.

Of course, the rail you lean against rests on landfill. As a toddler Melville never witnessed the grass and trees that now intervene between the house of his nativity and the promenade; it was all water then. But the view is much the same: ships, pleasure craft, birds, and people bumping into each other because they are gazing at the water. The home at 6 Pearl Street where Herman learned to walk has vanished and is now the site for an insurance company's skyscraper and a modest museum for city archaeology.

Melville died farther uptown, at 104 East 26th Street, in the Gramercy Park area. That home is also gone. He had returned to Manhattan after his Berkshire years (thirteen in all), and spent close to three decades ignored and virtually unknown, writing poetry and *Billy Budd*. Before his death in 1891, he would take the trolley with his granddaughter to Central Park to watch her run on the meadows and jump from rocks, and to listen to the flapping of her skirts. They sounded much like sails.

JOHN BRYANT
Writer, editor, and professor

1.6 Battery Park

Southernmost tip of Manhattan

This is the place in lower Manhattan that makes one forget all about that other, bigger, more central park to the north, especially if you are drawn to the water and especially if you happen to be a runner. Battery Park combines sweeping green lawns, lush flowerbeds, and a whiff of the city's energy from nearby Wall Street with a continuous view of the mighty Hudson. If you squeeze your eyes and look out between Roosevelt Island and Staten Island and the Statue of Liberty, you can almost convince yourself that you are alone in New York City, staring at your own private section of the Hudson River.

KATHLEEN DEMARCO VAN CLEVE
Author, screenwriter, and film producer

The Wilds of New York Nature Tour

In Manhattan:

1.7 **National Museum of the American Indian**
Alexander Hamilton U.S. Custom House
1 Bowling Green between Whitehall and State Streets
☎ 212 514 3700; www.nmai.si.edu

5.37 **Merchant's House Museum**
29 East 4th Street between Lafayette Street and Bowery
☎ 212 777 1089; www.merchantshouse.com

12.16 **Belvedere Castle**
Central Park, mid-park at 79th Street
www.centralpark.com

14.14 **Inwood Hill Park**
Northwest corner of Manhattan above Dyckman Street
www.nycgovparks.org

In the Bronx:

Orchard Beach
Pelham Bay Park (not on map)
www.nycgovparks.org

In Brooklyn:

Prospect Park
1873, Frederick Law Olmsted & Calvert Vaux
Between Prospect Park West and Flatbush, Parkside and Ocean Avenues (not on map)
www.nycgovparks.org

Old Stone House
Originally built, 1699; rebuilt, 1935
336 3rd Street between Fourth and Fifth Avenues, in James J. Byrne Memorial Playground (not on map)
☎ 718 768 3195; www.theoldstonehouse.org

The Salt Marsh Nature Center
Marine Park
Between Flatbush, Gerritsen, and Fillmore Avenues, and Jamaica Bay to the south (not on map)
☏ 718 421 2021; www.saltmarshalliance.org
Closed Wednesdays.

While many come to New York City to see its granite grandeur and the splashy commercialism for which it is so widely known, one shouldn't overlook the city's natural side. New York lies at the intersection of several migratory pathways and the juncture of several ecotypes. The city holds treasures and relics reflecting nearly a thousand years of human occupation; secreted within its emerald necklace of parks are various jewels containing fragments of its distinguished natural history.

Be brave and, in a car, trace the city's cultural and natural heritage. Start at the National Museum of the American Indian. Located at Bowling Green Park in lower Manhattan, the museum holds an incredible collection of artifacts from the various people who originally occupied this area. Then head north. If it's autumn, stop at Belvedere Castle in Central Park to see the hawk migration. Thousands of raptors pass over the park on cold fronts in September and October, and there is a ranger available to help you identify in-flight raptors, as well as eagles, falcons, harriers, and accipiters. Then, on to Inwood Hill Park (see p. 328) in upper Manhattan, where you will find the island's last great forest, surrounding a series of caves used for eons by Native Americans. Cross the Bronx and stop at Orchard Beach. If you walk all the way eastward on the boardwalk, you will come to a nature center that opens out onto a splendid beach, a back-bay salt marsh, and a beautiful upland forest that still contains vestige populations of American chestnuts. The beach sand was barged in from southern Long Island by Robert Moses, just so northern New Yorkers could have a beach as nice as any in Brooklyn or Queens. Have a seafood lunch on City Island and you'll think you're in Mystic. Head south across the Whitestone Bridge, take the BQE to Prospect Park, enjoying the park's sylvan scenery. It's worth your while to pause at the Old Stone House nearby for a taste of New York during the Revolutionary War. See where General Alexander badgered George Washington into a hasty retreat and listen to how four hundred Marylanders saved the Colonial Army so it could fight another day. Off again now, farther south to the shore. Stop in at the Salt Marsh Nature Center in Marine Park. Here is one of the great hidden treasures of the city: a nature center facing a vast marsh that turns bronze each fall and is always teeming with wildlife. It also hosts unique exhibits and creative programs prepared by park rangers and the National Geographic Society. Once you're back in Manhattan, wrap up this epic journey by stopping off at East 4th Street to visit the Merchant's House Museum (see p. 98). This cozy brown stone contains whale oil lamps, secret passages for the Underground Railroad, and great furnishings from the late nineteenth century.

ALEXANDER R. BRASH
Chairman, Habitat Committee in the EPA's Harbor Estuary Program

1.8 Bank of New York (originally Irving Trust Company)

1932, Voorhees, Gmelin & Walker
1 Wall Street at Broadway
www.nyc-architecture.com

The building is well known, but the "red room" banking hall, a superb blend of red terrazzo, dark purple marble, and sparkling red-to-orange-to-gold mosaic tiles, is one of the best surprises in New York. This masterpiece deserves a special trip, especially if you're looking for New York Art Deco.

DAVID M. CHILDS
Architect

1.9 Wall Street Wall

Steeped in city, national, and international history for nearly four centuries, the world's best-known address was actually once a wall. In 1653, the city's slaves were ordered to build a protective barricade with logs "twelve feet long, eighteen inches in circumference, sharpened at the upper end" from river (Hudson) to river (East) across Manhattan Island. Demolished in 1699, its first official market was an East River depot constructed in 1711 for the sale of slaves. In 1791, brokers and investors began meeting under a buttonwood (sycamore) tree at Broad and Wall Streets, and a year later founded a market for the buying and selling of stocks and securities.

CHRISTOPHER PAUL MOORE
Historian, author, and research coordinator for exhibitions, New York Public Library's Schomburg Center for Research on Black Culture

1.10 Trinity Church

1846, Richard Upjohn
Broadway at Wall Street
212 602 0800; www.trinitywallstreet.org

Trinity Church, the principal church of New York's first Episcopal parish, is worth a visit as much for its Wall Street context as for its extraordinary architecture. The most impressive nineteenth-century Gothic monument in New York, Trinity was completed in 1846 to the design of Richard Upjohn. The brownstone church and its graveyard seem to hold their own in the canyon of vintage skyscrapers at Broadway and Wall Street. The inside of the church, with its marble altar and reredos memorializing William B. Astor, completes this Gothic vision from the age of Melville.

PETER PENNOYER
Architect

A Perfect Evening

2.21 **The Peking Duck House**
28 Mott Street between Pell Street and Chatham Square
212 227 1810; www.pekingduckhousenyc.com

2.9 **City Hall**
1811, Joseph François Mangin and John McComb Jr.
City Hall Park between Broadway and Park Row
www.nyc-architecture.com

1.10 **Trinity Church**
1846, Richard Upjohn
Broadway at Wall Street
212 602 0800; www.trinitywallstreet.org

1.11 **George Washington Statue**
1883, James Quincy Adams Ward, pedestal by Richard Morris Hunt
26 Wall Street, in front of Federal Hall
www.nyharborparks.org

1.5 **Wall Street Bull (*Charging Bull*)**
1989, Arturo di Modica
Broadway at Bowling Green

1.4 **Staten Island Ferry**
South Street at the foot of Whitehall Street
718 815 2628; www.siferry.com
Ferry runs 24 hours.

Whenever friends come to town and go to see the Statue of Liberty, I feel deeply ashamed. I know New York the way I know my oldest friends, all the secret back corners and all the bad stuff, too, but the places I know least are the ones that visitors usually see. The closest I've been to the General Assembly of the United Nations is the pressroom, and the last time I took the Circle Line boat around Manhattan was twenty years ago, and then only because of a reporting assignment.

The New York I know and love is less eventful and more unremarked, less monument and boulevard and more row house and alleyway. And here is how I used to spend a perfect evening with my husband before we had children.

We would go to dinner at a place on Mott Street in Chinatown called the Peking Duck House, where you can eat Peking duck without ordering it in advance. We would browse in the little shops that sell cheap Chinese dishes, sandals, and fans.

We would walk south past the courts and the municipal buildings and into the pocket park that stands in front of the prettiest city hall in America, a graceful, oddly diminutive building with a beautiful floating staircase inside.

We'd continue toward the end of the island, passing through the area that was called Five Points when Manhattan was young, a neighborhood that two hundred and fifty years ago was a den of thieves, prostitutes, and streetgangs, all of whom have now moved largely uptown. We would pass the spire of Trinity Church (see p. 20), the neo-Gothic house of worship that was once the tallest point in the city, and cross over Wall Street, which is named after a wall the earliest immigrant New Yorkers, the Dutch, built to keep out the earliest New Yorkers, the Indians.

We would arrive at the giant statue of George Washington that commemorates his inauguration in New York and the giant statue of a bull that commemorates Wall Street's most recent incarnation. And suddenly we would run out of land at the point of Manhattan, where the ferry terminal stands.

So of course we would take the ferry to Staten Island.

We never stayed on Staten Island, just used its best-known, most romantic form of mass transit to see the city strung around us like a hive of hyperactive fireflies. (Staten Island actually has its own little aboveground subway system called the SIRT, which is as different from the rest of the subway as Staten Island is from the rest of the city. But that's another story.) Then we would take the ferry back again.

This constitutes a practically perfect experience, even better than taking the subway to Coney Island, looking at the beluga whales in the New York Aquarium, and having a hot dog and fries at Nathan's.

ANNA QUINDLEN
Author, journalist, and opinions columnist

1.13 Bridge Cafe

279 Water Street at Dover Street
212 227 3344; www.bridgecafenyc.com

There's nothing that will make you feel more like a real New Yorker than being one of the lucky few who know to head down to the Bridge Cafe the moment the first snowflakes of winter start to cover Manhattan's streets. Cozy up with an Irish coffee in the tin-ceilinged room and watch out the big windows as the snow dusts the two-hundred-plus-year-old cobblestone streets, and the lights on the Brooklyn Bridge, practically within touching distance, twinkle through the flakes. And think about what it was like when Water Street really fronted the East River and Prohibition-era guests slipped Irish whiskey into their coffees, right where you sit.

MARYELLEN GORDON
Founder, Stable of Content

1.14 Brooklyn Bridge

1867–1883, John A. Roebling & Washington Roebling
Park Row (Manhattan) to Adams Street (Brooklyn)

The Brooklyn Bridge celebrates the simple act of passage, elevating the commonplace to a ritual. Always a threshold to the city that is an island, the bridge normally is traversed by car, and during rush hours it is as rushed and full and bustling as any other downtown street. On the pedestrian walk, however, traffic is slowed to an almost stillness. The wooden platform stretches between two remarkable Gothic piers, pacing and dividing the excursion into three parts. The true privilege is in being able to use it this way, not as a special event but as an everyday occurrence.
FREDERICK BIEHLE
Architect

There is a component of Roebling's engineering design that I find so emphatically lyrical and marvelously beautiful that I almost prefer to keep it to myself. I have in mind a major structural feature that presents itself most dramatically from the Manhattan approach—namely, the great low-slung follow-through whereby the main cable, descending from the towers, sweeps down below the roadway only to sweep back up again without missing a beat, securing itself in the stone abutment. It strikes me as utterly modern—not pre-modern, but absolutely modern. I have long been convinced that this mathematical chord-like structural form inspired the governing motive of Albert Gleizes's curiously hearty 1915 Cubist painting, *Brooklyn Bridge*, now in the Guggenheim Museum.
JOSEPH MASHECK
Art historian

1.15 Former American Telephone & Telegraph Company

1923, William Welles Bosworth
195 Broadway between Dey and Fulton Streets

The lobby is a forest of Doric columns, in true hypostyle fashion, on an approximate fifteen-foot grid—an exquisite room, the way one should enter a grand and proud corporation. Beautiful craftsmanship and detailing, even though four panels created for this space by Paul Manship are no longer there. (Evelyn Beatrice Longman's *Genius of the Telegraph*, popularly known as "Golden Boy," once perched on the building's pinnacle, later was moved to AT&T's lobby in Philip Johnson's "Chippendale" tower at 550 Madison Avenue, and is now regretfully sentenced to their suburban New Jersey complex.)
DAVID M. CHILDS
Architect

1.16 Woolworth Building

1913, Cass Gilbert
233 Broadway between Park Place and Barclay Street
www.nyc-architecture.com

At seven hundred and ninty two feet, the Woolworth was the tallest building in the world until 1930, when the Chrysler Building surpassed it. The massing became a model for skyscrapers—a soaring, slender campanile of glazed terra cotta. Gilbert remarked, "a skyscraper, by its height, makes its upper parts appear lost in the clouds, whose masses must become more and more inspired as it rises." The lobby of this Gothic "cathedral to commerce" vibrates with mosaics, murals, and marble. Brendan Gill waxed that it was "one of the most sumptuous in the country... a bedazzlement of marble walls and gilt bronze doors with a vaulted ceiling of blue and gold mosaics." One whimsical carving includes caricatures of Gilbert with a model of the building and five-and-dime founder F. W. Woolworth counting his nickels.

FREDERIC SCHWARTZ AND TRACEY HUMMER
Architect and Writer

American Modernism

2.9 **City Hall**
1811, Joseph François Mangin and John McComb Jr.
City Hall Park between Broadway and Park Row
www.nyc-architecture.com

1.16 **Woolworth Building**
1913, Cass Gilbert
233 Broadway between Park Place and Barclay Street

It's 1913. Put together John Marin, the Woolworth Building, and City Hall, and you're right at the divide between safe Gothic skyscraper style and an insurgent American Modernism. Then jump twenty years to see Alfred Stieglitz, Modernism's major progenitor, promoting these insurgent impulses in Depression-era America.

First, go down to City Hall with a book of John Marin's city drawings. Stand on the steps of City Hall and look across Broadway to the ornamented Woolworth Building, then to Marin's drawings of the building, made in 1913, just after the then tallest building in the world opened.

The building itself has a regal look, quite proud of its height, design, and dripping ornament. But the drawings, a kind of abstraction, show the building bending, swerving, dancing. Marin said he made the building move because people move and people give it life, in itself a distinctly humanist expression of the Modernist impulse. Alfred Stieglitz hailed these drawings and immediately hung them at his gallery, 291 (located at 291 Fifth Avenue). One day

Cass Gilbert, the building's architect, came to see them. He walked in, looked around, and was so horrified that he stomped out—a perfect example of the clash between architecture's formalist entry into the twentieth century and painting's break-loose Modernist spirit.

Add twenty-one years to the same scene and you see Stieglitz, usually pigeonholed as elitist and formalist, striving to deepen Modernism's place in the American consciousness. It's May 8, 1934, sunny and spring-like. A crowd of two thousand looks up at the steps of City Hall, where Stieglitz, the main speaker, is standing with Lewis Mumford and John Dewey. The three, spokespersons for Artists for Democratic Action, a communist front, demanded of Mayor La Guardia a municipal center of art where artists and the people of New York might exhibit, teach, learn, socialize—and feed America's creative soul. The center never happened. But the next day Mumford and Stieglitz congratulated each other for the crowd's vision—and for their own performances.

JUDITH MARA GUTMAN
Writer

1.17 New York Telephone Company (Barclay-Vesey Building)

1927, McKenzie, Voorhees & Gmelin
140 West Street between Barclay and Vesey Streets
www.nyc-architecture.com

A favorite of Le Corbusier's and the frontispiece for his *Vers une architecture*, this trendsetting building, designed by a leading early Modernist, Ralph Walker, concretely illustrates the bold massing of the 1916 zoning laws as best rendered by Hugh Ferris in 1922. Massive, uplifting, uninterrupted skyward brick piers alternate with recessed vertical stripes of windows and spandrels capped by stone Art Deco motifs. Walker's preliminary massing studies predate the design of

Rockefeller Center. As the architect who introduced the "urban twist," he acknowledged the city's powerful grid by anchoring the parallelogram base to the local streets while twisting its tower for a citywide reading. Don't miss the Guastavino vaults under one of the city's only public sidewalk arcades.

FREDERIC SCHWARTZ
Architect

BATTERY PARK CITY

Battery Park City Esplanade

Battery Park City along the Hudson River from Chambers Street to Battery Place
212 267 9700; www.bpcparks.org; www.batteryparkcity.org

1.18 **The Real World**
1992, Tom Otterness

1.19 **Inscribed Writings**
1994, Mark Strand and Seamus Heaney

1.20 **North Cove Yacht Harbor Railing**
1986, Walt Whitman and Frank O'Hara
West of the World Financial Center
www.batteryparkcity.org

1.21 **Museum of Jewish Heritage**
18 First Place, Battery Park City
212 509 6130; www.mjhnyc.org

Run down Hudson River Park to the Battery Park City Esplanade along the river. Besides all the joggers and bicyclists, there's much to see. In the northeast corner of

Governor Nelson A. Rockefeller Park (at Chambers Street), there is the wonderful world of sculptures by Tom Otterness called *The Real World*. Groupings of funny Lilliputian animal-humans reflect our own world of work with humor and parody. Just above North Cove is the Lily Pool, with inscriptions by Mark Strand from *The Continuous Life*, and Seamus Heaney from *Death of a Naturalist*. Farther south at North Cove Yacht Harbor is a metal rail fence with the words of Frank O'Hara and Walt Whitman, and right past the Japanese gardens, where Robert F. Wagner Jr. Park begins, is the Museum of Jewish Heritage.
GAIL KRIEGEL
Playwright, librettist, and composer

1.20 North Cove Yacht Harbor Railing

1986, Walt Whitman and Frank O'Hara
West of the World Financial Center
www.batteryparkcity.org

At the beginning of a group of marble benches at the marina, you will see a rail resplendent with gold letters. Follow these words as you view the docked yachts and sailboats with Ellis Island as a backdrop. In these evocative phrases you may discover two of the most apt descriptions of New York City.

City of the world (for all races are here,
All the lands of the earth make contributions here;)
City of the sea!
City of wharves and stores—city of tall façades
of marble and iron!
Proud and passionate city—mettlesome, mad,
extravagant, city!
—Walt Whitman

For a different take on the city's charms, follow the words

on the other side of the marble stairs.

> *One need never leave the confines of New York to get all the greenery one wishes—I can't even enjoy a blade of grass unless I know there's a subway handy, or a record store or some other sign that people do not totally regret life.*
> —Frank O'Hara

THERESA CRAIG
Writer

1.22 Robert F. Wagner Jr. Park

1989, Olin Partnership; Machado & Silvetti; Lynden Miller
At the foot of Battery Park City
www.batteryparkcity.org

Robert F. Wagner Jr. Park is just steps from one of the city's oldest tourist locations, Castle Clinton in Battery Park, and one of its newest museums, the Museum of Jewish Heritage, which includes the Living Memorial to the Holocaust. Featuring a beautifully landscaped setting of well-tended flower gardens, lawns, and walkways, the waterfront Robert F. Wagner Park offers spectacular views of the harbor. At its center is Gigino (20 Battery Place, ☎ 212 528 2228), the perfect place for an al fresco lunch or dinner, where the loudest noise is not the backfire of a truck but the low rumble of passing tugboats. Joggers, skaters, and a few sunbathers complete the tranquil outdoor scene.

ROBERT COOK
Attorney

Ape & Cat (At the Dance)

1993, Jim Dine
www.batteryparkcity.org

In the middle of Robert F. Wagner Jr. Park is a circular English garden, a patch of beauty and serenity with a majestic brick pavilion and wide walkways that look out onto the river. In the winter, the frozen peaks of the waves are sublime. On the lawn, in front of the pavilion, is my favorite piece: two human-size, graceful bronze figures called *Ape & Cat (At the Dance)* by Jim Dine. I never tire of looking at the details of their clasped hands, their regal clothes, their kind faces. One can't help feeling tenderly toward this elegant "mixed" couple standing in the grass at the edge of the city.

GAIL KRIEGEL
Playwright, librettist, and composer

1.24 The Skyscraper Museum

2004, Skidmore, Owings & Merrill
39 Battery Place
212 968 1961; www.skyscraper.org
Closed Mondays and Tuesdays.

Founded in 1996, this can-do museum has put on exhibitions whose subject matter ranges from downtown New York to an international survey of the world's largest buildings. Thankfully, it has found a new high-concept permanent home, designed by Skidmore, Owings & Merrill, in the Ritz-Carlton Downtown located in lower Manhattan—the birth-place of the skyscraper.

WALTER CHATHAM
Architect

2
Clarkson St
W Houston St
King St
Charlton St
Vandam St
Spring St
Dominick St
Broome St
Varick St
Hudson St
Greenwich St
Washington St
Sixth Avenue (Avenue of the Americas)
Sullivan St
Thompson St
West Broadway
Wooster St
Greene St
Mercer St
SoHo
Holland Tunnel
Pier 34
Hudson River Park
Pier 32
West St
Canal St
Watts St
Desbrosses St
Vestry St
Laight St
Hubert St
Collister St
Beach St
St. John's Ln
Sixth Avenue
Howard St
Lispenard St
Walker St
White St
Franklin St
TriBeCa
N Moore St
Franklin St
Leonard St
Catherine Ln
Worth St
Pier 26
Harrison St
Staple St
Jay St
Thomas St
Pier 25
Duane St
Washington Market Park
Reade St
Chambers St
Nelson A Rockefeller Park
Church St
Warren St
Battery Park City
City Hall
Park Pl West
Murray St
Park Pl
City Hall Park
Barclay St
North End Av
Vesey St
Ann St
World Trade Center Site
Broadway
Fulton
World Financial Center
Dey St
John St
North Cove Yacht Harbor
Cortlandt St
Maiden Ln
Hudson River
Liberty St
Cedar St
Thames St
Albany St
Carlisle St
Pine St
Nassau St
Trinity Pl
Wall St
Esplanade
Rector Pl
Rector St
Exchange
Edgar St
W Thames St
Ward St
New St
14
13
12
11
9
10
7
8
3
4
5
6
2
1

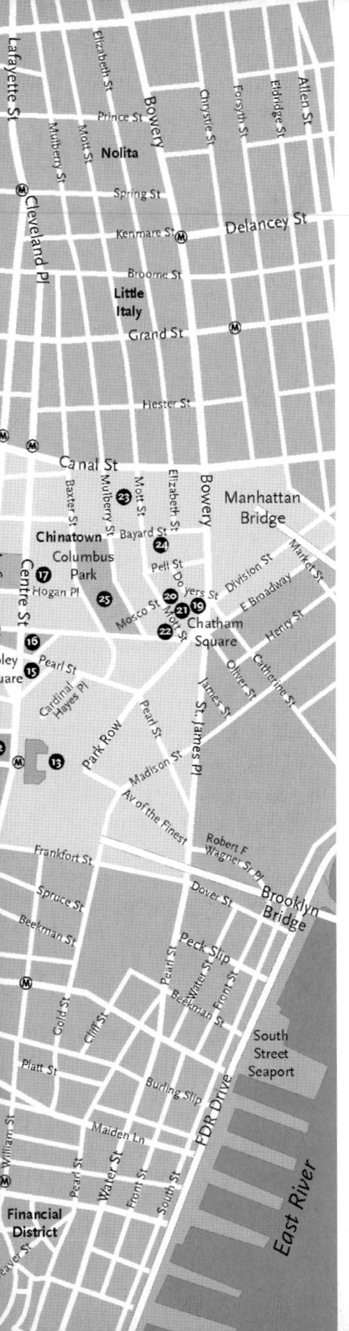

CHAPTER 2

TRIBECA

1 Hudson River Park
2 American Express Stables
3 Walker's
4 Ted Muehling
5 Taste of Tribeca
6 Washington Market Park (see p. 93)
7 Morgan's Market (see p. 92)
8 Odeon

CIVIC CENTER

9 City Hall
10 Old N.Y. County Courthouse
11 Emigrant Savings Bank
12 Surrogate's Court
13 Municipal Building
14 African Burial Ground
15 U.S. Courthouse
16 NY County Courthouse
17 Criminal Courts Building

CHINATOWN

18 Canal Street
19 Tunnel
20 Nom Wah
21 Peking Duck House (see p. 21)
22 Kam Kuo Food Corp.
23 Ten Ren's Tea Time
24 Chinatown Ice Cream Factory
25 Columbus Park

TRIBECA, CIVIC CENTER & CHINATOWN

TRIBECA

2.1 Hudson River Park

Along the Hudson River from 59th Street to Battery Park City
www.hudsonriverpark.org

At one time, downtowners wishing to run, skate, bike, or power walk had to go uptown to Central Park. Now the Hudson River Park, a long strip of interconnected parks and gardens from West 59th Street to Battery Park (and growing), provides traffic-free space and relatively fresh air filtered off the Hudson. Watch the ferries shuttling people between New Jersey and the Financial District while the Statue of Liberty looks on. Plantings along the path are in full bloom during the spring and summer, and in the winter Canada geese graze. Along the way are the famous Stuyvesant High School, an open field to rival Central Park's Great Lawn, a children's park, a pier where boats of the rich and famous dock, a wooden boardwalk where fishermen cast their lines year-round, and, right before Battery Park, the Museum of Jewish Heritage. A nearby set of steps provides a great view of the river and Ellis Island. Walk the steps slowly or run up like Rocky Balboa, on top of the world.

ADAM BERLIN
Writer

2.2 Former American Express Stables

1867
157 Hudson Street between Laight and Hubert Streets

The American Express Company was originally an express company; that is, it hauled things. Its headquarters were located in the then newly commercial part of New York west of Broadway and south of Canal, which today is once again residential. The company built a handsome marble-faced building at the southwest corner of Hudson and Jay Streets, now gone, though the present building on that site was also built by American Express in the 1880s. But American Express has left a small remnant where the keen-eyed observer can see it, at the northeast corner of Hubert and Collister Streets, and likewise at the southeast corner of Collister and Laight Streets. The handsome building that runs along Collister Street was the stable for its superb horses, and at either end of the building, high up in the steep gable, are circular reliefs with what are supposed to be dogs (the emblem of the company before that vapid centurion), surrounded by the words "American Express Co." The dog on Hubert Street looks more like a bear or a large cat with odd jaws; the dog on Laight is far more doglike, but oddly like a Chihuahua. They were supposed to be bulldogs, sources say, but neither one achieves proper bulldogginess. What's even odder is that they don't match. The building itself is a lovely brick composition, massive and confident, with splendid Palladian windows on the second floor.

ROBIN CLEMENTS
Teacher

Summer in New York

2.1 **Hudson River Park**
Along the Hudson River from 59th Street to Battery Park City
www.hudsonriverpark.org

3.11 **Kayak Rental**
The New York City Downtown Boathouse at Pier 40
On the Hudson River at West Houston Street
www.downtownboathouse.org

1.20 **North Cove Yacht Harbor**
West of World Financial Center, on the Hudson River
www.batteryparkcity.org

1.21 **Museum of Jewish Heritage**
18 First Place, Battery Park City
☎ 212 509 6130; www.mjhnyc.org

1.22 **Robert F. Wagner Jr. Park**
At the foot of Battery Park City
www.bpcparks.org

1.23 **Gigino**
In Robert F. Wagner Jr. Park
20 Battery Place
☎ 212 528 2228; www.gigino-wagnerpark.com

Take a bike and ride to the lower west side of Manhattan along the path that hugs the Hudson River and runs to the tip of Battery Park City. While this esplanade is still evolving and is by no means any competition for Frederick Law Olmsted, it attempts to open a new area of the city for exploration, allowing New Yorkers and visitors access to the Hudson River.

Starting at 23rd Street, this ride runs along the old piers of the lower Hudson River. It passes a variety of attractions along the way, including a boathouse for kayak rental, the ferry dock for rides to New Jersey, cafes and restaurants surrounding the yacht harbor at the World Financial Center, and the Museum of Jewish Heritage, before arriving at the jewel-like Robert F. Wagner Jr. Park at the foot of Battery Park City. Here one is thrilled by a magnificent view of New York Harbor and one of the great sculptural achievements of the nineteenth century—the captivating Statue of Liberty. This tiny park, designed by the firm of Machado & Silvetti, works beautifully.

A little cafe, Gigino, open in the summer months, with tables and umbrellas, is tucked gently into the base of the brick observation deck. Below stretches a plane of perfect green grass.

CAROLYN CARTWRIGHT
Feature-film set decorator and interior designer

2.3 Walker's

16 North Moore Street at Varick Street
212 941 0142

This is the requisite no-frills bar/restaurant in Tribeca. Walker's has three rooms, big windows, great fries, and a decently expanded menu that makes this the place to go when sophisticated restaurants with sophisticated pricing seem just too much of a hassle and what you really want is to be in a comfortable place with relaxed people and good food.

KATHLEEN DEMARCO VAN CLEVE
Author, screenwriter, and film producer

2.4 Ted Muehling

52 White Street between Broadway and Church Street
212 431 3825; www.tedmuehling.com

Although almost every fashionable woman I know owns at least one pair of beautiful earrings from Ted Muehling's elegant workshop on Howard Street, the origin of these treasures remains somehow mysterious. Maybe it's because ownership of a pair is like membership in an exclusive club. Or maybe because, like me, husbands refuse to tell their wives the location of this never-fail "get-out-of-jail-free" card. Whatever the reason, Ted Muehling has resisted the temptation to go "wide," and the quality and design remain unsurpassed. Though mostly abstract, these earrings, necklaces, bracelets, and pins find their inspiration in organic forms such as berries, rice, shells, nuts, and eggs.

The shop also carries beautiful ceramic pieces designed by Mr. Muehling and manufactured by the great Nymphenburg porcelain factory in Germany. Highly recommended as a source of simple beauty.

ROBERT KAHN
Architect

2.5 Taste of Tribeca

Duane Street between Greenwich and Hudson Streets
www.tasteoftribeca.com

In this annual event, world-class local restaurants and catering firms provide a mouth-watering outdoor buffet luncheon. Dozens of Tribeca's finest chefs prepare their signature dishes so that, on a late May Sunday from end of morning until mid-afternoon, they may be sampled by diners who stroll down Duane Street. Participating restaurants have included Boule, Nobu, Capsouto Frères, and Tribeca Grill, to name just a few. In terms of cuisine, no ordinary street fest. First held in 1996 in an effort to raise money for art in the neighborhood's public schools, Taste of Tribeca was conceived by its founders as a moment and place where, on a beautiful day in spring, their passion for great food and art and their children's education would converge.

JANE FISHER
Marketing consultant

2.8 Odeon

145 West Broadway between Duane and Thomas Streets
212 233 0507; www.theodeonrestaurant.com

Once the trendiest restaurant in the city (think long ago, like the '80s), this place has become a classic because they just do everything right: big dining area, great food, an atmosphere that remains comfortably chic but not off-putting. Odeon will probably continue to thrive for good reason.

KATHLEEN DEMARCO VAN CLEVE
Author, screenwriter, and film producer

2

Kayaking on the Hudson

646 613 0740; www.downtownboathouse.org
Seasonal and weather permitting.

3.11 **The New York City Downtown Boathouse at Pier 40**
On the Hudson River at West Houston Street

9.22 **The New York City Downtown Boathouse at Pier 96**
On the Hudson River at West 56th Street

Well off the beaten path psychologically, but easily accessible, is the Downtown Boathouse, which offers free kayaking in two locations in a city more known for crowded subways, noisy buses, rushing taxis, and busy sidewalks. Just show up on a summer weekend and you'll find a free kayak to use, basic instruction, and access to a relatively protected portion of the Hudson River. For more advanced kayakers, show up before 9 a.m. on the weekend (Pier 40 only) for a three-hour paddle to the Statue of Liberty or the *U.S.S. Intrepid*. Although there are often more people than boats for these longer trips, it's a great chance to get back to nature in a dramatically man-made city.

THORIN TRITTER
Historian

CIVIC CENTER

Civic Center Stroll

www.nyc.gov

2.9 **City Hall**

1812, Joseph François Mangin and John McComb Jr.
City Hall Park between Broadway and Park Row
www.nyc-architecture.com

2.10 **Old New York County Courthouse ("Tweed" Courthouse)**

1872, John Kellum and Thomas Little
52 Chambers Street between Broadway and Centre Street
www.nyc.gov

2.11 **Former Emigrant Industrial Savings Bank Building**

1912, Raymond F. Almirall
51 Chambers Street between Broadway and Elk Street
www.nyc-architecture.com

2.12 **Surrogate's Courthouse**

1907, John R. Thomas
31 Chambers Street at Centre Street
www.nyc.gov

2.13 **Manhattan Municipal Building**

1914, McKim, Mead & White
1 Centre Street opposite Chambers Street
www.nyc.gov

2.15 **U.S. Courthouse**

1936, Cass Gilbert and Cass Gilbert Jr.
40 Centre Street at Pearl Street
www.nyc-architecture.com

2.16 **New York County Courthouse (New York State Supreme Court)**
1925, Guy Lowell
60 Centre Street between Pearl and Worth Streets,
in Foley Square
www.nyc.gov

2.17 **Criminal Courts Building and Men's House of Detention**
1941, Harvey Corbett and Charles B. Meyers
100 Centre Street between Leonard and White Streets
www.nyc.gov

1.14 **Brooklyn Bridge**
1867–83, John A. Roebling & Washington Roebling
Park Row in Manhattan to Adams Street in Brooklyn

1.16 **Woolworth Building**
1913, Cass Gilbert
233 Broadway between Park Place and Barclay Street
www.nyc-architecture.com

I recommend an incredible group of buildings that I have often taken friends and students to visit. The tour can be completed in an hour unless one is detained by the many interesting aspects of this visit. It's best to go during business hours, as the interiors are of as much interest as the exteriors and are not open on the weekend.

I like to start at the front of City Hall, in the newly renovated City Hall Park. City Hall has an elegant 1812 French Renaissance façade by Joseph F. Mangin and John McComb Jr. and a dramatic interior hall with a twin circular stair and dome.

One used to be able to go out the back door to the "Tweed" Courthouse, on axis behind City Hall. In 1876, C. L. W. Eidlitz added a Romanesque cast-iron hall with glass walkways and a steel truss skylight that once held stained glass. You can leave Tweed Hall by the basement door in the front.

Across the street, on axis, is the former Emigrant Industrial Savings Bank Building, designed by Raymond F. Almirall in 1912. One can enter this interesting double tower building to see an impressive banking hall.

Just east on Chambers Street is the Surrogate's Court building (see p. 43). This Beaux Arts building has entries from both Chambers and Elk Streets. From Chambers, one passes through a double colonnaded entry to the center skylighted hall. There is an elegant and complex stair at the end of the hall that appears to be independent of its container. It begins with a symmetrical center entry and becomes asymmetrical as it rises above the skylit center court.

From here, one is confronted with the Arch of Constantine screen in front of the U-shaped Municipal Building. The Municipal Building is split by Chambers Street, with a vaulted space in the form of the entry to the Palazzo Farnese in Rome. This urban solution forced two lobbies and two elevator banks rising to the colonnaded top where stands the statue *Civic Fame*.

Now walk north on Centre Street; at Foley Square is the U.S. Courthouse, with its pyramided tower by Cass Gilbert and Cass Gilbert Jr. North of that is the New York County Courthouse, designed in 1912, but built fifteen years later. The hexagonal plan has a great interior hall surrounded by a colonnade.

Continue north to the Art Deco Criminal Courts Building and Men's House of Detention—"The Tombs" (see p. 44). Peek into the formidable center hall, then turn back to City Hall Park. This time, passing the screen of the Municipal Building under the south arm of Guastavino tile work, one can look down the axis of the Brooklyn Bridge.

Saving a walk over the bridge for another time, cross the park with eyes on the Woolworth Building (see p. 25). The delicate exterior is complemented by the glass mosaic lobby, which seems like a cross between a Byzantine street system and the proclaimed "cathedral of commerce."

JON MICHAEL SCHWARTING
Director of the graduate program in Urban and Regional Design, New York Institute of Technology

2.12 Surrogate's Court

1907, John R. Thomas
31 Chambers Street between Centre and Elk Streets
www.nyc.gov

The next best thing to seeing the Paris Opera House is a visit to the lobby of the Surrogate's Court. Open to the public during regular court hours, this spectacular granite building was begun in 1899 and completed in 1907. The courtrooms on the fifth floor, made of mahogany and English oak, are well worth the elevator ride. The building also houses the archives of the City of New York.

JAMES J. BRUCIA
Justice (retired), New York State Supreme Court

2.14 African Burial Ground Memorial

c. 1690
Corner of Duane and African Burial Ground Way (Elk Street)
Visitor Center: 290 Broadway, close to Foley Square and just north of City Hall
www.nps.gov/afbg

Unearthed during construction of the federal office building at 290 Broadway in 1991, the Colonial-era cemetery once spanned more than five acres or about five city blocks. Archaeologists estimate more than twenty thousand men, women, and children were once buried at the site, which included the preserved portion at the corner of Duane and Elk Streets.

CHRISTOPHER PAUL MOORE
Historian, author, and research coordinator, New York Public Library's Schomburg Center for Research on Black Culture

2.17 Criminal Courts Building and Men's House of Detention ("The Tombs")

1939, Harvey Wiley Corbett and Charles B. Meyers
100 Centre Street between Leonard and White Streets

Go to night court and listen to the pleas of a parade of pimps, prostitutes, petty thieves, and, every once in a while, a murderer. It's gritty and it's real. The Art Moderne design by Harvey Wiley Corbett is a poor man's Rockefeller Center. Named "The Tombs" after its Egyptian Revival predecessor across the street, it lived up to its name for decades as symbol of the deplorable condition of correctional institutions.
FREDERIC SCHWARTZ
Architect

CHINATOWN

2.18 Canal Street

This bustling, traffic-riddled crosstown thoroughfare originally functioned as a canal and is now virtually a linear flea market starting east at the Manhattan Bridge, running through the Lower East Side, Chinatown, Little Italy, SoHo, and Tribeca and ending west at the Hudson River. You can buy anything under the sun (and more), it seems, as vendors spill out on the sidewalks hawking their wares from sunrise to sundown. Brush up on your bartering skills before buying the knockoff handbags and watches that abound, and also watch your pockets. A great place to score the requisite NYC T-shirts and baseball caps at way below Midtown prices. Treat yourself to the best *café con leche* in New York at the West Side Coffee Shop (corner of Church and Lispenard).
FREDERIC SCHWARTZ AND TRACEY HUMMER
Architect and writer

Chinatown Walk

2.19 Tunnel
5 Doyers Street between Pell Street and Bowery
www.scoutingny.com/?p=1757; www.nychinatown.org

2.20 Nom Wah Tea Parlor
13 Doyers Street between Pell Street and Bowery
212 962 6047; www.nomwah.com

Head for Pell Street, where at No. 16 you'll find a bronze placard reading "Hip Sing Association." Pell Street has been home to the Hip Sing Tong, or association, since the 1880s. The Hip Sing were fierce rivals of the On Leong Tong (who were headquartered in the Pagoda on the southwest corner of Mott and Canal). From the late nineteenth century through the 1930s, the tongs would regularly erupt in battles over gambling turf and other interests of the day. These conflicts, referred to legendarily as the Tong Wars, were full of shootings and stabbings that spilled over from Pell Street onto adjoining Doyers Street. No. 5 Doyers, site of the Old Chinese Opera House, was the scene of an especially gruesome power play in 1906, when Hip Singers fired into an audience of On Leongers. The attackers made their getaway through Chinatown's network of ancient tunnels, and you can enter one of them at 5 Doyers Street today.

Take the staircase below ground and follow the tunnel until you exit at Chatham Square, farther to the south. What you'll encounter en route is a dingy arcade of small businesses. Still, it doesn't take too much fantasizing to conjure up images of blood, battle, and flight in this corridor a century ago. If you double back and exit on Doyers Street, you can stop for tea at Nom Wah (No. 13)—New York's oldest (1927) dim sum parlor.

JANE FISHER
Marketing consultant

2.20 Nom Wah Tea Parlor

13 Doyers Street between Pell Street and Bowery
212 962 6047; www.nomwah.com

Located on Doyers Street since 1920, Nom Wah is the oldest tea parlor in Chinatown. This is the real deal. The food is terrific, and extremely reasonable. Try the shrimp shumai—said to be the best in the city.

CLARISSA BLOCK
Fashion stylist and children's jewelry designer

2.22 Kam Kuo Food Corp.

17A Mott Street between Mosco and Worth Streets
212 233 5387

New York's Chinatown has grown tremendously in recent times, taking over the old Little Italy and reaching into the Lower East Side. In some ways, it is a city within a city and exploring it can be daunting. One good place to get started is the Kam Kuo Food Corp. From the street this looks like an ordinary small store, but once inside you'll realize that it's as large as a suburban supermarket and it has a second floor as well.

It's definitely not a tourist spot. Most people there are just doing their regular grocery shopping, and unless you ask for help, you will be left alone. Begin at the collection of bins in front. Mixed in with the usual bulk goods is more unusual fare, such as shredded squid, pickled tangerines, and preserved dry olives. One row offers six different kinds of ginseng, ranging from sixteen to sixty-three dollars a pound. There are some familiar brands on the shelves —Carnation, Nestlé—but these are products made for the Asian market, not the ones you see in America. Then there are the brands manufactured and sold in Asia, with Western names chosen to sound exotic in their target markets: Kewpie mayonnaise, Mickey Mouse haw candy, Bull-Dog Worcestershire sauce, Beefeater pukka tea.

2

Kam Kuo is a good source for hard-to-find foods from many Asian countries. They have a wonderful selection of ready-made foods; especially worth trying are the frozen steam buns. Try to leave with at least one product that you've never heard of before. It shouldn't be too difficult. On a recent visit some items to be considered were white fungus with pineapple, grass jelly drink, toddy palm seeds, shrink-wrapped preserved quail eggs, canned rambutan, sapote, jackfruit, "odour frying fish with chili," peanut gluten, salted croaker (a kind of fish), medlar-chrysanthemum drink crystal, honey-fritillary-and-loquat beverage, pickled *mayom*, as well as some foods whose names are translated only into Latin because there isn't an English equivalent.

Upstairs they sell mostly cookware and a few household appliances. You can find cheap, high-quality pots and utensils and beautiful dishes here. If you're having a banquet for fifty people, their banquet room has all sorts of little tables and chairs. And if you need an industrial-sized soybean drink press or a melon-seed cracker, you will find one here.

JANET B. PASCAL
Writer and production editor, Viking Children's Books

Mott Street Stroll

2.23 **Ten Ren's Tea Time**
75 Mott Street between Canal and Bayard Streets
212 732 7178; www.tenrenusa.com

2.24 **Chinatown Ice Cream Factory**
65 Bayard Street between Mott and Elizabeth Streets
212 608 4170; www.chinatownicecreamfactory.com

2.25 **Columbus Park**
Between Baxter, Mulberry, Bayard, and Worth Streets
www.nyc.gov

Most people think of Chinatown as a noisy, sprawling market of trinkets, gadgets, street vendors, and odd-looking food. But if you know where to go, you can enjoy the neighborhood at a slow pace, taking in its quiet moments in unexpected ways.

Enter the gateway to old Chinatown at the southern intersection of Mott and Canal Streets. Head south on Mott, where you'll soon see a cluster of new teahouses boasting the latest drink innovation: flavored tapioca teas or "bubble tea." These candy-colored teahouses are the new social clubs for young Asians, who are a few generations removed from the old benevolent societies their grandparents patronized. You may choose from a number of fruits and flavors, but all the drinks have giant black pearls of tapioca (hence the nickname, "bubble tea") bobbing on the bottom. Sucked up through a giant straw, the gummy beads pop into your mouth and require considerable chewing before you can swallow them (kids love this part).

Continuing south, just to the left on Bayard Street, is a tried-and-true institution, the Chinatown Ice Cream Factory. Forget about thirty-one flavors, the nearby Häagen-Dazs, or those two guys from Vermont; the ice cream here is made fresh daily, and many flavors, such as almond cookie, chrysanthemum tea, and lychee, are from ancestral Chinese recipes. Try these flavors you won't find in the supermarket freezer: ginger, taro, red bean, and green tea. Get a cone, or a dish, and continue your stroll down Mott Street until you reach Mosco Street. Follow Mosco to Columbus Park, an outdoor living room and salon for the community. The sounds of the city disappear here, not for the peace, but for the loud chirps of birds, the buzz of hundreds of people talking, and the clapping of mahjong tiles on the tables. Throngs of Chinese sitting on cardboard boxes and milk crates socialize here all year round, testing their skills and fortunes. They're young and old, male and female, but the activities seem to be segregated: the women play cards, the men play dominoes. Along the wire fence, fortune-tellers hang their red banners and point to mysterious battered books and long, thin reeds, devices used to divine the future. As few of the "wise women" speak English, having your destiny revealed may not come easy.

LANA BORTOLOT
Writer

3
Chelsea
Meat Packing District
West Village
Hudson River
Hudson River Park
Pier 51
Pier 42
Pier 40
Pier 34
Pier 32
W 14th St
Tenth Avenue
Ninth Avenue
Eighth Avenue
Seventh Avenue
Eleventh Avenue
Greenwich Avenue
Seventh Avenue South
W Houston St
Canal St
West St
Hudson St
Greenwich St
Washington St
Bleecker St
Sheridan Square

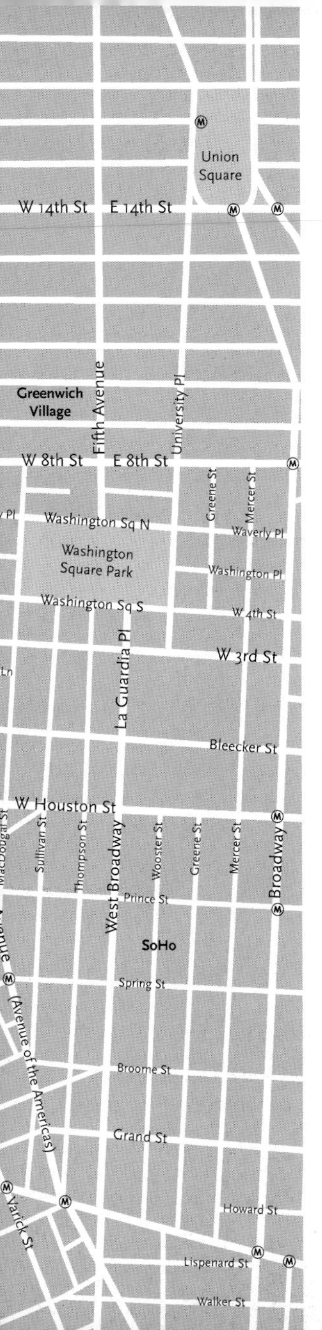

CHAPTER 3

WEST VILLAGE

🍴🍷 1 Pastis
🍴🍷 2 Corner Bistro
3 Village Vanguard
4 Smalls Jazz Club
🍴🍷 5 Mary's Fish Camp
🍴🍷 6 White Horse Tavern (see p. 66)
7 Grove Court (see p. 79)
8 St. Luke-in-the-Fields
9 Cherry Lane Theater
10 Home of St. Vincent Millay
11 Pier 40 (see p. 35, 39)

West Village

3.2 Corner Bistro

331 West 4th Street at Jane Street
212 242 9502; www.cornerbistrony.com

Located on the corner of one of the most maddeningly tangled sections of the West Village: the intersection of Eighth Avenue and West 4th and Jane Streets. It is, however, quite easy to find "the Bistro." Inevitably, there will be people pouring out of it, walking into it, and, depending on the weather, lounging outside of it. Forget everything you've heard about fancy service and sleek decor (there is a reason everything is so cheap) and order one of the Bistro's legendary hamburgers, fries, and a beer. A particular American species, Frat Boy, mistakenly believes it owns this place, but just push right by him and head for the back tables. You may look up one night (it doesn't close until the wee hours of the morning) and see Bruce Springsteen having dinner, right next to a bunch of businessmen, next to an in-love couple, next to a man who won't stop smiling. If it weren't always so crowded, it would be perfect.

KATHLEEN DEMARCO VAN CLEVE
Author, screenwriter, and film producer

3.3 The Village Vanguard

178 Seventh Avenue South between West 11th and Perry Streets
212 255 4037; www.villagevanguard.com

The legendary club that Miles Davis used to play in is dark, a little uncomfortable, and absolutely delightful.

ERIC STOLTZ
Actor

3.4 Smalls Jazz Club

183 West 10th Street between West 4th Street and Seventh Avenue South

📞 212 929 7565; www.smallsjazzclub.com

If Charles Mingus were ever to call me on the telephone and ask me to go to Minton's Playhouse up in Harlem, I would say, "But Charlie, Minton's is closed," and I would take him to Smalls. Smalls is a jazz club pinched between Seventh Avenue and West 4th Street, at the bottom of a stairwell that twists into the basement. The music at Smalls almost never stops. It starts every night at about 7:30 or 8 p.m., and flows like a glowing current of electricity until musicians can no longer honk, bleat, or swing, and sunlight cracks your eyes as you climb the stairwell and stumble back out into the street.

Sometimes on cold winter evenings, people will stand for hours holding plastic bags filled with imported beer or wine bottles, in a line so long that it wraps around the corner onto West 4th Street. They'll wait and wait until it's their turn to pay the ten-dollar cover charge to Mr. Borden, the man at the door, who is probably reading poetry or playing his violin. The inside of Smalls is smoky and very dark, and there's room for about fifty people. There's no stage, and musicians perform in the front of the club, in an area about the size of a phone booth. The club's brick walls are covered by black-and-white photos of jazz legends. Patrons sit at small, round, candlelit tables, on padded benches, or at the bar, which serves only fruit juice and iced tea. Musicians are paid entirely from the sale of CDs, but applause is also a valid form of currency. Mounted on the wall, behind where the drums are usually set up, is an old photograph of Louis Armstrong, sitting cross-legged on the ground, smiling gloriously because his ears are delighted.

ALEX FRENCH
Writer and journalist

West Village à la Carte

3.5 **Mary's Fish Camp**
64 Charles Street at West 4th Street
646 486 2185; www.marysfishcamp.com

5.11 **Pearl Oyster Bar**
18 Cornelia Street between Bleecker and West 4th Streets
212 691 8211; www.pearloysterbar.com

5.18 **Murray's Cheese Shop**
257 Bleecker Street at Cornelia Street
212 243 3289; www.murrayscheese.com

3.8 **Garden of the Church of St. Luke-in-the-Fields**
487 Hudson Street between Barrow and Christopher Streets, entrance on Barrow Street
212 924 0562; www.stlukeinthefields.org

5.12 **Blue Hill**
75 Washington Place between Sixth Avenue and Washington Square West
212 539 1776; www.bluehillfarm.com

5.13 **Washington Square Park**
At the foot of Fifth Avenue
www.nycgovparks.org

3.9 **Cherry Lane Theatre**
38 Commerce Street at Barrow Street
212 989 2020; www.cherrylanetheatre.org

3.1 **Pastis**
9 Ninth Avenue at Little 12th Street
212 929 4844; www.pastisny.com

Greenwich Village: the best place in Manhattan! Grab a lobster roll at Mary's or Pearl or a *panini* at my place, Murray's, and savor it in St. Luke's Garden. Have a late dinner on a summer evening at Blue Hill restaurant, then sit on a bench and watch the people go by in Washington Square Park (see p. 85). Catch a Sunday matinee at the Cherry Lane Theatre, and marvel at the most beautiful residential architecture in Manhattan. Stay up really late and have a bite to eat at Pastis in the meat market, then hit the local nightclubs.

ROBERT KAUFELT
Proprietor, Murray's Cheese Shop

3.8 Garden of the Church of St. Luke-in-the-Fields

487 Hudson Street between Barrow and Christopher Streets, entrance on Barrow Street
212 924 0562; www.stlukeinthefields.org

Walk through the street gate and follow the path to the walled garden. A walled garden—the kind so many of us imagined as children! In the center, a flowering tree, paths through lilac and tulips and roses (tended by bands of invisible volunteers), a few benches, squirrels, singing birds. It feels safe and sacred—a broken-off piece of paradise.

The garden is lovely in all seasons—in winter with snow falling, in spring when the first crocus comes up. People seem to talk softly and to smile and nod to one another as people do in churches, but it's also a good place for a kiss. I've seen commuters striding to the PATH train in the early morning stop and stare from the sidewalk, as if looking back into paradise from the fallen world.

MARIE HOWE
Poet

3.10 Former Home of Edna St. Vincent Millay

1873

75 1/2 Bedford Street between Morton and Commerce Streets
Not open to the public.

This house on Bedford Street is the smallest row house in Greenwich Village, once known as the "Edna St. Vincent Millay Doll's House" because the famous poet lived there with her husband Eugen Boissevain during the 1920s. It is said that the original house consisted of one narrow room on each of its floors, but it had the advantage of a closed-in backyard that gave easy access to a neighboring house occupied by Edna's one-time lover and lifelong friend, the poet Arthur Davison Ficke, then married to another dear friend, Gladys Brown.

EDMUND KEELEY
Author, critic, and translator

Stargazing

After several decades, the brick façades of many row houses built in New York during the Federal period began to fatigue and buckle, and it became necessary to "tie" the brick back to the joists with metal rods, which were then capped by iron plates on the outside walls. Early versions of these plates, which functioned like large washers, were made in straightforward utilitarian shapes—a couple of crossed iron strips, or perhaps a simple rondel. By the end of the Civil War, however, ironworkers began making them from melted-down cannonballs and casting them in the shape of stars to honor the enduring Republic. You'll find these utilitarian but beautiful symbols on brick walls throughout lower Manhattan and the Village—affecting examples of turning swords into plowshares.

ANGELA HEDERMAN
Publisher

Celebrated Women

6.21 **Home of Emma Goldman**
210 East 13th Street between Second and Third Avenues
Not open to the public.

3

3.10 **Home of Edna St. Vincent Millay**
75 1/2 Bedford Street between Morton and Commerce Streets
www.nyc-architecture.com
Not open to the public.

Two houses—one a tenement in the East Village, one a tiny town house in the West Village—still stand in lower Manhattan, much as they were in the early decades of the twentieth century, despite occasional renovations. Each memorializes the vibrant labors of a celebrated woman, each of whose creative accomplishments contributed to the exuberant spirit of an era.

At 210 East 13th Street, Emma Goldman (1869–1940), the anarchist organizer, feminist agitator, birth-control and free-love advocate who was tagged by FBI chief J. Edgar Hoover "the most dangerous woman in the world," lived for a decade. She moved to her "oasis in the desert," as she called it, in 1903, soon after she emerged from hiding, following President William McKinley's assassination in 1901 by a deranged anarchist whom Goldman was falsely accused of abetting. In the living room/bedroom, which also became her office, she launched her anarchist journal of art and politics, *Mother Earth*, in 1906; it appeared monthly for twelve years, interrupted only by occasional police interference. In that dashing era of the New Woman, Goldman's cold-water flat quickly became one of the city's liveliest centers of feminist agitation and radical thought. "There was always someone sleeping in the front, someone who had stayed too late and lived too far away or who was too shaky on their feet or needed cold compresses or who had no home to go to," wrote Goldman in her autobiography, *Living My Life*. The apartment was described by one friend as "a home for lost dogs," and lauded by another (Wobbly labor leader Big Bill Haywood) for its coffee "black asnight, strong as the revolutionary ideal, sweet as love."

Across town and some blocks south stands the house of Edna St. Vincent Millay (1892–1950), another New Woman. Her 1922 poem,

My candle burns at both ends;
It will not last the night;
But ah, my foes, and oh, my friends—
It gives a lovely light!

was taken up as the anthem of a generation. This celebrated poet, playwright, and advocate of women's sexual freedom was one of three famously beautiful sisters who took bohemian Greenwich Village by storm. They acted at the Provincetown Playhouse on MacDougal Street, sometimes in Millay's own plays. A decade after gaining national attention for a long poem she published at age twenty, Millay won a Pulitzer Prize in poetry in 1922, the first awarded to a woman. Her one-time lover, the influential critic Edmund Wilson, described her as "almost supernaturally beautiful" and her readings as "thrilling," noting ruefully that she was more interested in poetry than in men. After half a dozen years spent in various Village apartments with her sisters and sometimes their mother, Millay married in 1923 and moved for a while to the one-room-wide, three-story house—reputedly the city's narrowest—at 75½ Bedford Street. In her eighties, Millay's sister Norma told me that back during Prohibition the sisters would sometimes tend bar as a favor to their friend Lee Chumley, owner of Chumley's, a then popular speakeasy at 86 Bedford, diagonally across the street from Millay's house. If Lee Chumley was away, Norma confided, they invited their friends in for an evening of free drinks.

ALIX KATES SHULMAN
Writer

4
West Village
Greenwich Village
Washington Square Park
SoHo
Tribeca
Battery Park City
Hudson River
Hudson River Park
Nelson A Rockefeller Park
Pier 40
W 8th St
E 8th St
Fifth Av
Waverly Pl
Washington Sq N
Washington Pl
Washington Sq S
W 3rd
W 4th St
La Guardia Pl
W Houston St
Seventh Avenue South
Sixth Avenue (Avenue of the Americas)
Hudson St
West St
Canal St
Bleecker St
Christopher St
Perry St
Charles St
Charles Ln
W 11th St
W 10th St
Grove St
Bedford St
Commerce St
Jones St
Cornelia St
Gay St
Barrow St
Morton St
Leroy St
Clarkson St
Carmine St
Downing St
Weehawken St
King St
Charlton St
Vandam St
Spring St
Dominick St
Broome St
Watts St
Varick St
Washington St
Greenwich St
MacDougal St
Sullivan St
Thompson St
West Broadway
Wooster St
Greene St
Prince St
Grand St
Desbrosses St
Vestry St
Laight St
Hubert St
Beach St
N Moore St
Franklin St
Harrison St
Staple St
Jay St
Lispenard
Walker St
White St
Leonard St
Worth St
Thomas St
Duane St
Reade St
Chambers St
Warren St
Murray St
Park Pl
Park Pl West
North End Av
Church St
Sixth Avenue
14
13
12
11
9
10
7
8
3
5
6
4
2
1

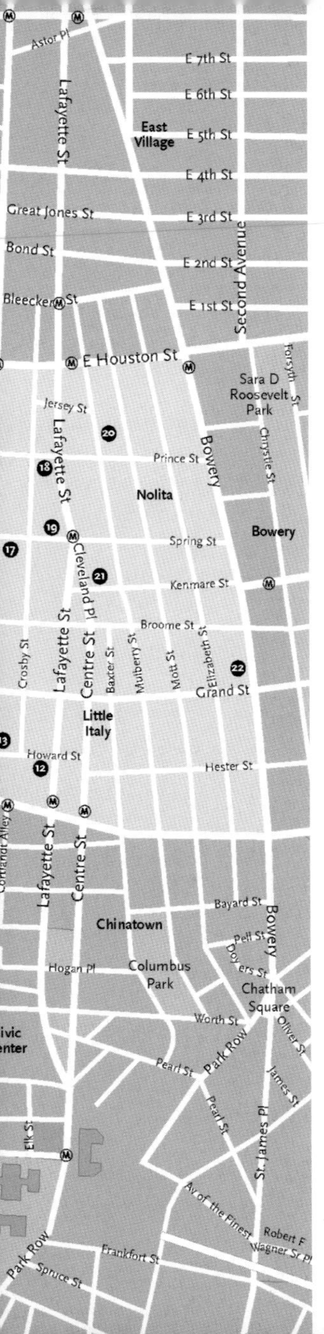

CHAPTER 4

SOHO

1 Film Forum
2 Joe's Dairy
3 St. Anthony of Padua
4 Pepe Rosso to Go
5 Pino's Prime Meats
6 Dia Center: *New York Earth Room*
7 Raoul's
8 Anonymous Hair Salon
9 Ear Inn
10 Dia Center: *Broken Kilometer*
11 Broome Street Bar
12 E. Vogel Inc.
13 Putnam Rolling Ladder Co.
14 Patina
15 Singer Building
16 Fanelli Cafe
17 Balthazar
18 Savoy
19 E. R. Butler & Co.

NOLITA & LITTLE ITALY

20 St. Patrick's Old Cathedral
21 Storefront for Art and Architecture
22 Bowery Savings Bank (p. 164)

SoHo, Nolita & Little Italy

SOHO

4.1 The Film Forum

209 West Houston between Sixth Avenue and Varick Street
212 727 8110; www.filmforum.org

Don't worry about what's on the bill at this intimate three-theater complex. Just trust the programmer's taste and go. Whether it's a quirky low-budget job, a pristine new print of an American classic, or a contemporary foreign film, these folks find and screen the best. The atmosphere is unpretentious, the crowd is smart and appreciative, and they have the best popcorn in New York.

GREGORY MOSHER
Theater director and producer

4.2 Joe's Dairy

156 Sullivan Street between Prince and West Houston Streets
212 677 8780
Closed Sundays and Mondays.

If you're a mozzarella snob or just like a good Italian sandwich, you will do well to make a stop at Joe's Dairy. It's a tiny, old-fashioned storefront, a vestige from the days when this neighborhood was the western half of Little Italy (split by what is now SoHo). Inside you'll find an ample cheese selection along with other dairy staples such as milk, mascarpone, and ricotta. Filling the shelves are a sampling of olive oils and dried pastas. But the real reason to make the pilgrimage is the mozzarella—unsalted, salted, and smoked. You may never taste better outside Italy. If you're lucky, you'll catch the cheese makers in action in the back, stirring and stretching the gooey white stuff in enormous soup pots. If you happen to walk by and see smoke billowing out of the place and the entire staff hanging around outside, don't bother calling the fire department . . . it's only the smoked mozzarella being made. Grab a half of a smoked for a tasty snack, or take an unsalted home for the perfect, rich, velvety accompaniment to a fresh tomato and sprig of basil. Joe's sells a nice mozzarella sandwich and also will grate your just-cut piece of Parmigiano Reggiano.

SARAH CAPLAN

Designer, graphic artist, and writer

Sullivan Street Stroll

4.3 **St. Anthony of Padua Roman Catholic Church**

c. 1888

155 Sullivan Street at West Houston Street

212 777 2755; www.stanthonynyc.org

4.4 **Pepe Rosso to Go**

149 Sullivan Street between West Houston and Prince Streets

212 677 4555; www.peperossotogo.com

4.5 **Pino's Prime Meats**

149 Sullivan Street between West Houston and Prince Streets

212 475 8134

4.8 **Anonymous Hair Salon**

105 Sullivan Street between Prince and Spring Streets

212 966 6806

There's a street, Sullivan Street, that was the spine of an Italian-American neighborhood now devoured by the advance of SoHo. But if you start at Houston and walk the three blocks south to Broome, a few places that remain can give you the flavor of what was.

Start at the church of St. Anthony of Padua. On a good Saturday you can catch an old-fashioned Italian-American wedding, with the chance of a horse and buggy or at least the longest white stretch limo you've ever seen. Walk past 150 Sullivan, which used to be Canapa's Bakery. Across the street is Pepe Rosso to Go, which used to be Rocky's Vegetable Store. The butcher shop's another leftover, with sawdust on the floor and a butcher block from years ago. Pino took over for Mario, but the flavor's the same. There used to be another butcher on this street, as well as two bakeries, two grocery stores, a club, some storefronts, and some stores that were just for rent to keep baby carriages and bicycles.

Cross Prince Street and keep walking and you'll come to a sign that reads "Anonymous Hair Salon." Go in on a Saturday morning and you'll be back in the old neighborhood. All the seniors come to get their hair washed and set and teased into bouffants that will hold all week. You'll get all the gossip: who died, who's sick, who's been naughty and who's been nice, plus you'll get a good haircut. Ask for Pat. She'll order you coffee and a sandwich at lunch-time. But be nice . . . you gotta be nice in the neighborhood. Then shop all you want in the SoHo everybody knows.

LOUISA ERMELINO
Writer and chief of reporters, InStyle

4.6 Dia Center for the Arts: *The New York Earth Room*

1977, Walter De Maria
141 Wooster Street between West Houston and Prince Streets
☎ 212 989 5566; www.earthroom.org
Closed Mondays and Tuesdays.

If the urban shuffle is making you pine for pastoral environs or if you just want a place to reflect, the Earth Room—a sanctuary in a SoHo loft—is the answer. Created in 1977 by American artist Walter De Maria, it is filled with two hundred and fifty cubic yards of rich, dark topsoil weighing two hundred and eighty thousand pounds and standing twenty-two inches high. Originally one of three Earth Rooms—the other two created by De Maria in Germany—this is the only one still remaining, sponsored and maintained by the Dia Center for the Arts. Prepare to be transported by an incredibly unique experience.

CHRISTINE MOOG
Graphic designer

4

4.7 Raoul's

180 Prince Street between Sullivan and Thompson Streets
212 966 3518; www.raouls.com

For someone who finds comfort in the gloriously faded past while being entirely immersed in the present, Raoul's is a godsend. I remember pulling up to the bar when I was a young writer and feeling as though I'd arrived home. Countless evenings have been spent enjoying long, winding discussions with friends, surrounded by straight talkers and abstract expressionists, gumshoes, and rock stars. Fifteen years after my first steak au poivre at Raoul's, I still look forward to every visit—every greeting from Eddie, maître d' and dear friend; every walk through the hectic kitchen to the back room; every journey up the precarious circular staircase leading to the restrooms. I've enjoyed dinners for fifteen in the front room settled comfortably into the seemingly ancient long banquette, as well as simple dinners for two, hidden away at a table under the skylight. Raoul's seems to get better every year, even though it hasn't changed a bit.

ANDY SPADE
Co-founder of Kate Spade New York, Partners & Spade, and Jack Spade,

Vintage Bars

4.9 The Ear Inn

326 Spring Street between Greenwich and Washington Streets
212 226 9060; www.earinn.com

4.16 **Fanelli's Cafe**
94 Prince Street at Mercer Street
212 226 9412
(see p. 122)

3.6 **The White Horse Tavern**
567 Hudson Street at West 11th Street
212 243 9260

Originally located on the banks of the Hudson River and originally known as the James Brown House, the Ear is one of the few remaining two-story, wood-framed, Federal-style buildings in Manhattan. One of the oldest taverns in the city (c. 1817), the Ear served as a halfway house for runaway slaves during the Civil War. Not only a beautiful and historic landmark, it's also the best meal for your money below Houston Street. The daily fresh fish special cannot be beat. A friendly, loud, and eclectic downtown neighborhood crowd that includes workers, bikers, artists, and musicians spills out on the sidewalk on summer evenings.

Though there is much debate about which is the oldest bar in the city (Fraunces Tavern, 1762; Bridge Cafe, 1794; Ear Inn, 1817; Pete's Tavern, 1864; McSorley's Ale House, 1854), Fanelli's is surely one of the oldest and best. Serving food and drink continuously since 1847, it operated as a speakeasy during Prohibition from 1920 to 1933. Perhaps the most beautiful back bar in the city, it faces a wall of original boxing photos and portraits dating from the turn of the century. Fanelli's was once my friendly local neighborhood watering hole, but as SoHo has changed, unfortunately so has the crowd (and boy, is it crowded). So, go very late at night after the tourists, shoppers, and the bridge-and-tunnel gang have gone to bed and try hard to engage Bob the bartender in conversation. A retired former prizefighter, he once fought Bob Chavalo for the Canadian heavyweight championship and was smart enough to turn down a fight with mean Sonny Liston. If you get

Bob going, then you're in for an education loaded with vicious one-liners and lots of laughs.

Once a speakeasy, the White Horse Tavern has been a favorite of locals, workers, artists, and writers since 1880 (including such neighborhood notables as Jack Kerouac, Norman Mailer, and Bob Dylan). Fact: in 1953, Dylan Thomas, on a two-day binge, drank himself to death here. ("I've had eighteen straight whiskeys and I believe that's the record.") Sit outside at the corner table on a lazy Saturday afternoon and watch Jane Jacobs's neighborhood stroll by. Stick to the beer, a good bacon burger, or my favorite, the tuna melt.

FREDERIC SCHWARTZ
Architect

4.10 Dia Center for the Arts: *The Broken Kilometer*

1979, Walter De Maria

393 West Broadway between Spring and Broome Streets

212 989 5566; www.brokenkilometer.org

Walter De Maria's five hundred-piece work is both the bright golden reflection you see and the silence you hear in the white room it inhabits: a weightless, drifting space. Looking left to right, the building's row of cast-iron columns gives comparison to scale, and divides the work into two rows of bars on one side, and three on the other. From foreground to background, all weight, dimension, and shape disappear into light. The rear bars float off the floor and the wall drops behind the horizon. The work's calm, mystical euphoria owes everything to its simple perspective in pictorial space. It feels huge and timeless and exists in a pure state of relativity. Seeing and understanding its specific physicality becomes a way of thinking while you are there, which is then claimed quickly by memory once you exit through the short maze and return to the outside.

JAMES L. BODNAR
Architect

4.11 **Broome Street Bar**
363 West Broadway at Broome Street
212 925 2086; www.broomestreetbar.ypguides.net

A wonderful no-frills restaurant located smack in the center of SoHo. After too much shopping at Prada and and too much walking and people-gazing and all the rest of the things people do in SoHo, go to the Broome Street Bar, sit back, order a beer, look out the window, and be so happy that there are places like this in the city where comfort reigns and pretension is permanently barred.
KATHLEEN DEMARCO VAN CLEVE
Author, screenwriter, and film producer

Howard Street

4.12 **E. Vogel Inc.**
19 Howard Street between Broadway and Lafayette Street
212 925 2460; www.vogelboots.com

4.13 **Putnam Rolling Ladder Co. Inc.**
32 Howard Street between Broadway and Crosby Street
212 226 5147; www.putnamrollingladder.com

While on Howard Street, look in on two establishments devoted to Old World craftsmanship. At No. 19, visit the three-story brick townhouse, home to E. Vogel, and order a pair of made-to-measure jodhpurs or a pair of custom dress shoes. You will be in good company; this fourth-generation establishment (thirty-two years in its present location, to which it moved from its 1879 Warren Street home) has made riding boots and shoes for General Pershing, Charles Lindbergh, Paul Newman, and Jacqueline Onassis, as well as for Olympic equestrian teams, and kings and queens.

At No. 32, you will find the Putnam Rolling Ladder Company. Their model Number 1—think library ladder sliding along a brass rail—has been in continuous production since 1905. The ownership is in its third generation, having taken possession of the company in 1946 when Mr. Putnam sold it to his longtime employee. The shop has been on Howard Street at its current whereabouts since the 1930s and nothing appears to have changed much. Even the sign above the shop is from Mr. Putnam's horse-drawn carriage. Current clients range from Diane von Furstenberg to Barnes & Noble.

ROBERT KAHN
Architect

NOTE: Ted Muehling's jewelry store, located on Howard Street for many years, has moved to 52 White Street (see p. 37).

4.14 Patina

451 Broome Street between Broadway and Mercer Street
212 625 3375; www.patinavintage.com

This unique SoHo shop features items that reflect the passions of its energetic owner, Lenore Newman. Hand-selected vintage clothing and accessories, unusual jewelry, ceramics, tableware, and glassware (both old and new) are available. Displays, in the form of amusing vignettes, are constantly changing, and new merchandise enters the store regularly. Perfect for that hard-to-find gift.

SUSAN TUNICK
Artist and writer

4.15 Singer Building

1904, Ernest Flagg
561 Broadway between Prince and Spring Streets

The two façades of Ernest Flagg's 1902–1904 Singer Building (the second façade pops out on Prince Street) rank among the most innovative structural and material expressions of New York architecture. Combining glazed and buff terra-cotta tiles, florid wrought iron and structural steel, and large panes of glass in different planes, the building is one of the most sophisticated responses to a strain of French architecture usually overshadowed by the Beaux Arts. It provided a richly suggestive direction for New York's high-rise architecture, yet had a disappointingly small progeny. Ten years later, Flagg offered a more refined variant on the theme in his building for Scribner's Bookstore (now a Sephora) on Fifth Avenue at 48th Street.

BARRY BERGDOLL
Philip Johnson Chief Curator of Architecture and Design, Museum of Modern Art

Savoir Fare

4.17 **Balthazar**
80 Spring Street between Broadway and Crosby Street
212 965 1414; www.balthazarny.com

4.18 **Savoy**
70 Prince Street at Crosby Street
212 219 8570; www.savoynyc.com

There are two restaurants that I rely on for sustenance. The busy, often crowded Balthazar is a terrific place for breakfast. When you walk in you can pick up *The New York Times*, bring it to your table, and read it over a cappuccino or a bowl of café au lait. You can also, if you wish, have delicious rolls—plain or sweet—or eggs Benedict or whatever pleases you. It is easily the most relaxed breakfast that I know. I sometimes go to Balthazar for dinner, and I like to be seated near the entrance. If I am early, I can catch the stylish and often outrageously attired guests making their entrance.

Perhaps my favorite place in which to eat, at least in downtown Manhattan, is the very intimate and not overly expensive Savoy. One has a choice of eating downstairs in a comfortable atmosphere, selecting a meal from a varied menu, or upstairs, in a smallish room with logs burning in the fireplace, where one eats from a prix-fixe menu. Whether one chooses downstairs or upstairs, the food will be delicious. The wine list is small but brilliantly selected. In all the years I have been eating there, I have not been disappointed with any meal. The people who work at Savoy are without question the friendliest yet least obtrusive of restaurant personnel. It is a great place to finish off the day.

MARK STRAND
Poet

4.19 E. R. Butler & Co.

53–55 Prince Street between Mulberry and Lafayette Streets
212 925 3565; www.erbutler.com
By appointment only.

Shopping at this hardware showroom is like a visit to Berry Brothers & Rudd Ltd., wine merchants to the Queen—you sit at a lovely mahogany table (in Butler's case, designed by the fine-furniture maker Chris Lehrecke) and the hardware is brought to you. It feels more like a museum of architectural hardware than a place to buy a latch set and a pair of hinges. Whether you are looking for a traditional, authentic early-American door handle or one designed by the philosopher Ludwig Wittgenstein, the Bauhaus master Walter Gropius, or the contemporary architect Richard Meier, you will find it here. If it exists, they have it; if it doesn't, they will make it for you, in any of seventy-five hand-finished metal patination formulas, including sterling silver. (And should you need to jot down a thought, the notepads are engraved.)

Behind this quiet and elegant showroom is a high-tech and sophisticated enterprise, including state-of-the-art CNC machines, prototype development, as well as antique conservation and restoration. There is even a library with five thousand rare trade catalogs, six thousand original drawings, and thousands of original hardware patterns.

The only catch (so to speak) is that the showroom is open to design professionals and their clients by appointment, and to the rest of you by pleading.

ROBERT KAHN
Architect

WNYC
820 AM or 93.9 FM

The best way to wake up and get your news—never too harsh or hyped, a gentle nudge into your day.

ERIC STOLTZ
Actor

NOLITA & LITTLE ITALY

4.20 St. Patrick's Old Cathedral

1815, Joseph Mangin
260–264 Mulberry Street between East Houston and Prince Streets
www.oldcathedral.org

Old St. Patrick's is a very charming brick church with a lot of greenery around it, an unexpected piece of the nineteenth century. Formally opened in 1815 to a crowd of more than four thousand worshippers and dignitaries, it was New York's first cathedral, the second Roman Catholic church in America, and the first house of worship in the United States to be dedicated to Ireland's patron saint, Patrick. The building was engulfed by a fire in 1866, which destroyed all but the outer walls, but was reconstructed in two years' time. It is surrounded on Mott, Prince, and

Mulberry Streets by a beautiful brick wall, built to protect the cathedral from the frequent brawls and street riots between Protestants and Catholics. When the Cardinal's seat was moved uptown to the new St. Patrick's Cathedral on Fifth Avenue, dedicated in 1879, the historic St. Patrick's downtown became a parish church.

JOAN SILBER
Writer

4.21 Storefront for Art and Architecture

1993, Steven Holl and Vito Acconci
97 Kenmare Street at Cleveland Place
212 431 5795; www.storefrontnews.org

On a small plot of land at the crossroads of SoHo, Little Italy, and Chinatown, a storefront façade uniquely defines its turf. In renovating a space to be dedicated to showing architectural schemes and urban plans, utopian or dystopian, Holl and Acconci conceived a wall that transforms itself from a blank surface into a geometric plane, hinged within to allow for bold opening sections that pivot out into the street. Windows and a door appear, then disappear, reverting to the planar surface from which they emerged. But the intellectual excitement of all this is in the realization of a kind of paper architecture in the very materials of the façade itself.

MARJORIE WELISH
Poet, artist, and art critic

The design of this gallery provides New York with a genuine stage for urban theater. The unfolding wall establishes a threshold that takes art into the street and brings people close to the exhibits.

IAIN LOW
Architect, and professor of architecture, University of Cape Town

5
W 16th St
E 16th St
W 15th St
E 15th St
W 14th St
E 14th St
W 13th St
E 13th St
W 12th St
E 12th St
W 11th St
E 11th St
W 10th St
E 10th St
W 9th St
E 9th St
W 8th St
E 8th St
Union Square W
Fifth Avenue
Sixth Avenue
Seventh Avenue
Sixth Avenue (Avenue of the Americas)
Milligan Pl
Patchin Pl
W 11th St
Perry St
Greenwich Avenue
Charles St
W 10th St
Waverly Pl
Christopher St
Gay St
W 4th St
Seventh Avenue South
Grove St
Sheridan Square
Washington Pl
W 4th St
Barrow St
Jones St
Cornelia St
Bleecker St
Commerce St
Morton St
Leroy St
Minetta Ln
Father Demo Sq
Minetta St
Winston Churchill Square
Carmine St
Bedford St
Downing St
W Houston St
King St
Charlton St
Vandam St
Spring St
MacDougal Alley
Washington Mews
Waverly Pl
Washington Sq N
Washington Sq W
Washington Square Park
Washington Sq E
University Pl
Washington Sq S
W 4th St
W 3rd St
MacDougal St
Sullivan St
Thompson St
La Guardia Pl
Bleecker St
W Houston St
SoHo
Sullivan St
Thompson St
West Broadway
Wooster St
Greene St
Green Vil
Washi
2
3
4
5
6
7
8
9
10
11
12
13
14
15
16
17
18
19
20
21
22
23
24
25
26
27
28
29
30
31
32
33
38
14
13
12
11
9
10
7
8
3
5
4
6
2
1

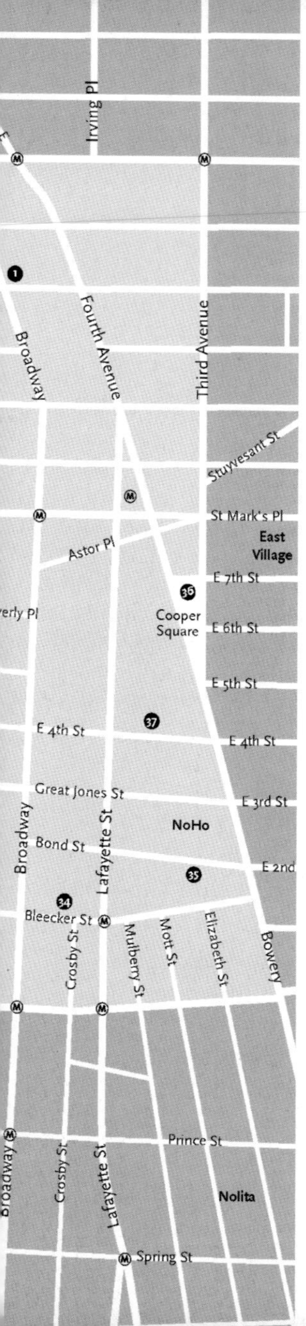

CHAPTER 5

GREENWICH VILLAGE

- 1 Strand Book Store
- 2 Forbes Magazine Building
- 3 Church of the Ascension (see p. 172)
- 4 Second Cemetery
- 5 Milligan Place
- 6 Patchin Place
- 7 Jefferson Market Library
- 8 Three Lives & Co.
- 9 Patisserie Claude
- 10 Home of W. H. Auden
- 11 Pearl Oyster Bar (see p. 54)
- 12 Blue Hill (see p. 54)
- 13 Washington Square Park
- 14 Provincetown Playhouse
- 15 Ottomanelli & Sons
- 16 John's Pizzeria
- 17 Cones
- 18 Murray's Cheese Shop
- 19 Faicco's Pork Shop
- 20 Rocco's Pastry Shop
- 21 Winston Churchill Square
- 22 Minetta Triangle
- 23 Father Demo Square
- 24 Minetta Lane
- 25 Joe's Pizza
- 26 Bagels on the Square
- 27 Trattoria Spaghetto
- 28 Da Silvano
- 29 Bar Pitti
- 30 'ino
- 31 The Grey Dog's Coffee
- 32 Village Comics
- 33 University Village
- 34 Bayard Building
- 35 Il Buco
- 36 Cooper Union
- 37 Merchant's House Museum
- 38 Former Asch Building

Greenwich Village

5.1 Strand Book Store

828 Broadway at East 12th Street

212 473 1452; www.strandbooks.com

For more than twenty years I've lived within a three minute walk to the Strand Book Store, which means I've had to contend with more than two decades of sheer temptation. The Strand's celebrated claim of "over eighteen miles of used books" certainly can no longer be true; I've purchased at least a mile's worth myself.

Now almost the last remnant in what used to be a thriving district of used-book and print shops, the Strand boasts a splendid selection of used books in all fields, along with extensive discounted offerings of review books. In addition, I will confess to enjoying a vicarious kick by purchasing discarded volumes from distinguished owners; my shelves contain books once owned by Elizabeth Hardwick, Aileen Ward, John Simon, and Joseph Alsop, among others.

Big, dusty, sometimes a bit confusing, often crowded, and resolutely unair-conditioned, the Strand remains a stalwart institution dedicated to the hopelessly addicted bibliophile.

RICHARD LAVENSTEIN
Architect

5.2 Forbes Magazine Building and Galleries

1925, Carrère & Hastings and Shreve & Lamb

62 Fifth Avenue at 12th Street

212 206 5548; www.forbesgalleries.com

The galleries are closed Sundays and Mondays.

The Forbes Building was built as the American headquarters for the British publisher, Macmillan. Architect Thomas Hastings of Carrère & Hastings (The New York Public Library) died before completion; the successor architects were Shreve & Lamb (Empire State Building). Elements of both firms' styles are visible here. The member of the Macmillan family who selected architects and oversaw construction was Harold Macmillan, who left publishing to go into politics when he returned to the U.K. and ended up Prime Minister. The building and adjacent 1840s brownstone were acquired by Forbes Inc. in 1964; the ground floor now houses the Forbes Magazine Galleries.

Shortly after the entire ground floor of the building opened as the Forbes Magazine Galleries in 1986, a friend of my father turned to him and laughingly observed, "Malcolm, that's the happiest sequence of non sequiturs I've ever experienced." Featuring a staggering archive of American historical documents, the earliest surviving renderings of the game Monopoly, an armada of toy boats, platoons of toy soldiers, inscribed trophies, and rotating exhibitions of paintings and photographs, the galleries are an evolving manifestation of the diverse collecting enthusiasms of three generations of Forbeses.

CHRISTOPHER FORBES
Vice chairman, Forbes Inc.

My vote for the best little jewel of a museum (and free to boot) is the Forbes Galleries in the lobby of the Forbes Magazine Building on Fifth Avenue. Apparently Malcolm Forbes's interests in collecting crossed many borders. Until recently, it featured the world's largest collection of Fabergé eggs. There is a fabulous collection of historical memorabilia, including the bill for Paul Revere's ride (who knew he was a consultant?) and Lincoln's opera glasses. The collection of toy tin soldiers and boats and the prototypes for the original Monopoly game are also wonderful.

MARIA MANHATTAN
Artist

5.4 Second Cemetery of the Spanish and Portuguese Synagogue

1805–1829

72–76 West 11th Street between Fifth and Sixth Avenues

In the middle of frenetic Manhattan, along one of the loveliest tree-lined streets in Greenwich Village, it is possible to miss one of the city's most unusual little gems if you walk too quickly. There, nestled along the south side of 11th Street, just a few feet from the streaming traffic along Sixth Avenue, is a tiny triangle that comprises one of the city's few Spanish-Portuguese-Jewish cemeteries. Scattered haphazardly on the small plot are a handful of simple weathered tombstones—somehow, in the midst of Manhattan's mad rush for development, this sacred corner of the dead survived intact. Today, occupying a tiny slice of real estate, this is a completely different stop for any city visitor. When finished, go to French Roast on the corner of West 11th Street and Sixth Avenue, and toast the dead with a good glass of house wine.

GERALD POSNER
Journalist and author

It is typical of New York that, unlike any other major city in the world, it does not have a recognizable and accessible cemetery. No Highbury, no Père-Lachaise, no San Michele. Maybe this lack of graveyard gravitas comes from the famous Gotham mercenary attitude; the lust for power and wealth have little to do with bones moldering six feet under.

There is, however, a tiny Jewish cemetery on West 11th. The men and women buried there came to New York in the early nineteenth century as refugees from South America in the wake of upheavals surrounding independence. There are a couple dozen headstones with Hebrew writing, two tombs, and an ivy-strewn brick walkway that meanders through the plots. But the walkway has nowhere to go. The cemetery is a triangle, no more than thirty feet in any direction, appallingly hemmed in on all sides by the city—by an apartment building, a brick wall, and a sidewalk. The hemming-in was so violent that more than one gravestone is a part of the brick wall that lies on its western and southern edge. The forces of real estate were so powerful that someone simply built walls through the gravestones.

The cemetery has a sad appearance, especially in a downpour, this forgotten place, no one to come to tend to the graves, and no one alive who knows any of the people resting there.

JAMES ZUG
Historian, journalist, and author

Greenwich Village Stroll

5.5 Milligan Place

1852

Sixth Avenue between West 10th and West 11th Streets

5.6 Patchin Place

1849

Off West 10th Street between Greenwich and Sixth Avenues

3.7 Grove Court

1854

Grove Street between Bedford and Hudson Streets

3.10 Home of Edna St. Vincent Millay

1873

75 1/2 Bedford Street between Morton and Commerce Streets
Not open to the public.

5.10 **Home of W. H. Auden**
7 Cornelia Street between Bleecker and West 4th Streets
Not open to the public.

6.23 **Home of W. H. Auden**
77 St. Mark's Place between First and Second Avenues
Not open to the public.

Let me take you away from the hurly-burly of Broadway, the elegant shops of Madison Avenue, and the dazzling corridors of art offered by the Metropolitan Museum. And where shall I lead you? Downtown on a ten-minute walk to some of the smallest and most poetic streets in Manhattan's Greenwich Village. Each is a gated cul-de-sac, tucked away from the furors of urban life and festooned in a quiet otherworldliness. The first and smallest is Milligan Place; you will need to look really sharp to espy it on the west side of the avenue, opposite Jefferson Market. There, inside the marked gate, a wee cluster of homes appears to belong to a private world. Built in the 1850s, they were conceived as boarding houses for Basque waiters and workers employed nearby. Farther west, off 10th Street, is Patchin Place—with two rows of diminutive dwellings dating from 1848; they, too, were built as boarding houses for toiling New Yorkers. At No. 4, near the gate, lived the poet E. E. Cummings, and at various times Patchin Place was the home of Djuna Barnes, Theodore Dreiser, and Padraic Colum. Continue west on 10th Street, turn south on Seventh Avenue, and west on Grove Street, mindful to keep looking sharp. Between Bedford and Hudson Streets you will come to Grove Court with its row of Victorian houses built in the mid-1850s, again for the working class. Compared with the heft of skyscrapers profiling the city, you will surely find the houses in each of these charmed groves doll-like in their proportions. You are also likely to comment on the irregularity of the early property lines that define them—no right angles here. Leon Trotsky, who arrived as an exile in New York in 1917 looking for working-class quarters and found them in the Bronx, characterized the dominant geometric pattern of New York's layout as "a triumph of Cubism." In an earlier century, Thomas Paine, the ex-corset maker from England turned eloquent revolutionary, found refuge during the final years of his life at various addresses amidst the wavering property lines of the West Village area. A brilliant proponent of American independence and author of *Common Sense* (1776), Paine died sad and lonely in the year 1809 in the back room of a frame dwelling on the site of what is now 59 Grove Street. But sadness will not be yours in the beckoning, small-street intimacy that defines the Village. There are colorful crowds, lively art galleries, and shops throughout, as well as cafés aplenty for a lingering cappuccino and conversation. Artists and writers who made—and still make—the Village their home are too numerous to mention, but you should take a look while you are in this area at the narrowest house in the Village located at 75½ Bedford Street (see p. 56). In the early 1920s, it was the home of the poet Edna St. Vincent Millay, who was moved to write that

> *The trees along this city street . . .*
> *Would make a sound as thin and sweet*
> *As trees in country lanes.*

W. H. Auden chose the Village as the locus of his several dwellings here and abroad, living at 7 Cornelia Street and then at 77 St. Mark's Place. In 1969 he declared,

> *My Eden landscapes and their climes*
> *Are constructs from Edwardian times.*

GLORIA DEAK
Writer

5.7 Jefferson Market Library and Garden

1877, Frederick Clark Withers and Calvert Vaux
425 Sixth Avenue at West 10th Street
☎ 212 243 4334; www.jeffersonmarketgarden.org

Smack in the middle of bustling, downtown Sixth Avenue, you will find a magnificent and elaborate concoction of a building, the Jefferson Market Library. Originally a courthouse (1876–1945) with an adjacent prison and market (both torn down in 1929 and replaced by a Women's House of Detention), this neighborhood library is a wonder of arches and turrets and stained-glass windows. It looks, as my daughter says, like a castle in a fairy tale. There is even a clock tower. In rare, quiet moments, you can hear the bell, which once summoned volunteer firemen, chime out the time.

The country's attention was focused on the original courthouse in 1906, when Harry K. Thaw was tried here for the murder of architect Stanford White. White's affair with chorus girl/model Evelyn Nesbit before her marriage to Thaw was the motive in this crime of passion, an episode captured by E. L. Doctorow in *Ragtime*.

Behind the library, largely hidden from view on Sixth Avenue, is the Jefferson Market Garden—a beautiful oasis in the middle of city gridlock. In the early 1970s, the Women's House of Detention on this site was closed, then demolished, creating the opportunity for this garden, now a beloved feature of the Greenwich Village Historic District. You will find wooden benches hidden among flowers, a small pond with fish and a fountain, and an arch with climbing vines marking the garden's perimeter path. Flowerbeds, dripping with color and scent, continue to change throughout the seasons. A luscious green lawn fills the middle—not to walk on, just to gaze upon.

The entrance to the garden is on Greenwich Avenue, and when the gates are open, there is a table with a volunteer or two, and a donation box, out front. Walk slowly along the garden path, and note the labels identifying the wide variety of flowers. If you are lucky, you may snag a bench for a little while. The city and its traffic never completely disappear, but they are held at bay in this garden, behind its lovely wrought-iron fence, a bequest of the Astor Foundation. 5

ELISSA STEIN
Graphic designer, illustrator, and writer

5.8 Three Lives & Co.

154 West 10th Street at Waverly Place
212 741 2069; www.threelives.com

Three Lives & Co. is one of the great small bookstores in the world. It is staffed by avid, eccentric readers, any one of whom, if asked, will recommend books on any subject. They are often books of which you have never heard; they are always revelations. Three Lives stocks a catholic selection of new books and a smattering of old ones, but trying to describe it in terms of its stock and even its remarkable staff is a little like trying to describe a face by offering the precise locations of the mouth, nose, and eyes. Three Lives is magical, utterly mysterious; it is enormously hospitable; it shines. I go there not only to buy books but sometimes simply to be reminded of why one writes books. I once asked the former owners if I could someday be buried there, under the floorboards in the southwest corner, but they told me they weren't zoned for that.

MICHAEL CUNNINGHAM
Writer

5.9 Patisserie Claude

187 West 4th Street between Sixth and Seventh Avenues
212 255 5911

Patisserie Claude is coincidentally owned and operated by a permanently taciturn man named Claude. Patisserie is the key word here: walk in and innocently ask for bread and Claude or one of his minions, if they are feeling kindly that day, will inform you that they know how to spell *boulangerie* and do you see *boulangerie* in the name of the store, you *américain stupide*? No bread, only pastry and maybe you should go away for a while.

First impressions can be telling. When I first met Claude some fifteen or so years ago, I was intimidated by his gruff manner and thought him to be cold, aloof, and disdainful. I now know that he *is* cold, aloof, and disdainful. Which doesn't mean a thing because Claude does make the best croissant, brioche, and *pain au chocolat* in the city. His fruit tarts are near equals to the tarts my wife's great aunt, Marie-Rose, used to cook up in Cannes, and to get them you don't have to sleep on that lumpy mattress and listen endlessly to Charles Trenet.

Claude has a simple rule. Less is more may fly in certain architectural circles, but not for Claude. Claude, like Albert Einstein, sought a central unifying theme to the universe. Unlike Albert, Claude found it, and it is called butter. More is better. Each croissant has at least a stick of butter in it and is the better for it. My visiting French relatives and friends generally drop their bags at the house and make a beeline for Claude's because they claim it is very difficult to get croissants, etc. that good in Paris anymore.

Claude's has a couple of perfunctory tables up front

where you can sip your coffee, look pensive in your beret, and eat the best patisserie in the city. But whatever you do, don't ask for bread.

ANDREW S. PAUL
Attorney

NOTE: Patisserie Claude is now owned and run by one of Claude's longtime employees; however, the patisseries are just as good as they were when Claude was in charge.

5.13 Washington Square Park

At the foot of Fifth Avenue
www.nycgovparks.org

"The Secret Worlds of Washington Square" would be an essay describing the multiple societies that coexist yet seldom interact in this treasured public space. Here are dog owners (large and small, separated by different exercise yards), chess players, musicians, amateur gardeners, students, lonely squirrel and pigeon feeders (each jealously guarding her bit of pavement), photographers, runners, bocce players . . . all dutifully recorded by busloads of tourists. As an N.Y.U. professor who has lived in the West Village for forty years, I pass through the park almost daily and love it as one who has seen—and participated in—its struggle against oblivion. Practically every book about the city repeats the facts and myths that have accumulated since the area was, first, a graveyard for slaves, then a drill ground for Revolutionary troops.

GEORGE C. STONEY
Filmmaker and Professor Emeritus, Tisch School of the Arts

When the city sizzles, and it's impossible to find a spot of concrete at any public pool, the Washington Square Park fountain offers a downtown oasis. With its wide seating area and five mighty water jets, it's one of the few fountains where jumping in and getting soaked is customary. The spot is never overcrowded (nearly empty before noon), and a midday splash is akin to a Midwestern run through the front yard sprinkler (though at a hundred times the power).

SCOTT HESS
Screenwiter, performer, and writer

Theater al Fresco

5.13 **Washington Square Park**
At the foot of Fifth Avenue

5.14 **Provincetown Playhouse**
133 MacDougal Street at West 3rd Street
www.nyu.edu/construction/provincetown

Washington Square Park is always alive, especially on the weekends, with music, acrobats, clowns, stand-up comics, people hanging out, every breed of dog being walked, kids on swings. In the summer nights you might stumble across a group of young actors doing a Shakespeare play by flashlight. And there's the statue of Garibaldi, reminding us that the leader of the Risorgimento, the revolutionary movement that united Italy, lived right here in New York and worked in Staten Island at a candle factory. Cut down MacDougal Street and look in at the Provincetown Playhouse, where modern American theater was born, thanks to Eugene O'Neill. (Until a couple of years ago the original set for *The Emperor Jones* was still part of the permanent structure of the stage.) Now you're in the Village, and it's still the best part of town.

JOHN GUARE
Playwright

Village Breadbasket

5.15 Ottomanelli & Sons
285 Bleecker Street between Seventh Avenue South and Jones Street
☎ 212 675 4217

5.16 John's Pizzeria
278 Bleecker Street between Jones and Morton Streets
☎ 212 243 1680; www.johnsbrickovenpizza.com

5.17 Cones
272 Bleecker Street between Jones and Morton Streets
☎ 212 414 1795

5.18 Murray's Cheese Shop
254 Bleecker Street at Cornelia Street
☎ 212 243 3289; www.murrayscheese.com

5.19 Faicco's Pork Shop
260 Bleecker Street between Morton and Cornelia Streets
☎ 212 243 1974

5.20 Rocco's Pastry Shop
243 Bleecker Street between Leroy and Carmine Streets
☎ 212 242 6031; www.roccospastry.com

5.21 Sir Winston Churchill Square
West side of Sixth Avenue where Downing Street meets Bleecker Street
www.nycgovparks.org

5.22 Minetta Triangle
Northeast corner of Sixth Avenue and Minetta Street
www.nycgovparks.org

5.23 Father Demo Square
Intersection of Carmine and Bleecker Streets and Sixth Avenue

🍴🍷 🎁 In the area popularly considered Little Italy, the Italian inhabitants are now only a memory. Except for a couple of tenacious survivors and a row of tourist restaurants, the area is now, for all practical purposes, part of Chinatown. If you want a sense of Little Italy as it used to be, go to Bleecker Street between Sixth Avenue and Seventh Avenue. From the turn of the century to the 1940s, this block, which has been called the "breadbasket of the Village," was choked with pushcarts selling provisions to the primarily southern Italian population. Following the passage of stricter sanitary laws, much of this commerce moved indoors; several stores established at that time still survive.

Beginning at Sixth Avenue, on the north side of Bleecker, is Ottomanelli & Sons, the butcher shop. The Ottomanelli family immigrated to New York from Bari in 1900 and established itself in the wholesale meat business. Their store opened on Bleecker Street in the 1940s. Since that time, it is substantially unchanged—it remains a real, old-fashioned butcher shop, with a long counter, huge hams and sides of beef hanging in the window, and personal service.

Across the street is John's Pizzeria. Founded in 1929 by John Sasso, John's famously does not sell single slices. But that's okay—the pizza is so good you'll want a whole one. The restaurant is now run by the nephew of the original John, and it's a good celebrity-spotting site, frequented by Woody Allen, Johnny Depp, Danny DeVito, Jack Nicholson, Mary Tyler Moore, and Matt Dillon, among others.

Next door is Cones. Self-described "ice-cream artisans" Oscar and Raul D'Aloisio make what is arguably not only the most authentically Italian gelato but the best ice cream of any kind in the city. The brothers come from Buenos Aires, where there is a large Italian community. Oscar says that when he tasted Häagen-Dazs ice cream, he thought, "This is the best America has to offer?" and decided to come over and show us what ice cream should be. The flavors, especially the fruit flavors, are startlingly intense and authentic. I also recommend the zabaglione.

Founded in 1940 as a wholesale vendor of butter and eggs, Murray's Cheese Shop used to be around the corner on Cornelia Street. The new, larger shop may not be as quaint as the old one, but it no longer has a perpetual line of waiting customers spilling out the door. They stock more than two-hundred-and-fifty different kinds of cheese from countries all over the world; if you've heard of a cheese, they have it. They also sell delicatessen fare such as olives, salami, prosciutto, and prepared foods.

Back on the south side of the street is another deli, Faicco's Pork Shop. As the blue pig on the storefront sign proudly announces, this store was founded in 1900, making it the oldest on the block (although it only moved from Thompson Street to its present location in the 1940s). Originally they sold only pork, and although they now sell a range of other Italian foods, too, their glory is still their pork sausage, which you can watch them make right in the shop.

For about eighty years, the Sixth Avenue end of the block was distinguished by its two side-by-side pastry shops—Bleecker Street Pastry and Rocco's. Bleecker Street Pastry was recently replaced by Pasticceria Bruno, and is now very elegant and upscale, although it retains the old decor. But Rocco's continues the same as ever. If you've ever been to Italy, the smell of anise as you walk in the door will take you right back. Everything in Rocco's is extraordinarily cheap and unself-consciously Italian, from the nuclear-blue and hot-pink decorations on some of the cakes to the hand-filled cannoli to the pink-and-green neon decor. Particularly noteworthy is their freshly baked, authentic tasting panettone—a hard-to-find treasure outside of Italy except during the Christmas season. In the summer they offer refreshing Italian ices, of which the hazelnut is especially good.

If you live near Bleecker Street, you can still do your shopping the old-fashioned way, with daily trips to the butcher, the baker, the dairy, and the greengrocer. If you're from farther away, try coming down on a nice day and assembling a picnic lunch as you walk down the block. Where Bleecker intersects Sixth Avenue, several tiny parks have recently been redesigned and offer restful places to eat. In the triangle formed by Downing and Bleecker Streets, Winston Churchill Square offers winding paths and benches around a sundial in the form of an armillary sphere. On the other side of the avenue, the even smaller Minetta Triangle has a few shady, secluded seats. Or if you prefer a more urban atmosphere, the older Father Demo Square between the two is an open brick plaza with trees, benches, and lots of street life and pigeons.

JANET B. PASCAL
Writer and production editor, Viking Children's Books

Father Demo Square

5.23 **Father Demo Square**
Intersection of Carmine and Bleecker Streets and Sixth Avenue
www.nycgovparks.org

5.21 **Sir Winston Churchill Square**
West side of Sixth Avenue where Downing Street meets Bleecker Street
www.nycgovparks.org

5.24 **Minetta Lane**
South of West 3rd Street, between Sixth Avenue and MacDougal Street

5.25 **Joe's Pizza**
7 Carmine Street at Bleecker Street
212 366 1182; www.joespizzanyc.com

5.26 **Bagels on the Square**
7 Carmine Street between Bleecker Street and Sixth Avenue
212 691 3041

5.27 **Trattoria Spaghetto**
232 Bleecker Street at Carmine Street
212 255-6752; www.trattoriaspaghetto.com

5.28 **Da Silvano**
260 Sixth Avenue between Bleecker and West Houston Streets
212 982 2343; www.dasilvano.com

5.29 **Bar Pitti**
268 Sixth Avenue between Bleecker and West Houston Streets
212 982 3300

Arrive hungry: you are at the threshold of great treats. But before you indulge, pause a few moments in this charming piazza. More triangle than not, this étoile stands at the crossroads of Sixth Avenue, Bleecker, Carmine, Downing, and Minetta Streets. Father Demo, the Italian-born pastor of nearby Our Lady of Pompeii Church, was lauded for his Herculean efforts during the famed Triangle Shirtwaist Company Fire of 1911 (see p. 100). In thanks, the Borough of Manhattan commemorated his life's work with this brick-paved homage.

Bordered to the southwest by the majestic single-domed church, the square spills onto Downing Street, at whose feet sits tiny, impeccable Churchill Square—a reference to the London abode of the only Prime Minister with a New Yorker mother. Folded into an adjacent corner of the park is a typical neighborhood playground, complete with whimsical frog and seal sculptures for climbing. (Discover, in a few paces's stroll along Downing Street, some of lower Manhattan's most interesting single-family residences.) Your bench on the east side of the piazza will provide an inimitable view north of both Jefferson Market Library and the Empire State Building. Also of note: Minetta Street, where Al Pacino's Serpico lived; and on the southeast corner of Bleecker Street and Sixth Avenue, the Little Red School House, an enduring neighborhood private school made famous by both Auntie Mame and the Rosenbergs.

And now you may eat, for Father Demo Square is home not only to Joe's Pizza and Bagels on the Square—both Village classics—but also Trattoria Spaghetto, where the finest bowl of minestrone soup on the island can be consumed. And if there's time for a proper meal, then by all means cross Sixth Avenue to the south and invest a couple of hours sitting outside at either Da Silvano or Bar Pitti. Known fondly to regulars as "first-class and coach," the relationship is as magnetically charged as that of Paris' Café de Flore and Les Deux Magots. Silvano costs more and takes major credit cards; Pitti is cheap and takes only cash. Both are delicious. Whichever you choose, you will not be sorry.

RACHAEL HOROVITZ
Film producer and co-founder of the Cinema School

Best Tuna

5.30 **'ino**
21 Bedford Street between Sixth Avenue and Downing Street
212 989 5769; www.cafeino.com

2.7 **Morgan's Market**
13 Hudson Street at Reade Street
212 964 4283

2.6 **Washington Market Park**
Greenwich Street between Chambers and Duane Streets

5.31 **The Grey Dog's Coffee**
33 Carmine Street between Bleecker and Bedford Streets
212 462 0041; www.thegreydog.com 5

As one who loves the city deeply, I offer you this favorite thing (of many) about New York: the tuna sandwich.

I want to omit any mention of tuna "steak," the slabs of rare tuna on toast (the Odeon! my favorite; see p. 38). What I prefer to recommend are tuna salad sandwiches, those that originate in a can and are easy to eat with one hand while turning pages of a book or properly folded newspaper. Here are three personal favorites:

1. The tuna *tramezzini* at 'ino. Tuna in a bit of oil with caperberries and black olive pesto on Pullman bread with the crust removed. Two subway cars side by side could just fit into this little room with a scuffed floor on an aging side street. Have wine and coffee with your sandwich and, after lunch, stumble left to the Village or right into SoHo.

2. Tuna with lettuce on a pita at Morgan's Market in TriBeCa. Kind of creamy, kind of plain, kind of perfect tuna salad. There's no place to sit down here (it's a market). You can carry your lunch bag a block down Reade Street to Washington Market Park, a nice patch of tree-lined grass with a playground and benches. Hudson River Park (see p. 34), only two long blocks west, is right on the water.

3. The No. 8 at Grey Dog. Dense, happy tuna with lettuce and tomato and one secret ingredient—relish—on sponge-sized slabs of big fresh bread. Order your sandwich at the counter and find a little table. FM music and doggie biscuits; it's loud and dimly lit, in a good way, with moms

and writers and the occasional EMS girl or well-known actress, a little-known painter, a suit, a teacher, a couple of kids. Ain't life grand; it's that kind of place.

STACY COCHRAN
Filmmaker

5.32 Village Comics

214 Sullivan Street between Bleecker and West 3rd Streets
212 777 2770

There are comics stores in New York such as Forbidden Planet that cater to the superhero, alternative, and weirdo-comics aficionado, and then there's Village Comics, which appeals to the rest of us. Though not a big comic-book fan myself, I have a voyeuristic interest in the countercultures that comprise this fan base.

Village Comics is something of an epicenter for the underground, overground, and middle earth of comics. It sells the usual fare of DC and Marvel, the unusual oddities by the likes of Chris Ware, and for this voyeur, comic models—plastic, resin, and dolls galore. But don't let the *habitués* hear you say the word "dolls": they prefer the state-of-the-art term "action figures."

The store is fully stocked with action figures that you'll never see at Toys "R" Us, representing troops from the Civil War, World War II (German and American), Vietnam, members of SWAT teams, special forces, and more. The avid recreationist who builds large dioramas and vignettes in which these figures play will find a wall covered with doll clothes and miniature weaponry. Also in stock for the art enthusiast are resin models, samples of which are precisely constructed and displayed in glass reliquaries. Models on hand run the gamut from classic Revel snap-togethers of cars, ships, and planes to variations of odd comics characters in revealing, if not kinky, garb. There is also the requisite Adults Only section, which I have never dared enter, given the fact that whenever I'm in the store, I feel just like a kid.

STEVEN HELLER

Art director, writer, and co-chair of MFA/Design, The School of Visual Arts

5.33 University Village

1966, I.M. Pei & Partners

From Bleecker Street to West Houston Street, between LaGuardia Place and Mercer Street

Escape the hodgepodge of Greenwich Village into I. M. Pei's urban utopia. The three simple concrete towers stretch above the neighboring horizon, injecting light, air, and space into the otherwise crowded cityscape. Follow the rough-cut stone drive from Bleecker Street to a central square. Here you will be greeted by an enormous, thirty-six-foot-high cast-stone-and-concrete *Portrait of Sylvette* by Pablo Picasso. (This enlargement of Picasso's much smaller sculpture is the 1970 work of Carl Nesjar.) The combination of massive forms, idealism, and simplicity is truly impressive. A visit to this austere oasis never fails to leave me at peace.

GEORGIA O'NEAL

Owner, Tree and Leaf Farm

5.34 Bayard Building (originally Condict Building)

1899, Louis Sullivan

65 Bleecker Street between Broadway and Lafayette Street

This is the only Louis Sullivan building in New York and is pretty and calming to look at. I have always thought of it as the wedding-cake building. When it was built, architectural critic Carl Condit (not to be confused with the building's

first owner, Silas Condict), supposedly said, "Who would expect an aesthetic experience on Bleecker Street?"
JOAN SILBER
Writer

The only building in New York designed by Louis H. Sullivan is best viewed from the corner of Houston and Crosby on a sunny day when the filigreed terra-cotta-clad façade beams white. On the skyscraper of his time, Sullivan wrote: "It must be tall, every inch of it tall. The force and power of altitude must be in it." Commanding all of thirteen stories, the supporting columns indeed shoot skyward, giving way to arches, porthole windows, and heavy-handed ornamentation. Bring your binoculars to catch the dragonfly women—with arms and wings outstretched. They're the high altitude caryatids that carry the cornice and were reportedly added to the design against Sullivan's wishes.
FREDERIC SCHWARTZ AND TRACEY HUMMER
Architect and Writer

5.35 Il Buco

47 Bond Street between Lafayette Street and Bowery
212 533 1932; www.ilbuco.com

One of the most gracious dining experiences in Manhattan is, without doubt, Il Buco. In the capable hands of its proprietor, Donna Lennard, I have eaten many of my most memorable New York dinners. This unassuming gem serves an Italian cuisine in a cozy, yet lively setting. Ask for tips on the wine menu, as their steward is most knowledgeable and insightful. Octopus carpaccio is nicely paired with a glass of *prosecco* to start, moving on to roasted baby beets and goat cheese followed by any number of fish or pasta dishes accompanied by a beautiful, hot, crusty fresh bread soaked in deep green, first-press olive oil. Ask to eat in the wine cellar, which served as the inspiration for Edgar Allen Poe's *The Cask of Amontillado*. Call early for reservations, as this treasure has been discovered.

CAROLYN CARTWRIGHT

Feature-film set decorator and interior designer

5.36 The Cooper Union for the Advancement of Science and Art Foundation Building

1859, Frederick A. Peterson

7 East 7th Street at Cooper Square

212 353 4100; www.cooper.edu

Cooper Union is steeped in history. On February 27, 1860, Abraham Lincoln spoke in the Great Hall, effectively beginning his first presidential campaign. Abolitionist and women's rights activist Frederick Douglass spoke several times in the same hall. As a child, my maternal grandmother walked in yellow lamplight through a snowstorm with her parents, from her house on West 10th Street to Cooper Institute, to catch a glimpse of Lincoln. That walk still takes a visitor past some of New York's oldest and most charming houses.

PETER BURCHARD

The late Peter Burchard was an author, designer, and illustrator.

Although he had little formal education himself, the industrialist and philanthropist Peter Cooper envisioned a college of the first rank for the working-class and immigrant children of New York City. Strategically and symbolically placed between the Bowery and the more prosperous neighborhoods uptown, the tuition-free college was intended by its founder to break through the class boundary. As pointed out in a characteristic passage by Horatio Alger Jr., the building has entrances uptown and downtown, but the clock and its light face the Bowery.

A national and city historic landmark, the Italianate Foundation Building was designed by Frederick Peterson and, in 1859, was the tallest building in New York City. As the first thoroughly fireproof structure in the city, it set a standard for public safety in construction. It also included the round shaft requested by Peter Cooper in anticipation of the invention of the elevator. When the interior of the building was completely rebuilt in the 1970s, modern technology permitted the old rectangular elevator to be replaced by a cylindrical one.

Abolitionist William Lloyd Garrison and feminists Susan B. Anthony and Victoria Woodhull rallied against the injustices of their time and spearheaded great change in their speeches in the Great Hall of the Foundation Building, and it was there that Albert Einstein presented his transcendent ideas in physics.

GEORGE CAMPBELL JR.
Former president (retired), The Cooper Union for the Advancement of Science and Art

5.37 Merchant's House Museum

1832
29 East 4th Street between Lafayette Street and Bowery
212 777 1089; www.merchantshouse.com

In 1835, for eighteen thousand dollars, the merchant Seabury Tredwell bought an elegant three-year-old Greek Revival/Late Federal-style house on the outskirts of New York, at East 4th Street, and moved in with his large family, including five daughters and two sons. Five years later, his last daughter, Gertrude, was born. Seabury, whose ancestors had come over on the *Mayflower*, was a stern and devout man, and when Gertrude wanted to marry an Irish

Catholic doctor, he forbade her. She never married and continued to live in the house her whole life, first with her parents, then with three spinster sisters, and finally, when her money was gone, with paying guests. She died in the house in 1933 at ninety-three years of age. By then the area had changed from a wealthy and respectable suburb to one of the Lower East Side's crowded tenement neighborhoods, known for its bars and brothels. Outside the house, the world was altered completely, but inside, time stood still. Except for a very few modernizations, the house remained as it had been when Gertrude was young. According to one legend, Gertrude's haunting story was the inspiration for Henry James's *Washington Square*.

After her death, the house was given to the city, and it has been a museum ever since—one of the few places where you can see, not a re-creation of Victorian life, but the real thing. The lower floor houses the pantry, the family dining room, and the kitchen, where dishes and cookware still sit. The room is dominated by the black woodstove (which replaced the original fireplace). The sink is worked by a pump connected to a cistern filled with rainwater. Next to it stands the little round tub the family used for bathing. The legs on the pie safe are corroded where they were stood in glasses of water to keep vermin from the baked goods.

Visitors came to the elegant ground floor, containing the dining room and formal parlor decorated with columns, elaborate plasterwork, and magnificent marble fireplaces. To satisfy the Greek Revival desire for symmetry, the parlor was built with two heavy wooden doors—one to use, and a dummy that opens onto a blank brick wall, revealing the structure of the walls. Mrs. Tredwell redecorated in the 1860s to show the family's prosperity—she was trying to marry off six daughters. (Only two ever married.) The piano the girls used to entertain their guests, with an extra pedal meant to imitate an organ, stands by the window.

Upstairs are a small guest room and two separate bedrooms for Mr. and Mrs. Tredwell, connected by a private passageway. Mrs. Tredwell's mirror is lit by gas jets shaped to look like morning glories twining around the edge. The effect is very pretty, but it's a little frightening to imagine her doing up her hair just inches from two open jets of flame. Although the rooms are large and expensively decorated with gilded pressed-tin ornamentation, there are no closets. Houses were taxed according to the number of rooms, and closets counted as rooms. After Gertrude's death, the magnificent red damask bed curtains were found to be too decayed to salvage, but there was no need to try a modern re-creation; bolts of the original fabric were still stored in the attic.

There is a charming little garden in back, which now looks out on brick walls and barbed wire, but once backed onto the Vauxhall Pleasure Garden. You can see the domed top of the cistern, fed by a drainpipe from the roof, but the outhouse has been removed.

If you want to pretend you're a Victorian, the Old Merchant's House is the place to do it. And if you want to be reminded why you're glad you're not a Victorian, consideration of the throne-like mahogany commode in the bedroom, the small hand-filled and hand-emptied bathtub, or Gertrude's terrifyingly narrow corset should do it.

JANET B. PASCAL
Writer and production editor, Viking Children's Books

5.38 Former Asch Building, now the Brown Building

29 Washington Place at Greene Street

On March 25, 1911, a fire in the Asch building, one block east of Washington Square, took the lives of a hundred and forty-six garment workers, most of them young women, some little more than children. The Triangle Shirtwaist

Company occupied the top three floors of the ten-story building. The company's vast workrooms were packed with seamstresses and flammable materials. It was nearly quitting time when fire broke out on the eighth floor and spread swiftly to the upper floors. Flames blocked the only unlocked exits. A *New York Times* reporter wrote: "The girls rushed to the windows and looked down at Greene Street, a hundred feet below them. One poor little creature jumped. Then they all began to drop. A girl, who waved her handkerchief at the crowd, leaped from a window. Her dress caught on a wire and the crowd watched her hang there until the dress burned free and she came toppling down."

Social worker and reformer Frances Perkins, who was in the neighborhood when the fire alarms were sounded, rushed to Greene Street, where she saw heaps of broken bodies lying on the slate sidewalk. Outraged by the carelessness and greed that had made escape impossible, Perkins joined a campaign to eliminate the irresponsible and cruel labor practices that had led to the disaster. Workers like Rosie Yussum, who survived the fire, made it impossible to forget the people who had perished. Rosie said, "They didn't want to jump. They was afraid. They was saying their prayers first, and putting rags over their eyes so they should not see."

PETER BURCHARD

The late Peter Burchard was an author, designer, and illustrator.

6
Stuyvesant Park
E 14th St
E 13th St
E 12th St
E 11th St
E 10th St
E 9th St
St Mark's Pl (E 8th St)
E 8th St
E 7th St
E 6th St
E 5th St
E 4th St
E 3rd St
E 2nd St
E 1st St
E Houston St
Third Avenue
Second Avenue
First Avenue
Avenue A
Avenue B
Avenue C
Stuyvesant St
Shevchenko Pl
Tompkins Square Park
East Village
Bowery
Bleecker St
Mott St
Elizabeth St
Chrystie St
Forsyth St
Eldridge St
Allen St
Orchard St
Ludlow St
Essex St
Norfolk St
Suffolk St
Clinton St
Attorney St
Ridge St
Pitt St
Stanton St
Rivington St
Prince St
Lower East Side
Nolita
Delancey St
Spring St
Kenmare St
Broome St
Grand St
Cleveland Pl
Mulberry St
Sara D Roosevelt Park
Little Italy
Hester St
Seward Park
East Broadway
Jefferson St
Canal St
Rutgers St
Division St
Henry St
Madison St
Baxter St
Bayard St
Pell St
Chinatown

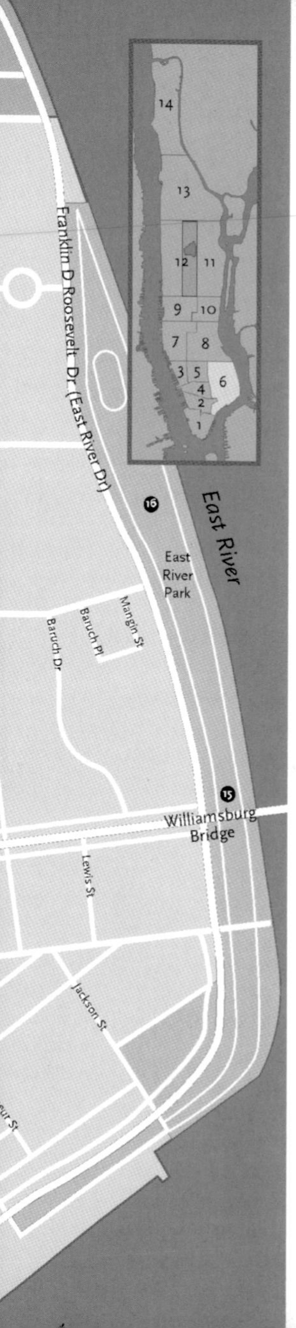

CHAPTER 6

LOWER EAST SIDE

1 Orensanz Foundation
2 Russ & Daughters
3 Katz's Delicatessen
4 Orchard Corset Center
5 Economy Candy
6 El Castillo de Jagua
7 First Roumanian Synagogue
8 Rosario's Pizza
9 Sara D. Roosevelt Park
10 Yonah Schimmel's Knishes
11 LES Tenement Museum
12 Williamsburg Bridge
13 Doughnut Plant
14 Eldridge Street Synagogue
15 East River Park Tennis Courts

EAST VILLAGE

16 East River Park
17 Tompkins Square Park: Fountain
18 Tompkins Square Park: Dog Run
19 Russian Turkish Baths
20 Monday Night Magic
21 Home of Emma Goldman (see p. 57)
22 St. Mark's-in-the-Bowery
23 Home of W. H. Auden (see p. 80)
24 Gem Spa Newsstand
25 McSorley's Old Ale House

Lower East Side & East Village

LOWER EAST SIDE

6.1 Angel Orensanz Foundation

1850, Alexander Saeltzer

172 Norfolk Street between Stanton and East Houston Streets

212 780 0175; www.orensanz.org

Designed under the spell of Hegel, Schinkel, Schiller, Heinrich Heine, and the German Romantic movement, this building was erected at the time of the great buildings of central Berlin of the 1840s—the Altes Museum, the Neue Museum, the Berlin Opera, the Berlin Concert Hall, Humboldt University, the Friedrichswerdesche Kirche, and others. The German-Jewish community that arrived in Manhattan in the 1840s asked Berlin architect Alexander Saeltzer to build a synagogue on Norfolk Street that would replicate the glory of the Cologne cathedral and the humanistic splendors of central Berlin. From here, the Jewish Reform movement would transform the cultural horizon of New York and the country.

Angel Orensanz Foundation, formerly the Congregation of Ansche Chesed, has a neo-Gothic main space of about seven thousand square feet with fifty-foot-high blue cathedral ceilings and soaring balconies. There is also an Assembly Room of about four thousand square feet. In 1986, the Angel Orensanz Foundation, established by sculptor Angel Orensanz, rescued the building from demolition. Some of New York's most creative recent projects have been staged here, including *City, Garbage and Death* by Rainer Werner Fassbinder; Alexander McQueen's first American fashion show; Mandy Patinkin's *Mamaloshen*; and George Frideric Handel's *Esther*, in its first full staging since the eighteenth century. This unique, breathtaking space has been used by a diverse group of people in the arts: Philip Glass, John Zorn, Lou Reed, the Kronos Quartet, Whitney Houston, Mariah Carey, Spike Lee, Cecil Taylor, Elie Wiesel, Maya Angelou, and Erica Jong, among others. As a space for culture, spirit, and high learning, the Orensanz Foundation sustains the vision and dream of those ninteenth-century reformers and humanists.

AL ORENSANZ
Director, Angel Orensanz Foundation

Loisada

6.2 **Russ & Daughters**
179 East Houston Street between Orchard and Allen Streets
212 475 4880; www.russanddaughters.com

6.3 **Katz's Delicatessen**
205 East Houston Street at Ludlow Street
212 254 2246; www.katzdeli.com

6.6 **El Castillo de Jagua**
113 Rivington Street between Essex and Ludlow Streets
212 982 6412

6.7 **First Roumanian-American Congregation Synagogue**
c. 1860
89-93 Rivington Street between Ludlow and Orchard Streets
212 673 2835

6.8 **Rosario's Pizza**
173 Orchard Street at Stanton Street
212 777 9813

6.9 **Sara D. Roosevelt Park**
East Houston Street to Canal Street between Chrystie and Forsyth Streets
www.nycgovparks.org

6.10 Yonah Schimmel's Knishes Bakery
137 East Houston Street at Forsyth Street
212 477 2858; www.knishery.com

For every American of Jewish descent there is a one-in-three chance that they had an ancestor who, upon arrival in this country, lived in the Lower East Side. One in three Puerto Ricans who have settled in the continental U.S. has a relative who has lived in that crowded corner of Lower Manhattan. The same one-in-three odds also apply to parents all over the U.S. who may have had a child run off to New York to be an artist. Unlike many sections of Manhattan where ethnic or cultural groups come and go, usually leaving nothing more than a few plaques or cleverly named coffee shops to commemorate their presence, the Lower East Side (LES), or Loisada if you're Latino or "down," still pulsates with the energy of each of these groups.

Begin at Houston Street (pronounced HOW-stun) and Orchard, which used to be the center of the Lower East Side when its boundaries extended north to 14th Street. (The blocks between Houston and 14th Street east of the Bowery are now called the "East Village," a designation begun in the 1950s to compete with the hip West Village.) Now Houston and Orchard is the northernmost part of the LES. Though there is no official signpost, two neon fish glowing over 179 East Houston Street can serve as your markers. They're perpetually swimming over Russ & Daughters, the last and best of the smoked fish and delicacy stores that used to dot the neighborhood. Though the space has remained small and unassuming, Russ & Daughters' selection and quality make stores like Zabar's and Dean & DeLuca look like, as my grandmother would say, "they don't know from fish." The place is a true microcosm of the LES, with Latin countermen who can banter with customers in Spanish-laced Yiddish (Spiddish) and the owner of the store, Mark Russ Federman, who manages it all with his Colombian wife, Maria. More Jews swear by their whitefish salad than they do by the Torah. Order a bagel to go, or get a few pounds of Gaspé salmon packed in ice and a tub of their incomparable whipped cream cheese. With one foot in 1900 and another in the present, you can grab an old-fashioned licorice whip and a cappuccino as you walk out the door.

A block east, on the corner of Ludlow, is Katz's Deli. Since 1888, Katz's has been churning out the best pastrami and corned beef in the city. You'll be given a ticket as you enter—your bill, which you will be expected to produce when you leave. Start at the counter on the far right with a hot dog, so you have something to nosh while countermen with flashing knives prepare your sandwiches. When a chunk of pastrami flies your way, it's not a mistake, you're being offered a taste (be sure to tip). You can even eat your sandwich in the same spot where Meg Ryan faked an orgasm in *When Harry Met Sally* (or the same chair in which my Uncle Irving did not fake it in 1944 over a particularly good brisket on rye).

Take a right upon leaving Katz's and stroll south down Ludlow. Remarkably, the thirty or so new bars that have sprung up over the past few years have not seriously impacted the authentic tenement feel of the street. Many original shop signs remain, though the stores they advertised are long gone. Have a drink at any of these hipster bars. There's a fifty-fifty chance that the grungy-looking kid sitting next to you is either an artist you just read about in *The Times* or an N.Y.U. student cutting class.

A couple of blocks south at 113 Rivington Street on the corner of Essex is one of the best inexpensive Latin restaurants in the city, El Castillo de Jagua. As a paroled friend of mine once said, "Any place where you can frequently find six or seven Latin cops eating has to be good." If matzo ball soup can cure a cold, their chicken (*sopa de pollo*) could raise the dead. It's just how your Jewish grandmother would have made it if she were Dominican, and yucca and cilantro had been available anywhere near Kiev. Castillo is especially known for seafood, so try their paella Valencia (yellow rice with seafood). And be sure to spend at least a dollar on the jukebox to get a crash course on the hottest salsa music. Unlike many other bars and restaurants in the city, you will have no problem hearing your selections playing, even a couple of blocks away. Any Jewish patrons feeling guilty from too much roast pork or *arroz con longosta* can walk a few blocks west to 89 Rivington to the First Roumanian-American Congregation Synagogue. Though not packed the way it would have been ninety years ago, there's rarely trouble getting a minyan for the 5 p.m. daily services.

About a block north on the corner of Stanton and Orchard is Rosario's Pizza, a neighborhood institution for more than thirty-eight years. The place is run by Salvatore Bartolomeo, who will also be heating up your slice, the best in the city. You'll recognize Sal because the walls of Rosario's are covered with photos of him, taken by numerous appreciative neighborhood photographers whom Sal feeds late into the night, even after he's posted the "Closed" sign.

Now take a slice three blocks west and one north to Sara D. Roosevelt Park, which runs from Houston to Canal between Chrystie and Forsyth. On the way, stop into any of the neighborhood bodegas and brown-bag a 40-ounce beer. Make it a malt liquor. Plant yourself on a park bench within this island of towering trees and basketball courts. You can watch a game of pickup or read Henry Roth's *Call It Sleep* and let the Yinglish of the kids in the book who played in the neighborhood eighty years ago mingle in your mind with the Spanglish of today's inhabitants.

For dessert, walk about twenty steps east to 137 Houston, since 1910 home of Yonah Schimmel's Knishes. As you

ascend the step into the doorway of the shop, you'll see an interior barely changed since its opening. You could be in Poland or Russia of a hundred years ago, except for the fact that punk rockers were probably having sex in that very doorway only hours before. Substitute Cossacks for punks and cross the threshold. Order a cheese knish. It's as though you've stepped into an Isaac Bashevis Singer novel, but better. In the shtetl you wouldn't hear motorcycles revving outside of the Hells Angels's headquarters a few blocks north or the Puerto Rican man on the corner, scraping a huge block of ice to make mango-flavored snow cones.
DAVID BAR KATZ
Writer and director

6.4 Orchard Corset Center

157 Orchard Street between Rivington and Stanton Streets
212 674 0786; www.orchardcorset.com

If you get your thrills wearing daring little pearl thongs, this is not the place for you. If, on the other hand, you prefer more serious support, then pay a visit to Ralph Berk at the Orchard Corset Center. Berk has an uncanny talent for serious bra counsel: from the outline of your shirt he'll guess your size with remarkable accuracy. And the prices! Wacoals—those French gifts to D-cups—are always on sale.
DANY LEVY
Founder, DailyCandy.com

6.5 Economy Candy

108 Rivington Street between Ludlow and Essex Streets
800 352 4544, www.economycandy.com

Started in the midst of the post-Depression era when candy still came in barrels, Economy Candy is a rickety little Lower East Side spot owned by Jerry Cohen, a grizzly New York City native with an auctioneer's voice and an attitude to match. This vintage candy warehouse brims floor to ceiling (literally—a stepladder is required) with jawbreakers, licorice whips, chocolate-covered raisins, root beer barrels, Chiclets, Pixy Stix, kosher gourmet jellybeans, and other Willy Wonka-like delicacies. A favorite of Jerry Lewis, Red Buttons, and Tony Curtis, Economy Candy was described by *Gourmet* magazine as "the penny-candy store elevated to an art form."

Other favorites include rock-candy swizzle sticks (red, blue, amber, yellow, pink, and green), Jordan Almonds, Atomic Fireballs, candy necklaces, eighteen kinds of halvah, chocolate-covered pretzels (milk, dark, and white), and Pez in every imaginable size and form. In fact, the only candy you won't find here is Chunky. "It's my favorite," says Cohen. "I don't sell it because I'd eat it all day long." At least the man shows some restraint.

DANY LEVY
Founder, DailyCandy.com

6.11 Lower East Side Tenement Museum

108 Orchard Street between Delancey and Broome Streets
212 431 0233; www.tenement.org
Guided tours only.

This is a breathtaking discovery, perfectly preserved on a busy Lower East Side street. You can touch and smell the world of the original immigrants and see what was overcome to succeed in New York City.

Here is the Lower East Side as gateway to America: the heart of this museum, the tenement at 97 Orchard Street, was home to an estimated seven thousand people from more than twenty nations between 1863 and 1935. It is now a National Historic Landmark. Visit and tour carefully-restored tenement apartments of actual past residents: German Jews (1870s), Eastern European Jews (1900s), and Italian Catholics (1930s). There is also a living-history program

focusing on Sephardic Jews from Turkey (1916). There will soon be apartments that interpret an 1893 sweatshop and an Irish family in residence during the Civil War.
JOHN PENOTTI
Founding partner, GreeneStreet Films

This museum is not your conventional installation of precious objects. Instead its apartments are more like a collection of time capsules ranging from the Civil War era to the early part of the twentieth century, each bearing witness to succeeding generations of immigration into the Lower East Side. Furnished with authentic period furniture and artifacts, these humble shelters for the genteel working poor give the visitor an almost eerie sense of association with the families who called these apartments home.

Be sure to take the complete tour with one of the very knowledgeable and enthusiastic guides. Any wait time can be put to good use wandering the narrow old streets nearby and maybe heading for one of the few remaining ethnic delis for some New York specialties. You'll feel like you're on the set of the *The Godfather*.
EVELYN AND PETER KRAUS
Proprietors, Ursus Books and Prints

6.12 Williamsburg Bridge

1903, Leffert L. Buck
From Delancey and Clinton Streets in Manhattan to Washington Plaza in Brooklyn

South Passage
Manhattan entrance at Delancey and Ridge Streets
Brooklyn entrance at Broadway and Roebling Street

In a rapidly gentrifying city, this temporary metal mesh cage provides a glimpse of the gritty, graffiti-covered dystopia of the 1970s. Built to protect bikers and pedestrians during the bridge's interminable reconstruction, this poor man's Pompidou offers the river and skyline to the south and the wheels and sparks of the adjacent J train to the north.

SEBASTIAN HARDY
Urban planner

6.13 Doughnut Plant

379 Grand Street between Essex and Norfolk Streets
212 505 3700; www.doughnutplant.com
Open Tuesdays to Sundays, from 6:30 a.m. until the doughnuts sell out.

Sandwiched between a thrift shop and a row of brick apartments, Doughnut Plant's storefront is easy to miss. But what lies within puts the franchise doughnut stores to shame.

One day, while sifting through boxes, Mark Isreal happened on some of his grandfather's recipes, so he whipped up a batch of doughnuts and tried selling them to his local coffee shop. The orders poured in literally overnight, and today Mark's doughnuts grace the counters at, among others, Dean & Deluca, Zabar's, and Balducci's. But for the real experience, head down to Grand Street and meet the man behind the doughnut.

This is not your average cop food. Flavors range from classic vanilla bean to ginger, lime, pistachio, and rose water, all hand-cut, hand-rolled, and fried in canola oil. Best of all, each doughnut measures roughly the size of a human head. In the words of *The New York Times*' Florence Fabricant, "a plusher chocolate doughnut than his Valrhona would be hard to find."

DANY LEVY
Founder, DailyCandy.com

6.14 Eldridge Street Synagogue

1887, Peter Herter & Francis Herter
12 Eldridge Street between Canal and Division Streets
The Museum at Eldridge Street
212 219 0888; www.eldridgestreet.org

Completed in 1887, Eldridge Street was the first synagogue in America built by Eastern European Jews. Which is to say, this synagogue is a link to an older New York that everybody knows about, some have family ties to, and hardly anyone has any contact with. The building itself, with seventy-foot ceilings, Moorish design, and a vast skylight, is beautiful. The fact that it still stands, and, amazingly, is still used for worship, is incredibly moving. The Museum at Eldridge Street hosts readings, concerts, and educational events at the synagogue; volunteer docents lead tours, complete with details that summon the old neighborhood and the synagogue's central place in its life. Imagine: mounted policemen were required for crowd control on the high holidays; people paid rent to reserve their seats in the pews. After exploring the synagogue, which also has a display of signs advertising rabbinical services and a collection of plaques depicting the Ten Commandments under the guard of carved lions—made by the same craftsmen who made the elaborate carousel horses then popular—take a look around the neighborhood. Part of Chinatown now (albeit far off the tourist track), it continues to serve new arrivals and provide an anchor for the next generation of New Yorkers.

MARTHA SCHULMAN
Writer and teacher

6.15 East River Park Tennis Courts

FDR Drive north of Delancey Street
212 533 0656; www.nycgovparks.org

For me, the quintessential New York experience must involve playing tennis. Where Delancey Street meets the river, there are twelve outdoor hard-surface courts at the Brian Watkins Tennis Center, in East River Park under the Williamsburg Bridge.

The most amazing thing about the experience of playing there, aside from seeing the same cronies every time (the guy who never has a racket or tennis shoes, but beats anyone and everyone, the "coach" who gives lessons but looks like he's too large to move around the court, the rooster who feeds on platters of rice and beans) is the incredible urban context in which the courts are situated. To one side is the East River with its stream of maritime traffic; above, the never-ending road-and-rail din of the Williamsburg Bridge; to the south, gatherings of family and friends, with music of the Caribbean islands, Puerto Rico, and the Dominican Republic often blaring from loudspeakers; and to the west, the East River Drive, a frequent route for fire engines and police cars.

With all this around you, it's imperative you work out some type of sign-language system with your partner for communicating (you can forget about even trying to hear the ball bounce!). Yet, despite the dissonance, one whiff of "sea" breeze can relax even the most stressed-out New Yorker.

All it requires is a fifty-dollar permit (good for one season, April 15 to October 15, at any city park court), available online, at Paragon Sporting Goods (867 Broadway between 17th and 18th Streets, 212 255 8036), and the courts in Central Park. Get there at least forty-five minutes before the hour to secure a court. If the winter is mild,

the nets don't come down and you can play all year long. Diehards have been known to show up with their own.
STEFANIE SILVERMAN
Architect

EAST VILLAGE

6.16 East River Park

East 12th Street to Montgomery Street between the East River and FDR Drive
www.nycgovparks.org

Grand Street Park, as it was known back then, was enlarged in 1946 when Marshall Plan Aid was taking food to bombed-out Europe. They needed ballast on the way back for the empty boats. When they got back to New York, they had to get rid of the ballast. The cheapest way was to dump it in the East River, off Grand Street Park, and enlarge the park. This kind of thing has been done for three hundred years, you know. Manhattan had about ten percent less acreage back in those days, maybe even less. Now when kids hopscotch in the park, they're doing it on Hitler's bunker.
PETE SEEGER
Songwriter

6.17 Tompkins Square Park

1834
East 7th Street to East 10th Street between Avenues A and B

Slocum Memorial Fountain
Mid-park near 9th Street
www.nycgovparks.org

When you walk through Tompkins Square Park, you pass clusters of old Ukrainians, old Italians, and old Slovaks; young Latino families, picnickers, skaters, people walking their dogs (or vice versa), "artsy" kids paying eighteen hundred dollars a month or more for studios in Old Law tenement buildings in the neighborhood, and a multitude of homeless folk.

If you walk east through the park on the path closest to 10th Street, until you are almost all the way to Avenue B, you will come to a small Parks Department building. If you look north through the walkway of this building, you will see a rose-colored eight-foot marble stela with a small lion-head fountain and a shallow relief image of children looking out to sea on its south face. The inscription on this face reads: "They were earth's purest children, young and fair."

The stela was "dedicated by the Sympathy Society of German Ladies" in "the year of Our Lord MCMVI . . . in memory of those who lost their lives in the disaster to the Steamer *General Slocum*" on June 15, 1904.

In 1904, Tompkins Square was in the very center of a neighborhood called Kleindeutschland or Little Germany. The neighborhood was home to more than a hundred and fifty-thousand Germans and German-Americans; a German free library, hospital, town hall, and schools; numerous German Socialist organizations; and the thriving congregation of St. Mark's Evangelical Lutheran Church on East 6th Street.

On June 15, 1904, St. Mark's Evangelical Lutheran Church leased the *General Slocum* to take the women and children of the congregation to their annual Sunday school picnic in Locust Grove, Long Island. Somewhere around 125th Street, the boat caught on fire. It is still not known what caused the fire, although various sources cite a galley fire, illegally stowed hay placed too near kerosene, a cigar smoked near oil cans, and a fallen match or cigarette. What is known is that the captain did not heed the warnings that the boat was on fire until it was too late to pull into safe harbor at one of the many working piers along the way, the crew had not been trained in emergency procedures, the boat's original hoses had never been replaced and were no longer functioning, its six lifeboats had been painted and wired to the ship and could no longer be pried free, its life vests crumbled and sank when used, and—although scores of people saw the burning boat and battled the East River currents and the intense heat from the flames to try to reach it—by the time the *Slocum* pulled into North Brother Island, at least one thousand and twenty-one women and children had been drowned, killed by the churning wheel of the steamship as they tried to escape the boat, or burnt to death.

Almost every family in Kleindeutschland lost a family member to the disaster and within a very short time Kleindeutschland was no more. The Germans moved uptown to the previously smaller German community of Yorkville, where they could be both closer to the cigar factories where many of them worked and far away from the devastating memories of June 15, 1904—making numerous apartments between the East River and the Bowery, and between Division, Grand, and 14th Streets, available for the next wave of immigrants, some of whose now aged children can be found sitting and chatting in the park today.

There are a few mementos left of the old German neighborhood: the sign for the free German library ("Freie Bibliothek u. Lesehalle") above the doorway of the Ottendorfer Branch of the New York Public Library on Second Avenue between St. Mark's Place and 9th Street, and the sign for the German hospital ("Deutsches Dispensary") above the doorway of Cabrini Medical Center's Stuyvesant Polyclinic next door. But the Germans themselves are long gone, and today fewer and fewer people know about either the *Slocum* disaster or the monument to its victims in Tompkins Square Park.

KATE HARTNICK
President, Hartnick Consulting

6.18 Tompkins Square Park Dog Run

9th Street entrance, near Avenue B

One of the best dog runs in the city, complete with a giant wooden statue of a bone.

ERIC STOLTZ
Actor

6.19 Russian Turkish Baths

268 East 10th Street between First Avenue and Avenue A
212 674 9250; www.russianturkishbaths.com

You've been tramping around the city and it's finally beginning to get to you: the noise, the traffic, the constant press of human beings. You want to do something that will put you in a completely different frame of mind. Go to the Russian baths. You are surrounded mostly by people in their sixties, seventies, and eighties, many of them speaking Russian. You sit in a hot steam room and every once in a while you leave and jump into a cold pool.

There are small surrounding rooms where you can get different types of massages. The most unusual is the one using branches of oak leaves. You lie on a slab in the main steam room and an attendant rubs and massages your body and beats you with wet oak leaves; as you heat up from the steam, the attendant pours cool water on you and continues to beat and rub. I sent a friend of mine who described it as a religious experience.

MARGOT ADLER
Correspondent, National Public Radio

Go up the red steps. At the register, deposit your money and jewelry into a safe-deposit box. Go behind a curtain, take a cotton robe and a pair of plastic slippers, and put your clothes, along with your modesty, into a locker. Don your robe and slippers and go down a flight of steps to the Russian Turkish baths, where you may enter a traditional sauna, a sauna with a pull-chain shower, a steam room, an ice-cold pool, or—best of all—the radiant heat room. The first time I went into the radiant heat room, I was handed a bucket of icy water. Puzzled, I entered a stone room lined with two tiers of wooden benches. I have never experienced such intense heat. Within seven minutes I had overturned the bucket on my head; it was wonderful. For a modest fee you can spend hours at leisure. Founded in 1892, the baths are a rare New York treat, but the days and hours vary for single-sex and co-ed bathing; call to be sure.

MARGARET A. BRUCIA
Latin teacher and scholar

6.20 Monday Night Magic

Theater 80
80 Saint Marks Place between First and Second Avenues
212 615 6432; www.mondaynightmagic.com

Fun! Thrills! Comedy! Magic! Imagine a different full-length magic show presented each week in an intimate setting and you've got Monday Night Magic, where the best magicians from all over the world come to perform for an appreciative and enthusiastic audience. In addition to performances on the stage, with no seat more than four or five rows away, intermission features close-up magic where the miracles happen right in front of your disbelieving eyes. In addition to magicians, you'll often find sideshow performers, escape artists, comedy-magicians, jugglers, and Wild West whip-crackers on the bill. This is New York's longest-running magic show.

MATTHEW FIELD
Editor, Magic Circular magazine

6.22 St. Mark's-in-the-Bowery Church

1795–1799; 1828, steeple designed by Martin E. Thompson and Ithiel Towne

131 East 10th Street at Second Avenue

The Poetry Project: 212 674-091; www.poetryproject.com

When it was completed in 1799, St. Mark's-in-the-Bowery was already more than a hundred years old, having started in 1660 as a Dutch chapel on Peter Stuyvesant's farm. It stands today as the second-oldest site of worship in New York City after St. Paul's Chapel. The Bowery, to the left of St. Mark's, was the road leading to the New Amsterdam governor's farm.

If slightly weary from all the changes around it, St. Mark's is still the most vocal member of the community. The old bronze bell tolled for John F. Kennedy and Martin Luther King, and rang to celebrate the end of the Vietnam War. Cracked in the fire of 1978, it now sits in the courtyard. After years of fundraising, the church was restored and rededicated in 1983.

There is a sublime simplicity to St. Mark's. The inside of the church looks more Quaker than Episcopalian. The sun streams into the large white room over wooden floors—a place where one is as likely to hear the voices of poets as prayers. There is little sign of the arboreal splendor that marked the Stuyvesant farmland, but beautiful trees still grace the courtyard with a skyline of green. With your back to Stuyvesant Street, you can imagine the small colonial town of 1650. Just as easily, you will feel the history of community involvement and countercultural movements. Always a forum for common and radical beliefs alike, St. Mark's is a symbol of peaceful acceptance as well as protest.

St. Mark's has been home to the Poetry Project, scene of the only joint reading by Robert Lowell and Allen Ginsberg, since its founding in 1966. Readers have included Amiri

Baraka, John Ashbery, Yoko Ono, Kenneth Koch, Adrienne Rich, and many adventurous unknowns. A small dogwood in the courtyard honors Allen Ginsberg, who wrote: "The Poetry Project burns like red hot coal in New York's snow." Nearby, flowering trees memorialize W. H. Auden, Paul Blackburn, and Frank O'Hara. A brass plate on the Parish wall quotes Auden: "Thousands live without love, not one without water."

I love St. Mark's for the two women eating lunch on the porch and the man practicing tai chi in the courtyard, the gravel barely moving under his light but deliberate steps. Growing up, we used the vault markers as bases. I walked quickly past Peter Stuyvesant's bust as if he were the authoritative parent of a friend. I kissed my first kiss amidst the charred stones. St. Mark's church—eternal home to seven generations of Stuyvesants—reminds us that among the hustle and bustle of Second Avenue, poetry thrives and New York, with its gritty past, is still beautiful.

LAURIE DUCHOVNY
Teacher

6.24 Gem Spa Newsstand

131 Second Avenue at St. Marks Place
212 995 1866

In my opinion this Manhattan newsstand serves the best version of that world-famous concoction of milk, seltzer, and syrup that is often described as the quintessential New York beverage. Once you've got the proportions and ingredients right, the trick to a great egg cream is using very, very cold milk, and Gem Spa keeps theirs in an ice-cream freezer. The mixologists at Gem Spa have one fault, however. They will ask you what flavor you want. Scoff at them. Any real New Yorker knows that egg creams only come in chocolate.

MICHAEL MISCIONE
Manhattan Borough Historian

Best Old Barrooms

6.25 **McSorley's Old Ale House**
15 East 7th Street between Second and Third Avenues
212 473 9148; www.mcsorleysnewyork.com

4.16 **Fanelli's Cafe**
94 Prince Street at Mercer Street
212 226 9412

8.12 **Old Town Bar and Restaurant**
45 East 18th Street between Broadway and Park Avenue South
212 529 6732; www.oldtownbar.com

McSorley's Old Ale House, the "wonderful saloon" chronicled by Joseph Mitchell and painted by John Sloan, may be the last remnant of a New York we all dreamed about long ago. "To a devoted McSorley customer, most other New York City saloons are tense and disquieting," Mitchell wrote. "It is possible to relax in McSorley's. For one thing, it is dark and gloomy, and repose comes easy in a gloomy place.... Also, there is a thick, musty smell that acts as a balm to jerky nerves; it is really a rich compound of the smells of pine sawdust, tap drippings, pipe tobacco, coal smoke, and onions." Despite a few modifications, including the first female face behind the bar, McSorley's is much as it was when Mitchell brilliantly captured it for *The New Yorker* almost sixty years ago; much as it was when the doors first opened in 1854. Dim and crowded (avoid it at all costs on Saint Paddy's Day), it has the same bar taps, the same pot-bellied stove, and it serves just two kinds of beer—McSorley's own light and dark.

If McSorley's is the place to be pleasantly melancholy, then Fanelli's is the place to be happy. It's practically the last genuine establishment left in SoHo, once a gritty factory neighborhood and now full of relentlessly trendy shops. The beautifully intact speakeasy interior hasn't changed much since the repeal of Prohibition. And even though the gallery-goers and local loft-dwellers who dart in and out may whip out Palm Pilots at the drop of a hat, Fanelli's remains without pretensions, offering generous drinks and plates of honest grub at fair prices. A friend once compared it to the bar in *Cheers*, but to my mind it's more like the bar in *Northern Exposure*: completely nonjudgmental. Prada and Yohji Yamamoto rub elbows with well-worn workshirts and the seersucker jacket and madras tie on the gentleman to your left.

If you've seen the opener of *Late Night with David Letterman*, with that grand sweep of mahogany bar (it seats forty), then you've seen the Old Town. It's pretty great. And when it comes to being conducive to talking (or eavesdropping), there is nothing like it. Go early, when the serious drinkers are there, and slide into one of the intimate booths opposite the bar. There's a good selection of brew on tap, but there's something about the tone of the place that makes the choice of Bud in a bottle almost automatic. And the food—burgers, real bar sandwiches, terrific fries—is popular with neighborhood loyalists.

JANE DANIELS LEAR
Food and travel writer

7
W 42nd St
W 41st St
Dyer Av
W 40th St
W 39th St
W 38th St
W 37th St
W 36th St
W 35th St
W 34th St
W 33rd St
W 31st St
W 30th St
W 29th St
W 28th St
Chelsea Park
W 27th St
W 26th St
W 25th St
W 24th St
W 23rd St
W 22nd St
W 21st St
W 20th St
W 19th St
W 18th St
W 17th St
W 16th St
W 15th St
W 14th St
Meat Packing District
Little W 12th St
W 13th St
Horatio St
W 4th St
Greenwich Avenue
Port Authority Bus Terminal
Garment District
Madison Square Garden
Chelsea
Pier 83
Pier 64
Lincoln Tunnel
West Side Hwy (Joe DiMaggio Hwy)
Twelfth Avenue
Eleventh Avenue
Tenth Avenue
Ninth Avenue
Eighth Avenue

CHAPTER 7

CHELSEA

1 Starrett-Lehigh Building
2 General Theological Seminary
3 Chelsea Market
4 Port Authority Commerce Building
5 La Taza de Oro
6 El Quijote
7 Biricchino
8 Capitol Fishing Tackle Co.

GARMENT DISTRICT

9 Greenwich Savings Bank (see p. 164)
10 Drama Book Shop
11 Tinsel Trading
12 New York Public Library
13 Bryant Park
14 Books Kinokuniya (see p. 181)
15 Empire Theater

W 46th St
E 46th St
W 45th St
E 45th St
W 44th St
E 44th St
W 43rd St
E 43rd St
Vanderbilt Avenue
Grand Central Terminal
W 42nd St
E 42nd St
Bryant Park
New York Public Library
E 41st St
Sixth Avenue (Avenue of the Americas)
W 40th St
E 40th St
W 39th St
E 39th St
W 38th St
E 38th St
W 37th St
E 37th St
W 36th St
E 36th St
W 35th St
E 35th St
W 34th St
E 34th St
Fifth Avenue
Madison Avenue
Park Avenue
E 33rd St
E 32nd St
E 31st St
E 30th St
E 29th St
E 28th St
E 27th St
Park Avenue South
E 26th St
E 25th St
E 24th St
Madison Square Park
Madison Avenue
E 23rd St
Flatiron
E 22nd St
E 21st St
Broadway
E 20th St
E 19th St
E 18th St
E 17th St
E 16th St
Union Square
E 15th St
E 14th St
Sixth Avenue (Avenue of the Americas)
Fifth Avenue
E 13th St
E 12th St
Greenwich Village
E 11th St

Chelsea & Garment District

CHELSEA

7.1 Starrett-Lehigh Building

1931, Russell G. Cory & Walter M. Cory, and Yasuo Matsui
601 West 26th Street between Eleventh and Twelfth Avenues

The streamlined Art Moderne Starrett-Lehigh Building anchors a full city block like a hulking dry-docked tanker. Russell and Walter Cory and Yasuo Matsui designed the 2.5 million-square-foot shipwreck for the Starrett Brothers (contractors for the Empire State Building) and the Lehigh Valley Railroad. An early Modernist landmark work of the Machine Age, its gently curved corners are wrapped with nine miles of strip windows and brick. Freight train cars were ferried across the Hudson River, rode the elevated High Line rail inside and were hoisted to the upper floors fully loaded by super-powered Otis elevators. For a brief moment, the former factory and warehouse housed hundreds of dot.coms. Remaining tenants include the do-it-yourself diva Martha Stewart, who delights in driving door-to-door (via the freight elevator) to her empire designed by architect Dan Rowan.

FREDERIC SCHWARTZ AND TRACEY HUMMER
Architect and Writer

7.2 General Theological Seminary Garden

175 Ninth Avenue between West 20th and West 21st Streets
☎ 212 243 5150

Stroll past the bookstore and onto the grounds of the oldest seminary of the Episcopal church in the U.S.

(founded in 1817 and a New York City landmark since 1826). You'll find a central garden or "close," with expansive lawns and towering trees, that is an absolute surprise. Wander in for a bit of Boston in New York. It's beautiful, peaceful, and free.

ERIC STOLTZ
Actor

7

Skybridges

West 15th Street between Ninth and Tenth Avenues
Tenth Avenue between West 15th and West 16th Streets
East 60th Street between Lexington and Third Avenues

The autogyros and skyline freeways of Hugh Ferriss's Metropolis of Tomorrow never appeared, and dirigibles don't moor at the spire of the Empire State Building. However, these simple bridges cantilevered over Manhattan's streets serve both the prosaic purpose of linking showroom and warehouse and providing a sliver of the romantic comic book city of Gotham amid Manhattan's relentless grid.

SEBASTIAN HARDY
Urban planner

7.3 Chelsea Market

75 Ninth Avenue between West 15th and West 16th Streets
www.chelseamarket.com

The old Nabisco Factory where the original Oreo Cookie was made in 1912 is once again a center for good food. Since 1995, it has housed the Chelsea Market complex of shops. The factory building fills the entire block between Ninth and Tenth Avenues and 15th and 16th Streets. Developer Irwin Cohen drew on the area's history as New

York's meatpacking and wholesale produce district at the end of the ninteenth century and came up with a design that lightheartedly recalls the building's industrial past. A corridor, originally part of the railroad that carried supplies from the Hudson River, runs through the center, lined with shops like the main street of a village. Halfway through, a factory pipe has been made into an indoor waterfall. All along the walk, gears, bits of old brick, and other machinery now serve as sculptures. (There is also, somewhat oddly, a series of stone carvings of various parts of the human body.) The shops do a large part of their business wholesale, using the original loading bays. Each also sells retail from a storefront, offering the same products used at many of New York's most elegant restaurants at excellent prices. In a particularly nice touch, the wholesale kitchens are all on display behind glass, so you can watch huge batches of cookies, breads, and soups being made. The old factory still contains many bakeries, among them the famous Sarabeth's Bakery and Amy's Bread. Other shops offer meat, wine, fresh milk in glass bottles, soups, freshly squeezed fruit juices, Thai food, imported Italian goods, and produce, including some hard-to-find fruits and vegetables. A kitchen supply store sells both new and used kitchen equipment, including some huge professional ovens and restaurant fixtures. There is a flower shop, a hardware store, and a gift basket creator. Several places offer free samples. Many establishments include small restaurant areas, and there are also benches along the central corridor, so you can assemble a picnic and eat it right there. The market and the shops in it sponsor occasional events such as food and wine tastings, and on Saturday evenings there is free tango dancing (Triangulo, ☎ 212 633 6445; www.triangulonyc.com).

JANET B. PASCAL

Writer and production editor, Viking Children's Books

The Renaissance Street Singers

www.streetsingers.org

On a Sunday somewhere in the five boroughs, you may come upon a small semicircle of musicians singing fifteenth- and sixteenth-century a cappella motets on the sidewalk. These are the Renaissance Street Singers, a group founded in 1973 by John Hetland. The concerts are always free (and the group returns any donations people try to leave for them), given simply for love of the music and as a gift to the City of New York. For twenty-eight years, the group has sung in any public space they can find (unless someone kicks them out). Some favorite spots are the corner of Christopher and Bleecker Streets in Greenwich Village, Chelsea Market (see p. 127), the corner of Henry and Montague Streets in Brooklyn Heights, and Cleopatra's Needle in Central Park. They perform two or three Sundays a month, usually from 2 p.m. to 4 p.m. If you're interested in tracking them down, the location of the forthcoming Sunday's concert can be found on their website.

JANET B. PASCAL
Writer and production editor, Viking Children's Books

7

7.4 Former Port of New York Authority Commerce Building

1932, Abbott, Merkt & Co

111 Eighth Avenue between West 15th and West 16th Streets

In this full-block structure, find an elevator large enough for semi tractor-trailers, ramps for same, an elevator machine room straight out of Charlie Chaplin's *Modern Times*, and a circular elevated helicopter landing pad with a giant red "x" raised above the roof.

TERENCE RILEY
Architect

If you tilted this muscular 1930s Art Moderne behemoth on its end, it would rise as tall as the Woolworth Building. With more than two million sprawling square feet of space, this is the fourth-largest building in New York City. Its enormous footprint (two hundred by eight hundred feet) encompasses one of the city's biggest blocks and merits its own subway entrance. This was formerly the Port Authority's headquarters, where six giant elevators once hoisted trucks to thirty loading docks in the sky.

TRACEY HUMMER
Writer

7.5 La Taza de Oro

96 Eighth Avenue between West 14th and West 15th Streets
212 243 9946
Closed Sundays.

There is really no reason to pay all that money at Starbucks when you can get such a superior product at this popular Puerto Rican diner. A dollar flat will get you a generous cup of *café con leche*. The brew is foamy and rich, with more than enough caffeine to get you through a morning's worth of Chelsea gallery-hopping or a shopping expedition at Jeffrey. If you need more fuel, sit down to a plate of delectable roast chicken with rice and beans.

MARY CLARKE
Editor

7.6 El Quijote

226 West 23rd Street between Seventh and Eighth Avenues
212 929 1855; www.elquijoterestaurant.com

You wouldn't say there's a scene to make at El Quijote, but the place is generally crowded with actual New Yorkers there to eat the excellent lobster and paella, to drink some sangria or Marques de Riscal, and to spend some time in the very cool atmosphere of this handsome and sturdy seventy-year-old Spanish restaurant. The Quijote is a survivor, and the better part of its patrons—writers, models, hospital workers, legitimately eccentric denizens of the Chelsea Hotel—appear to be among those who have gone too far down their chosen road to contemplate turning back. The Dulcinea Room and the Cervantes Room are attractive, in a slightly Miss Havishamesque way, but the main dining room, with its terra-cotta walls painted with duotone Quixote murals, is the best spot to take in the underlit defunct elegance of the place. Owner Manny Ramirez says he's a direct descendant of Don Quixote, a claim worthy of the Man of La Mancha himself. Dig into the big portions and the red wine.

CHRISTOPHER CAHILL
Author, and director of the American Irish Historical Society

Most people go to El Quijote, the oldest Spanish lobster palace in the city, for its generous portions of paella, and the staggering surf-and-turf platters. Few go for the bar, which is one of the best spots for revisiting the New York of fedoras, furs, and cigarettes cases. It's one of those places where "old" New York isn't re-created—it simply never left. The bartenders wear uniforms with undersized bow ties and engraved nameplates on their vests. Exceedingly polite and formal, it's clear they consider restaurant service an honorable profession—just one of the many subtleties that places the restaurant in another era. The bar is old-fashioned, too, with its large frosted glass etched with lobsters, and backlit a pale blue. Quixote figures form an odd parade along the bar, filling every space not occupied by bottles. The spirits collection includes crème de menthe, Dubonnet, and sloe gin—things you'd think no one has ordered in years until the night you come in here for a perfect Manhattan and you see a woman of tattered beauty—maybe a 1948 Miss Nassau County or a former showgirl—nursing one of those retro drinks in the curve of her arm. Hemmed into her space by the couples from Jersey or the Island, the guy with slicked-back hair and the well-toned date, and the art types from the Chelsea Hotel, she's a character type that's all but forgotten.

From the bar you have the perfect vantage point from which to see the dining room. Red banquettes line the walls, which in turn are lined with the original black-and-white and burnt-sienna murals depicting Quixote's adventures. Windmills turn slowly along the back wall—the only sluggish element in this bustling place, where waiters hustle at breakneck speed, swooping into the dining room with large trays overhead.

There's no pretension here. There's no kitsch, no irony, and no attitude. It's earnest, authentic, delicious—and you'll get a perfect Manhattan at an old-fashioned price.

LANA BORTOLOT
Writer

7.7 Biricchino Northern Italian Restaurant

260 West 29th Street between Seventh and Eighth Avenues
212 695 6690; www.biricchino.com
212 736 7376; www.salumeriabiellese.com

Go to Biricchino (don't be put off by the decor) and try a sample appetizer of five of their sausages. The sausages and salamis are made fresh by Salumeria Biellese, their deli next door, and are served at New York's finest restaurants including the Four Seasons and Alain Ducasse. When there's a game at Madison Square Garden, people with season tickets also appear to have reservations for tables at the restaurant, until exactly 7:20 p.m. The place stops serving at 9 p.m., so go early.

LIONEL TIGER
Darwin Professor of Anthropology, Rutgers University, and Co-research Director, Guggenheim Foundation

7.8 Capitol Fishing Tackle Co.

132 West 36th Street between Broadway and Seventh Avenue
212 929 6132; www.capitolfishing.com

🎁 I've attempted to fish only a few unsuccessful times in my life. But whenever I happen to walk by Capitol Fishing Tackle, I find myself stopping in to browse the extensive array of fishing paraphernalia and equipment. The beauty, humor, and inventiveness of the vast inventory of lures is astonishing. Their line-up of reels may not rival in diversity the Metropolitan Museum's collection of early weaponry, but it does provide an impressive display of variations on a theme—a kind of simple mechanical beauty either eliminated or hidden in most current product design. For the avid fisher or anyone who likes cool stuff, it's worth a visit. They also carry a decent collection of T-shirts emblazoned with all kinds of piscine imagery.

BILL KOMOSKI
Artist

GARMENT DISTRICT

7.11 Tinsel Trading

1 West 37th Street between Fifth and Sixth Avenues
☎ 212 730 1030; www.tinseltrading.com

🎁 The family story of Tinsel Trading is hidden from the casual shopper on this Garment District street. But it's hard to ignore the extraordinary nature of the trims and ribbons sold in this store. Marcia Ceppos inherited this business from her grandfather Arch Bergoffen. In the 1930s, Mr. Bergoffen sold gold trim for military uniforms. He gradually expanded to include many trims using metal thread, handmade raffia flowers from Italy, and straw trims from Switzerland. When things went out of style, he put them away. When Ms. Ceppos found this treasure trove, some of which had not been looked at in fifty years, she decided to keep the business not only going, but in the family.

CHARLES SUISMAN AND CAROL MOLESWORTH
Co-authors of Manhattan User's Guide

7.12 The New York Public Library

1911, Carrère & Hastings
Fifth Avenue and 42nd Street
212 340 0833; www.nypl.org

Rose Main Reading Room

Restoration 1998, Davis Brody Bond
General Research Division, third floor

Salomon Room

Third Floor

Newly renovated, the Main Reading Room of the New York Public Library is one of the premier public spaces in the city. Take a morning to visit the library, perhaps to order a fine or obscure book from the stacks for perusing at one of the long reading tables. Then, walk across the hall to the Salomon Room (now a wireless reading and study room), where you'll find curious or arresting exhibits drawn from the library's collection of books, manuscripts, and papers. Afterwards, lunch or dine at the Bryant Park Grill behind the library and stroll along the park path, taking in the sculpture and the people.

PAUL KANE
Poet and professor of English, Vassar College

Children's Center

Ground Floor, Room 84

Stop in at the Central Children's Room and you'll discover an old friend in a glass case (they say it's bulletproof). It's the world's most famous teddy bear, Winnie-the-Pooh. Given to the New York Public Library in 1987 and part of a *cause célèbre* when a member of the British Parliament tried unsuccessfully to extradite him in 1998, he waits for fans old and young to pay homage.

JOHANNA HURWITZ
Author of children's books

7.13 Bryant Park

1871; 1934, redesigned by Lusby Simpson
Sixth Avenue between West 40th and West 42nd Streets

Bryant Park Grill
25 West 40th Street between Fifth and Sixth Avenues
Upper terrace, behind the library
212 840 6500; www.bryantpark.org

One of the best ways to spend an hour in Midtown is in Bryant Park, the oasis behind the New York Public Library—by some miracle restored rather than replaced like its counterparts in London and Paris. Ask to see the outdoor roof garden at the Bryant Park Grill. You'll be shown a dark, hidden staircase that takes you to the roof with a wonderful wide view of the elegant park ringed with skyscrapers. Tired from reading, your eyes take in the grassy rectangle below, edged by rows of lush perennials and greenery, partially shaded by rows of tall, graceful trees, and anchored by kiosks selling drinks, tickets, and fresh flowers.

LAURIE LISLE
Journalist and biographer

7.10 Drama Book Shop

250 West 40th Street between Seventh and Eighth Avenues
212 944 0595; www.dramabookshop.com

If you're interested in the theater, don't miss the Drama Book Shop. You'll see stars of tomorrow stretched out in chairs and on the floor, reading scripts for auditions and not buying. The management doesn't mind.

JOHN GUARE
Playwright

7.15 Former Empire Theater, now AMC Empire 25

Façade 1912, Thomas W. Lamb

234 West 42nd Street between Seventh and Eighth Avenues

212 398 7843

How can a vast new twenty-five-screen multiplex on 42nd Street be called a city secret? What makes the AMC worth a careful look is the way the building expresses that it is the largest structure in New York City ever to be physically moved. The remaining signs of that 1998 move are fascinating.

As a boy, I spent happy days on old West 42nd Street, visiting magic shops and Hubert's Flea Circus. The exterior of the new AMC was there then. It was built in 1912 as the Eltinge Theater, named after Julian Eltinge, a famed cross-dressing actor of the era—a work by theater architect Thomas W. Lamb, who in New York also did the lost Strand, Ziegfeld, Rialto, Rivoli, Capitol, and Loew's 72nd Street, and the still extant Cort and Mark Hellinger theaters. Over the decades, the building's function changed from comedy playhouse to burlesque theater to cinema, and its name changed to the Empire in 1954, after it became a second-run movie house. When 42nd Street was rebuilt in the last few years, it was decided to transform the Empire into a multiplex. The single auditorium space became superfluous, but the building façade and elements within were thought worth preserving as major historic constituents of what eventually became an internally linked, mixed old and new architectural ensemble.

The front of the Eltinge/Empire that in 1998 rolled a hundred and seventy feet west from its original position weighed 7.4 million pounds, including its temporary structural reinforcement. (Though preparations had taken months, the distance was covered in a single day.) What's architecturally interesting is how the completed design expresses the assemblage of parts, the old façade providing an ad hoc component for the amalgamation. The dome over the lobby, visible behind exterior glazing, covers a surprisingly kinetic space when one walks in. Two transparent-sided escalators merrily penetrate what used to be the old proscenium arch, carrying customers out of the ticketing area into the hinterland of screened auditoriums and eateries. All this can be visited and viewed without buying a ticket.

The lobby interior's largely scenographic decoration includes a restored mural uncovered before the move. It depicts three muses, probably the likenesses of Julian Eltinge in drag. A final transformation for you, sir!

NATHAN SILVER
Architect, critic, and writer

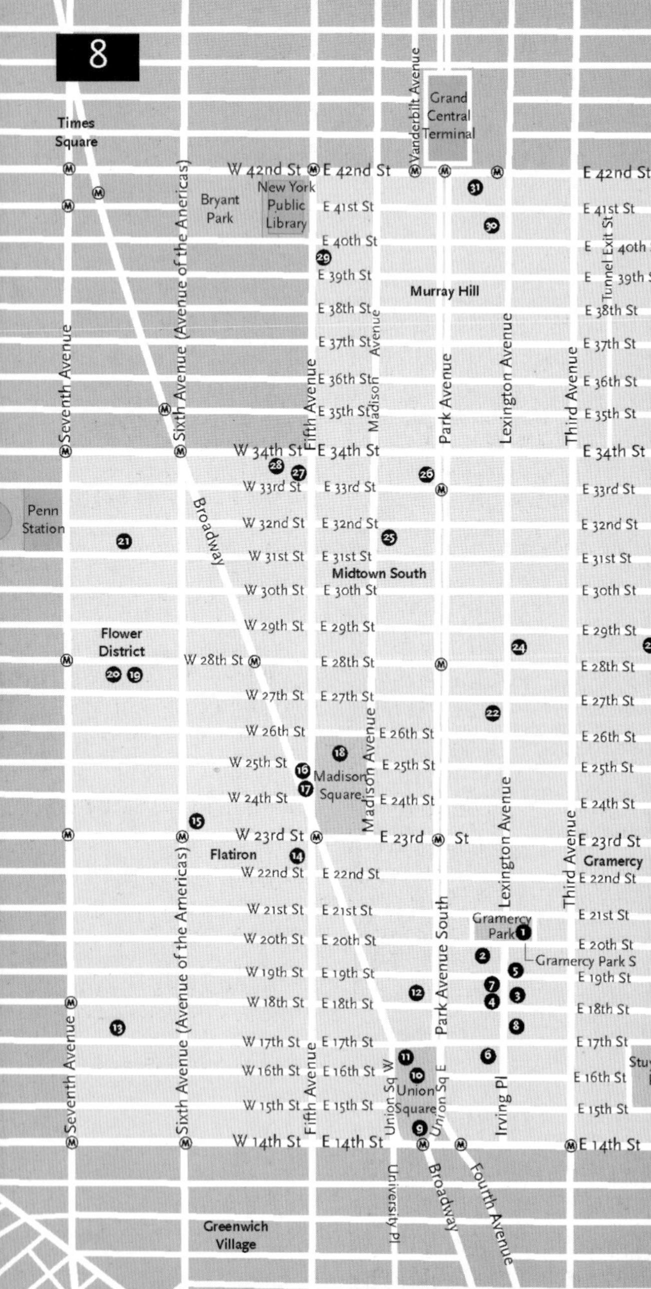

8
Times Square
Grand Central Terminal
Vanderbilt Avenue
W 42nd St
E 42nd St
New York Public Library
Bryant Park
E 41st St
E 40th St
E 39th St
Murray Hill
E 38th St
E 37th St
E 36th St
E 35th St
Tunnel Exit St
Seventh Avenue
Sixth Avenue (Avenue of the Americas)
Fifth Avenue
Madison Avenue
Park Avenue
Lexington Avenue
Third Avenue
W 34th St
E 34th St
W 33rd St
E 33rd St
Penn Station
Broadway
W 32nd St
E 32nd St
W 31st St
E 31st St
Midtown South
W 30th St
E 30th St
W 29th St
E 29th St
Flower District
W 28th St
E 28th St
W 27th St
E 27th St
W 26th St
E 26th St
W 25th St
E 25th St
Madison Square
W 24th St
E 24th St
W 23rd St
E 23rd St
Flatiron
Gramercy
W 22nd St
E 22nd St
W 21st St
E 21st St
Gramercy Park
W 20th St
E 20th St
Gramercy Park S
W 19th St
E 19th St
W 18th St
E 18th St
Park Avenue South
W 17th St
E 17th St
W 16th St
E 16th St
Union Square
Union Sq W
Union Sq E
Irving Pl
W 15th St
E 15th St
W 14th St
E 14th St
University Pl
Fourth Avenue
Greenwich Village
1
2
3
4
5
6
7
8
9
10
11
12
13
14
15
16
17
18
19
20
21
22
23
24
25
26
27
28
29
30
31

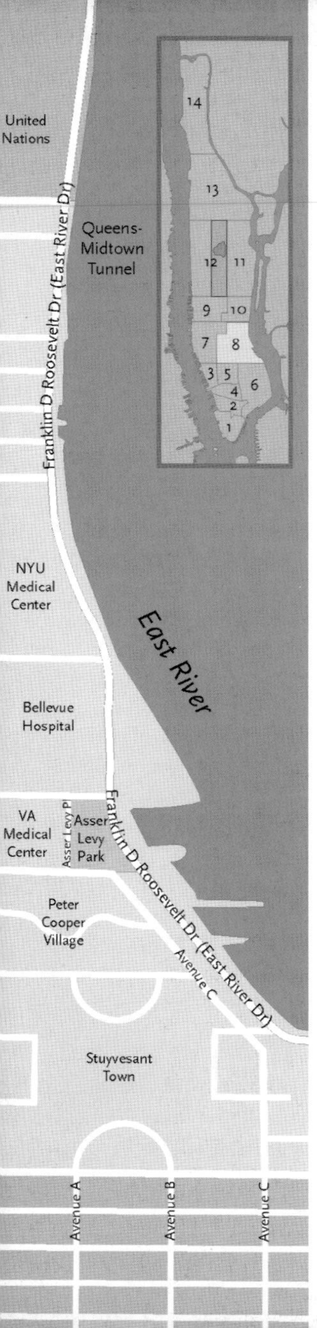

CHAPTER 8

GRAMERCY

1 Gramercy Park
2 The National Arts Club
3 Pete's Tavern
4 71 Irving
5 80 Irving Place
6 Yama
7 Chosi
8 Inn at Irving Place

FLATIRON DISTRICT

9 Arts for Transit
10 Union Square Park
11 Union Square Greenmarket
12 Old Town Bar (see p. 122)
13 Housing Works
14 Eisenberg Sandwich Shop
15 Masonic Hall
16 Water Supply Maintenance Cabin
17 General Worth Monument
18 Madison Square Park
19 TADA!
20 Flower District

MIDTOWN SOUTH

21 Church of St. Francis of Assisi
22 I Trulli
23 Paddy Reilly's Music Bar
24 Kalustyan's
25 Paul J. Bosco
26 Della Robbia Bar
27 Empire State Building
28 Louis Tannen Inc.

MURRAY HILL

29 Mid-Manhattan Library
30 Bronze Architectural Plaques
31 Bowery Savings Bank

Gramercy, Flatiron District, Midtown South & Murray Hill

GRAMERCY

8.1 Gramercy Park

1831, Samuel Ruggles
East 20th to East 21st Street between Park Avenue South and Third Avenue
Open to the public on Christmas Eve.

It may look like a London square, but Gramercy Park is a microcosm of old and new New York. Though most of the houses that surround it were built in a subdued Greek Revival style in the 1840s and '50s, most were updated, enlarged or—on the north and east sides, especially—replaced over the years, so that today the place is a little museum of local architectural history up to about 1930.

The red brick house (No. 5, dated 1843), at the corner of 20th and Gramercy Park West, gives the best impression of the original type. It would have had a wrought-iron veranda like that which its elegant neighbors at Nos. 3 and 4 (dated 1847) still have. The house at No. 2 later received an additional story, paired pilasters, and a balustrade. Two houses purchased by Samuel Tilden at No. 15 were "Victorianized" inside and out by Vaux & Radford in 1884; they are now home to the National Arts Club (see p. 141). After the actor Edwin Booth bought a house with Gothic trim next door (No. 16) in 1887, Stanford White converted it to a clubhouse for the Players. The houses at Nos. 13 and 14 were remodeled in the 1930s with large casement windows, but because one is still red brick with its classical cornice intact, it passes for being older. Their now

International Style neighbor—painted white with bright yellow trim on the windows— had its cornice removed to emphasize the flat roof. The apartment houses that rose on the other edges of the park include: the polite Federal-style tower of duplexes at 24 Gramercy Park; the Gramercy (No. 34), a Queen Anne fortress dated 1883; the neo-Gothic terra-cotta extravaganza (1910) at No. 36 (complete with metallic-colored knights guarding the door); the collegiate Tudor tower at No. 44; the vaguely Deco building at No. 45; Emery Roth's 1928 New York apartment house with Spanish trim at No. 60; and the massive brick building at 1 Lexington Avenue.

JAYNE MERKEL
Architectural historian and critic

8.2 The National Arts Club

1884, Calvert Vaux

15 Gramercy Park South between Park Avenue South and Irving Place

☎ 212 475 3424; www.nationalartsclub.org

This magnificent former residence of Samuel Tilden is now a national landmark and home to the hundred-year-old National Arts Club. Overlooking Gramercy Park, the Victorian mansion is a cynosure from a bygone era in one of the city's loveliest neighborhoods. Although the club is private and its finest rooms are open only to members, the space can be rented for functions, and most of the art galleries are open to walk-in visitors. If possible, sneak a peek at the glorious blue bubble-glass ceiling above the bar. It's a jewel by John La Farge, Louis Comfort Tiffany's great rival.

ALEXANDRA STYRON
Writer

Irving Place Stroll

8.3 **Pete's Tavern**
129 East 18th Street at Irving Place
212 473 7676

8.4 **71 Irving Espresso and Tea Bar**
71 Irving Place between East 18th and 19th Streets
212 995 5252; www.irvingfarm.com

8.5 **80 Irving Place**
At East 19th Street

8.1 **Gramercy Park**
1831, Samuel Ruggles
East 20th to East 21st Street between Park Avenue South and Third Avenue
Open to the public on Christmas Eve.

8.6 **Yama**
122 East 17th Street at Irving Place
212 475 0969; www.yamarestaurant.com

8.7 **Choshi**
77 Irving Place at East 19th Street
212 420 1419; www.sushichoshi.com

8.8 **The Inn at Irving Place**
56 Irving Place between East 17th and East 18th Streets
212 533 4600; www.innatirving.com

If not for Gramercy Park, Lexington Avenue would storm right down to 14th Street. Luckily, the park deflects Lexington at 21st Street, leaving a six-block oasis in its stead: Irving Place. A tree-lined, quiet, two-way street, Irving radiates a unique feeling. One senses the absence of an avenue where an avenue should be, and the particular tranquility created by this vacuum.

Pete's Tavern, at the corner of 18th, is the heart of Irving Place. Founded in 1864, it is the longest continuously operating saloon in New York. Two staples of the American literary canon were created in this corner pub: O'Henry's "The Gift of the Magi" and Ludwig Bemelmans's *Madeline*. Bring a pen and maybe you'll get lucky; clearly something magic is in the beer. Today Pete's draws mostly young corporate types, but don't let that scare you off. In the pantheon of old New York gin mills, it holds a hallowed niche between the dusty Irishness of McSorley's and the Dylan Thomas romanticism of the White Horse Tavern.

Across the street percolates a fun little cafe called 71 Irving. They have fresh bread they'll toast and butter for you, and you can have the satisfaction of buying coffee from a small-business person rather than a huge multinational. Across, at 19th, stands a wonderful house (No. 80) —home to Sigourney Weaver's character in the movie *Working Girl*, but truly triumphant because of its two-car garage. Living in Manhattan, one gets inured to trappings of luxury, but a two-car garage still impresses.

At 20th is Gramercy Park (see p. 140), the only private park left in New York. You can wander around the wrought-iron gates, looking inside at the kids with their nannies and the octogenarians on the benches. This is actually the best way to see Gramercy Park; everything shines brighter when you're on the outside looking in.

A brick house on the corner of 17th has a plaque suggesting that Washington Irving once lived there. Irving, creator of "Rip Van Winkle" and "The Legend of Sleepy Hollow," certainly gave his name to the street, but my sources doubt that he ever called that address home. However, in the basement, the sushi restaurant Yama serves up fist-sized pieces of yellowtail and *toro*, so delicious that the horseman would wish he had a head, so sublime they would wake Rip Van Winkle. So yummy, in fact, that the line is often around the corner. If it is, go up the block to Choshi.

Their portions aren't as generous, but they have a pleasant outdoor seating area and I recommend their Kinoko sauté, a delicious blend of Asian mushrooms in soy sauce and butter.

If you're looking for a place to stay and you don't feel like dealing with the madness of Midtown, try the Inn at Irving Place. The luxuriously cozy bed and breakfast occupies a double-wide town house between 17th and 18th Streets, a perfect base from which to enjoy the charms of Irving.

SAM HOFFMAN
Filmmaker

FLATIRON DISTRICT

8.9 Arts for Transit: *Framing Union Square*

1998, Mary Miss & Lee Pomeroy
www.mta.info/mta/aft

If you visit the grand outdoor greenmarket at Union Square, spend some time exploring the archaeological layers of the subway station, brilliantly elucidated by artist Mary Miss and architect Lee Pomeroy. Three stations, built in 1904, 1914, and 1930 for now-intersecting lines, are joined and have been recently renovated. Pomeroy and Miss have revealed the layers and history of the site through bright red enameled frames in 115 locations. Framed vertical slits, some with faceted mirrored interiors, indicate the workings of the system (electrical panel boxes, message slots, telephone wiring, ceiling light fixtures, holding cells, mesh and wire grates, concrete arches between the columns, cables), or cut through the walls of one level to another so visitors can view the passage of trains. Red horizontal frames border details that were excavated during construction (particularly bands of patterning and lettering in earlier styles). There are massive hunks of freestanding wall decorated with mosaics and glazed, cast ceramic eagles along an upper-level corridor, outlined with red girders to draw our attention. In fact, this signature red is used throughout on signs, pipes, railings, and poles as a marker, even alternating with white diagonal stripes along the train walls; in this way, infrastructure is highlighted through a contemporary graphic process.

JOYCE KOZLOFF
Artist

Lower Midtown Squares

8.10 **Union Square**
1839; redesigned 1872 by Frederick Law Olmsted and Calvert Vaux; restored in 1985
East 14th Street to East 17th Street between Union Square West (Broadway) and Union Square East (Park Avenue South)
212 460 1200; www.unionsquarenyc.org

8.1 **Gramercy Park**
1831, Samuel Ruggles
East 20th to East 21st Street between Park Avenue South and Third Avenue
Open to the public on Christmas Eve.

8.18 **Madison Square Park**
1847, Ignatz Pilat
East 23rd to East 26th Street between Fifth and Madison Avenues
www.madisonsquarepark.org

8.11 **Union Square Greenmarket**
Union Square Park
212 788 7476; www.grownyc.org

I love the "necklace" formed by Union Square, Gramercy, and Madison Square parks so much that I have chosen to conduct my entire personal and professional life around those jewels. It's Manhattan at its most civilized scale, and no neighborhood better combines beautifully preserved historic architecture with a dynamic sense of modern style. One could say that this is where "Ladies' Mile" meets "Silicon Alley." Architects, publishers, and new-media executives commingle with young family residents, greenmarket farmers, and the city's densest population of excellent restaurants. The trick to any stroll through this zone is to look up. Each building brings an animated story to the streetscape, and many have been lovingly restored and given meaningful, modern uses. The Union Square Greenmarket—open Monday, Wednesday, Friday, and Saturday, but at its abundant and bustling best on Wednesday and Saturday—is New York's closest thing to a vital Italian piazza. It is perhaps the only place in the city where New Yorkers choose to slow down, smell the smells, and talk to each other.

DANNY MEYER

Restaurateur and cookbook author

8.13 Housing Works Thrift Shop

143 West 17th Street between Sixth and Seventh Avenues

718 838 5050; www.shophousingworks.com

A treasure trove in Chelsea. Like thrift shops everywhere, the merchandise is donated, but here the stuff is fabulous. Antiques, furniture, art, collectibles, jewelry, and tchotchkes, often comparable to those found in Madison Avenue antique shops, are to be had at less-than-flea-market prices. There are also racks of gently worn designer and vintage clothing, and from time to time some top-notch designers donate samples. And as if this weren't rewarding enough, all proceeds go to AIDS assistance. Housing Works also operates the terrific used-book store and cafe at 126 Crosby Street.

BINNIE KIRSHENBAUM

Writer, and chair of the M.F.A. program, Columbia University

8.14 Eisenberg Sandwich Shop

174 Fifth Avenue between West 22nd and West 23rd Streets
212 675 5096; www.eisenbergsnyc.com

Step in the front door here and leave the new millennium behind; inside, it's 1942. To your left, a long row of swiveling stools. To your right, a few tables if you're dining *à deux*. If you're alone, slide onto a stool and peruse the menu, which hangs from wooden plaques on the wall that look like they've been there since, well, 1942. Choose corned beef or pastrami at a fraction of the price of the snob uptown delis, meatloaf (always a special—alas, now served with instant mashed potatoes), or matzo ball soup bobbing with namesakes bigger than tennis balls. Wash it all down with a Dr. Brown's cream soda. When you're done, there's no check; just tell the cashier what you had. No one running the place seems to be Jewish anymore—the countermen are Hispanic, the cashiers Asian. No matter. In a happy, plastic McDonald's world, Eisenberg's is the real deal.

SUSAN WYLAND
Magazine consultant

8.15 Masonic Hall

1910, Napoleon Le Brun
71 West 23rd Street at Sixth Avenue
212 337 6602; www.nymasons.org

One of the finest edifices in New York is the Masonic Hall and home of the Grand Lodge of Free and Accepted Masons of the State of New York, as well as Holland Lodge No. 8. Founded in 1787, Holland Lodge's many distinguished members have included Samuel Fraunces (famous tavernkeeper), Baron von Steuben, John Jacob Astor, and F. D.R. The building is of granite and its construction in the early 1900s cost more than a million dollars. Its frontage on 23rd Street is a hundred and forty feet, and its height to the capstone is two hundred and forty feet. The principal entrance on 23rd Street is through a Doric portico; at the entrances to the lodge rooms are plaster columns of the Egyptian order emblematic of "strength and beauty" and representative of the two great pillars set up at the appointed entrance of King Solomon's Temple at Jerusalem. The inside is also beautifully decorated.

GORDON J. WHITING
Managing director, Angelo, Gordon & Co.

8.16 Water Supply Maintenance Cabin

c. 1935, attributed to Aymar Embury II
Worth Square, at the intersection of Fifth Avenue, Broadway, West 24th and West 25th Streets

Just across Fifth Avenue from Madison Square, this gem of a self-effacing little black hut is easily mistaken for a disused comfort station. It was erected in 1935 or soon after for the City of New York Department of Water Supply, Gas and Electricity, in order to replace an "eyesore" of a wooden cabin. Short and chunky, flat-roofed as well as flat-faced, this little one-story structure turns its back to downtown and to the adjacent monument of General Worth, with a single bronze window in either short side, while its curved, northerly face bows segmentally out from end to end, inflected only by a central bronze door. The whole, diminutive as it is, is faced with great large rectangles of black granite, with the corner joints sealed by a kind of Chanel-style piping along the seams. Fine materials and radically simple form. This is a stunningly fine, plain little honed box. Upstaged by the general's ho-hum obelisk (1857), it is a little unsung hero.

JOSEPH MASHECK
Art historian

8.17 General Worth Monument

1857, James G. Batterson

Worth Square, at the intersection of Fifth Avenue, Broadway, West 24th and West 25th Streets

Researching a novel set in a fictional version of my hometown of Hudson, New York, I came across a complicated figure born there, General William Jenkins Worth. He was born in 1794 and made his name in the War of 1812 (the Seminole and Mexican wars), specializing in the massacre of Native Americans. His other claim to fame was as a dancer; the "General Worth Quickstep" was all the rage in the early 1830s. But his arrogance defeated him, and he died of cholera in San Antonio in 1849. Fort Worth and Lake Worth are named after General Worth, as is Worth Street in lower Manhattan. He is buried under this obelisk, which is hard to get close enough to, to really inspect, but if you dare, you can see all his victorious battles carved on the stone—Chapultepec, Vera Cruz, Churubusco, Florida, Lundy's Lane, Puebla, Monterrey, Perote—exotic names, some barely remembered anymore. *Sic transit gloria*, although the inscription on the monolith says *Ducit amor patriae*, "Love of Country."

SAMUEL SHEM

Psychiatrist, author, and professor of psychiatry, Harvard Medical School

8.19 TADA!

15 West 28th Street between Fifth and Sixth Avenues

212 252 1619; www.tadatheater.com

As you walk along West 28th Street, surrounded by the jungle-like greenery of the wholesale plant district, a bright red banner flying above might catch your eye. The banner heralds TADA!, a not-for-profit children's theater company where talented New York kids perform original musicals. The performers range in age from seven to eighteen and come from all different cultural, economic, and social backgrounds. They work for an intensive six-week rehearsal process, and the results are often spectacular. The ensemble sparkles, the songs are catchy, and the performances always seem to have an energy and freshness that simply comes from the actors being kids. TADA! puts on a winter, spring, and summer show; the tickets are cheap and it's easy to make reservations.

CAITLIN PETRE
Journalist

8.20 Flower District

West 28th Street between Sixth and Seventh Avenues
The shops are open Mondays to Saturdays from 4:30 a.m. to early afternoon.

If you are an early riser and want to feel the city hum at daybreak, jump on the subway and head to 28th Street. Follow your nose east to New York's sweetest spot, the wholesale Flower District. (The parking police are unrelentingly vigilant on noncommercial vehicles; do not take your car.) While shops spill a few blocks up and down Sixth Avenue, the premier vendors are squeezed between Sixth and Seventh Avenues on 28th Street. Monday through Saturday, cut-flower vendors open as early as 4:30 a.m., and a bustling business peaks between 5:30 and 7 a.m. French tulips with individual netted caps; Gerber daisies, their heads arranged like bubble-gum-colored checkerboards, and lotus blossoms plucked from island lagoons arrive daily from across America and around the world—California and Canada, South Africa and Holland, New Zealand and Australia, Israel and Italy. Double-parked trucks are unloaded and loaded again at a dizzying speed, while men, shouldering piles of yard-long boxes labeled in multiple languages, maneuver, hips swaying hula-style, through the crowded sidewalks. Other men hose the topiary-lined pavement and sweep up dead flower heads, their fragrance ripened into heady perfume. Inside the shops, rub shoulders—literally, as quarters are notoriously cramped—with the city's foremost party-meisters, floral designers, and flower-shop owners and listen as they vie for five-foot, true-blue delphiniums or tiny nosegays of violets, majestic Stargazer lilies, or rainbows of sweet peas. While the market is strictly wholesale, carry a little cash in your pocket and quietly pick up a bouquet of garden roses, fit for Redouté's brush, for a few dollars.

STARR OCKENGA
Garden photographer and writer

MIDTOWN SOUTH

8.21 Church and Friary of St. Francis of Assisi

135 West 31st Street between Sixth and Seventh Avenues
212 736 8500; www.stfrancisnyc.org

The Great Mosaic

1930, Rudolph Margreiter (design) and Joseph Wild (construction)

The lovely Church of St. Francis of Assisi is a peaceful haven in one of the most bustling areas of New York. The original church, built in 1844, was demolished and rebuilt in its present form in 1892. Embellished with Italian marble, the church also incorporates Vermont marble, Mexican onyx, and white oak into its design. Its most impressive feature, however, is the huge mosaic in the sanctuary. Unveiled in 1925 and known as the Great Mosaic because it was the largest mosaic in America at the time of its execution, it covers more than sixteen hundred square feet. It features Mary and includes scenes from the life of Saint Francis and famous Franciscan saints.

Saint Francis founded an order of friars dedicated to leading a simple life and to helping the poor. Those ideals were put into action in Manhattan shortly after the stock market crash of 1929. The friars of St. Francis organized the distribution of bread and alms to the poor and hungry of New York. The number of alms-seekers grew as the Depression continued until it was not unusual for more than four thousand people to receive assistance each day.

Today, many New Yorkers take a short detour from wherever they are headed and pause in the courtyard of the church to touch the bronze statue of Saint Francis. Kneeling in prayer with head tilted upward, the right heel, hand, and knees of the statue are shiny from rubbing.

JAMES J. BRUCIA AND MARGARET BRUCIA
Justice (retired), New York State Supreme Court. The late Margaret Brucia was a schoolteacher.

8.22 I Trulli

122 East 27th Street at Lexington Avenue
212 481 7372; www.itrulli.com

I Trulli is one of the few restaurants in New York to specialize in the food of Puglia, and Nicola Marzovilla and his family make sure it tastes that way. Nicola's mother comes in every morning to make pasta by hand—not because she has to, but because she "has" to. Unless you're lucky enough to have a mother who makes homemade pasta for you, this shouldn't be missed.

I Trulli is also the only restaurant in New York where you will find a *panzerotti*. When you translate the southern Italian slang, you'll find it means "busted gut." I won't even try to describe what *panzerotti* is. You'll have to go find out for yourself.

FRANK PUGLIESE
Playwright, screenwriter, and director

8.23 Paddy Reilly's Music Bar

519 Second Avenue at East 29th Street
212 686 1210; www.paddyreillysmusicbar.us

In much of Manhattan, you can barely stumble down a block without encountering an Irish pub; in some places, several. But not even in Ireland will you find a drinking establishment that serves nothing on its taps but Guinness, as is the case at Paddy Reilly's Music Bar. In fact, it was only at the urging of the sales reps from Guinness that pub owner Steve Duggan, a former Gaelic footballer, agreed to offer wine, liquor, and even other beer in bottles. But the nine shining taps that stand sentry over his chipped oak landmark bar bleed the bitter only, and thanks to Duggan's care in storing the suds at exactly forty-one degrees, I challenge you to find a better cup of it this side of the Atlantic.

But that's only the beginning of what sets Paddy's apart from New York's other Irish pubs (and from the nondescript strip of Second Avenue on which it's located). This relatively small bar—which gets downright cozy at night with its old copper lanterns looming down from the bar ceiling and candles glowing on the tables—is well-known in music circles as an incubator of the finest Irish music talent on the East Coast. Catch it here seven nights a week, starting around 10:30 p.m., when the place fills with locals, music lovers, the occasional celebrity, and the lively sound of the old country.

JULIAN RUBINSTEIN
Author and journalist

8.24 Kalustyan's

123 Lexington Avenue between East 28th and East 29th Streets
212 685 3451; www.kalustyans.com

The best source for ingredients for the cuisines of Greece, Turkey, Indonesia, Morocco, and India—all of Asia and the Middle East, in fact—is Kalustyan's, a souk of sorts tucked away in the aromatic neighborhood of Little India. Enter this bright and orderly store and prepare yourself for the widest and highest-quality array of exotic products in Manhattan.

Upon entering, a shopper spies large, zippered bags of basmati and jasmine rice and, above them, beautifully designed metal tins of saffron, dec ffed with a nineteenth-century engraving titled "The Gathering of Saffron." Next, take a look at the piles of delectable dried fruits and nuts, including lemon pistachios, masala cashews, and cinnamon-sugar-honey almonds.

The meticulously organized shelves along the right wall are devoted to condiments. The first section holds chutneys (lime-pickle, mango, lime and ginger, mixed-pickle). Next, you'll find a stunning array of oils, curry pastes, marinade- and cooking sauces, including fish sauces. Supposedly

Cambodia's is the best in the world; a splash enriches almost any soup, as does a dash of the *muhamma* hot-pepper dip. Four shelves of hot sauces include my personal favorite, Linghams from Malaysia. *Harissa*, the Moroccan hot sauce, is available in a tube. I consider another item, *zhoug*, a Yemenite chili paste with coriander, a magic ingredient when spread on a fish fillet.

On a low shelf you'll find three dozen varieties of dried beans with irresistible names, including rattlesnake, European soldier bean, Steuben yellow, Jacob's cattle bean, calypso, Jackson wonder, rice bean, and scarlet runner. Then move into the lentils, couscous, and rices. Something called brown *teff* is "the smallest grain in the world," according to the label.

There are beverages, too: Arab sorrel tea, which the Bedouins drink to quench their thirst in the desert, as well as the beautiful pink hibiscus flower tea. Then there's the simply named Mountain Tea, a peasant drink from Greece, as well as many varieties of coffee. Some of the syrups here, including flavors such as quince-lemon and sun-baked pure mulberry, can be added to sparkling water for refreshing drinks; I haven't tried Rooh Afza, "the summer drink of the East."

The freezers hold an abundance of fresh frozen items, such as Kafir lime leaves, lemongrass, banana leaves, and *galangal*, a sort of ginger root, for Thai soups. Preserved lemons, essential for Moroccan cooking, are available here, too. There are delicious samosas and other prepared foods, as well as interesting-sounding ice creams, including fig and saffron-pistachio.

In the bakery department is a sweet bread filled with dates, which can be found alongside naan, tahini bread, and Zaatar bread.

The housewares are beautiful objects in themselves. The copper beakers are lovely, as are the brass spice grinders.

There are small iron woks with loopy metal handles, Indian sifters with four interchangeable screens, a rolling pin for chapati, and a wooden hand mixer that looks like a giant champagne aerator. There are strings of dried okra, cosmetics, and many, many more things.

Upstairs, you'll find more housewares as well as a small snack bar with a couple of tables overlooking the street where you can have a delicious lunch of food made on the premises. Order a portion of olives, or wash down a *basturma* sandwich (air-dried beef in a pita with cumin, pepper, tomatoes, and yogurt hot sauce) with a passion-fruit drink or a ginger beer.

HELEN MARDEN
Artist

8.25 Paul J. Bosco

149 Madison Avenue, entrance on 32nd Street
Closed on Sundays.
212 758 2646; www.pauljbosco.com

The owner, Paul Bosco, has been collecting coins and medallions for more than forty years. The currency spans ancient coins to modern subway tokens. The medallions (struck to commemorate people and events) range from the Renaissance to the present day. Here you can find a portrait of an Italian noble by the early Renaissance artist Pisanello—the first and finest of the medallists—or perhaps the official medal from the 1925 Exposition des Arts Décoratifs from Pierre Turin, the Art Deco master. Although Mr. Bosco caters to serious collectors, including museums, there is plenty here for the rest of us. It is possible to find a coin or medallion covering almost any subject—actually, the place is "organizationally challenged," so that it is almost impossible to find anything without Mr. Bosco's help. Among the hundreds of themes covered are world fairs and world wars, bridges and bunny rabbits, cemeteries and cathedrals, magic and mythology. I have bought subject-specific gifts for architects and doctors as well as playwrights and actors (although in the last instance, any shiny object with a reflective surface would have done the trick). Mr. Bosco also has an assortment of objets d'art, mostly acquired because he just couldn't say No. The last time I was there, he handed me an old letter opener with a decorative handle and asked if I knew what it was. After a few minutes, I answered that it looked as if the entire object was made from a single piece of carefully twisted metal. He then handed me its leather case, which read, "Compliments of John A. Roebling's Sons Company"; it was a nineteenth-century "giveaway" from the inventors of the steel cable and designers of the Brooklyn Bridge.

ROBERT KAHN
Architect

8.26 Former Della Robbia Bar

1913, Warren & Wetmore
4 Park Avenue at East 33rd Street

A remarkable space has survived in the former Vanderbilt Hotel. The hotel has a beautiful ceramic rathskeller, which was originally known as The Crypt, and later the Della Robbia Bar, and now Wolfgang's Steakhouse. The ceilings are embellished with polychrome terra-cotta ornaments made by the renowned Rookwood Pottery (Cincinnati, Ohio) and surrounded by Guastavino tiled arches. The room was declared a New York City Landmark on April 15, 1994, and is one of the rare restaurant interiors with such a distinction.

SUSAN TUNICK
Artist and writer

8.27 Empire State Building

1931, Shreve, Lamb & Harmon
350 Fifth Avenue at West 34th Street
www.esbnyc.com

Yep. It's worth it. Especially right before closing time, at around 10:30 at night. Take a date, it's stunning.
ERIC STOLTZ
Actor

Viewed from the south at sunset, the parallel lines of stainless steel trim catch the light, gleaming with a red-orange glow that shimmers along the thousand-foot shaft to the wings of the crown and television mast above. Surprisingly, lightning travels *up* the building as well as down, and often before it hits, a spiral of fire jumps up from the top of the tower to guide the electric current to the clouds above. The mysterious Saint Elmo's fire, the hovering light seen on ships at sea, is also a phenomenon of the upper realms of the tower, and when it appears, it is accompanied by a hissing sound. On the 102nd floor, a solid gold rivet tops off the steel structure, driven in by then governor Al Smith.
ALEX GORLIN
Architect

Although the Empire State Building is no secret, there are secret times to visit. My favorite is in the morning after a snowstorm, when the air is crisp and clean and all of New York City's rooftops are covered with snow. The building creates peculiar wind currents and there are times when it snows up rather than down. Rain, on the other hand, travels around the building sideways and sometimes when it is raining at the top, the street below is completely dry. When the clouds conceal the city beneath, you feel like you're floating, weightless, above land.

Back down to earth, try to find out when the fluorescent lobby lights are scheduled for their yearly cleaning. When the cleaners remove the translucent panels that cover them, the lobby's original decoratively painted ceiling is exposed and you can see where the original chandeliers once hung. It's like being transported to the great Art Deco days of the 1930s.

RONNETTE RILEY
Architect

City Lights

As New Yorkers, we instinctively chafe at playing second fiddle, gathering our "bests" and "firsts" and "largests" honors as a matter of birthright and taking umbrage when other cities have the temerity to make a claim to fame that we think really ought to be ours. Some distinctions are of little interest: the St. Louis Arch? Don't want it.

Staffordshire thinks of itself as the ceramics capital of the world? Let them have it. Paris's boast, though, that it's the City of Lights, was bound to be seen as a gauntlet thrown, and one advertising executive decided to take it up.

Douglas Leigh was known for masterminding kinetic billboard ads that included the Times Square smoking Camel sign and one for Pepsi with a block-long waterfall. Having spent enough time in Times Square to see the light, he decided to brighten up some of the city beyond the theater district.

Mr. Leigh knew that the Empire State Building, opened in 1931, had remained short of tenants as a result of the Depression. He had the idea of getting Coca-Cola to take the top floors and proposed that the tower have changing lights that would serve as a weather forecast. Coke would package bottles with a small guide to decipher the colors. By late 1941, Coke had agreed, but following Pearl Harbor, the lights of the city were darkened. The government suddenly needed a lot of office space, filling up much of the Empire State Building, and the Coke deal fell by the wayside. After the war, they decided to use a different, simpler lighting scheme.

More immediate success in creating a night skyline is in evidence with his designs for the Crown Building, Citicorp, John Jay College, New York Life, 90 West Street, and 2 Park Avenue. Among his most successful is one for the Helmsley Building at 230 Park Avenue. When the decision was made to illuminate the building, the owners agreed to add plenty of gilding (including the sculptures and the clock) to enhance the effect, and a gold band around the lower part of the pyramid roof. The yellow (high-pressure sodium) light is focused on the tower from beneath and glows through the balustrades and onto the cupola. It gives a spectacular focus to the vista down Park Avenue.

More than three decades passed before Mr. Leigh had another crack at the Empire. In 1976, he was made chairman of City Decor to welcome the Democratic Convention and visitors for the Bicentennial. This time, he suggested to the ESB's owners that the lights be colored red, white, and blue. It was an instant success, and they were left that way until the end of that year. Mr. Leigh then offered the idea of tying the lights to different holidays, rather than the weather, which is the fundamental scheme still in effect today.

The great Broadway lighting designer Abe Feder also made an enormous contribution to the city at night when he was asked to light Rockefeller Center from four sides. He decided to project light up the building (about eight hundred and fifty feet), but the bulbs he used in the theater only projected eighty or so feet. Bulbs used in sports arenas projected greater distances, but they were meant to be on for a shorter period of time and were already big in size. In the end, he took these as a prototype and developed a bulb that had the power wattage increased from four hundred watts to fifteen hundred watts without increasing its size. In all, three hundred and forty two lights now illuminate Rockefeller Center from many locations, and Mr. Feder focused each one individually. The lighting was unveiled on December 3, 1984, at 5:15 p.m. before the lighting of the Christmas tree.

Bright lights in the big city are also on display at the Chrysler Building, the Four Seasons Hotel, Park Avenue Tower, Met Life, Con Ed, the Woolworth Building, and American International. For an exhilarating rush of warm light, though, it's hard to beat crossing the street at Fifth Avenue and 55th Street. Two hotels, the St. Regis and the Peninsula, straddle the thoroughfare, so pause as long as you can in the middle of it and look up. The luminosity from both buildings merges mid-avenue in such a great wash that even if New York isn't the City of Lights, its burnished glow stays with you.

CHARLES SUISMAN AND CAROL MOLESWORTH
Co-authors of Manhattan User's Guide

8.28 Louis Tannen Inc.

45 West 34th Street between Broadway and Sixth Avenue
Sixth floor

212 929 4500; www.tannens.com

You might never guess that this smallish shop is the largest magic store in the country, but then, nothing here is what it appears to be. You may see a silvery orb float inexplicably through space, a borrowed object vanish . . . only to re-appear in your pocket, or a card you have visualized rise, slowly and unaided, from its deck. But, of all the tricks—and there are hundreds of them displayed behind glass cases—the most amazing is the transformation of suspicious adults into bewildered children and vociferous children into speechless beings of pure joy.

The salesmen perform their legerdemain with enthusiasm and aplomb and, of course, as a means of selling the illusions. The customers—celebrities and CEOs, teachers and cops—watch in total amazement. The more magically advanced discuss and compare techniques against a learned history of prestidigitation and, maybe, show off their own variations.

Beware: this is a lifelong addiction. You may walk in to pick up some magician's wax or to discuss the "perfect Faro shuffle," when, before you know it, you have purchased all eight volumes of the *Tarbell Course in Magic*, first published in 1927, and presto... your money has vanished.

ROBERT KAHN
Architect

MURRAY HILL

8.29 Mid-Manhattan Library

455 Fifth Avenue at 40th Street
212 340 0833; www.nypl.org; www.digitalgallery.nypl.org

Picture Collection
Third floor

The Picture Collection at the Mid-Manhattan Library started out in 1915 as a modest collection of pictorial images. Today it is a huge circulating and reference archive containing more than five million images—illustrations clipped from books, magazines, newspapers, catalogs, and pamphlets, as well as postcards, linecuts, prints, and photographs—organized into nearly twelve thousand subject categories. In this unique collection, history is served up visually, in images that reflect the constant evolution of popular taste and trends. This archive is an unparalleled resource for research and brainstorming, and it is turned to regularly not only by designers, illustrators, and picture researchers, but also by visual artists, historians, students, writers, and professionals from advertising, interior design, book publishing, theater, fashion, and film. You can borrow any useful image, and people do, at the rate of half a million pictures loaned out each year.

MUNTADAS
Artist

8.30 Bronze Architectural Plaques

1996, Gregg LeFevre

Block encompassing 41st Street (south side, towards Lexington), Park Avenue (east side) and 40th Street (north side, towards Lexington)

Few people would think of shifting their gaze downward to view Midtown's famous towers, but doing so in the block of Park Avenue bounded by 40th and 41st Streets allows you to see the rich details of Midtown's skyscrapers without straining your eyes or craning your neck. Go to the east side of the Pershing Square overpass and start looking down. Seventeen bronze plaques are imbedded along the sidewalk, each depicting a famous building in the immediate vicinity. Artist Gregg LeFevre, well known for his public art, was commissioned to create the plaques, which celebrate the Grand Central area's rich architectural heritage.

The Modernist buildings—the Seagram, Pan Am, and Lever House—don't translate well to the medium; their geometry is better appreciated when you're standing in front of them. But the Art Deco jewels—particularly the Chanin, French, G.E., and the Daily News buildings—are beautifully rendered in bronze, with details that you can't see from the street. In particular, note the Egyptian styling of the French Building, showing mythical animals and lounging figures in high relief; the decorative detail in the fiery crown of the G.E. Building; the Aztec geometry of the Chrysler Building doorway; and the original decorative elements of the Bowery Savings Bank portal (some of which have been removed from the building). Some of these buildings are within a two-minute walk, so after you see them in bronze, you can see them for real.

Or, opt for a free guided tour with an urban historian, sponsored by the Grand Central Partnership (☎ 212 883 2468; www.grandcentralpartnership.org).

LANA BORTOLOT
Writer

Historic Savings Banks

In Manhattan:

4.22 **Bowery Savings Bank**
1895, Stanford White of McKim, Mead & White
130 Bowery between Grand and Broome Streets
www.nyc-architecture.com

8.31 **Former Bowery Savings Bank, now Cipriani's 42nd Street**
1923, York & Sawyer
110 East 42nd Street between Park and Lexington Avenues
www.nyc-architecture.com

12.29 **Former Central Savings Bank, now Apple Bank for Savings**
1928, York & Sawyer
2100 Broadway at West 73rd Street

7.9 **Former Greenwich Savings Bank, now Republic National Bank**
1924, York & Sawyer
1352–1362 Broadway at West 36th Street

In Brooklyn:

The Dime Savings Bank of New York
1908, Mowbray & Uffinger; 1932, expanded by Halsey, McCormack & Helmer
9 DeKalb Avenue, off Fulton Street (not on map)

Former Williamsburgh Savings Bank Tower, now Republic National Bank

1929, Halsey, McCormack & Helmer

1 Hanson Place at Ashland Place (not on map)

The ATM has made them an endangered species, but from the 1890s to the 1930s the explosion of savings banks eager to house the pennies of New Yorkers created spaces that surpass many of the city's civic buildings and churches in awe-inspiring splendor. Hurry to see them before 3 p.m. closing and before yet another one becomes a Duane Reade drugstore (it happened at the corner of West 96th Street and Amsterdam Avenue) or a Gap (East 85th Street). In most cases the grand but solemn exterior hardly prepares one for the luxury of both space and materials that greets you within. We instinctively become quiet, as if in a church—the only place, it seems, where Americans are hesitant to talk up about money. Moralism and patriotism are also good incentives for squirreling away your cash—be sure and read the inscriptions on the benches provided at my personal favorite, downtown Brooklyn's Dime Savings Bank, before you sit down to wait for your turn at the teller's booth.

BARRY BERGDOLL

Philip Johnson Chief Curator of Architecture and Design, MoMA

9

Hudson River
West Side Hwy (Joe DiMaggio Hwy)
Freedom Pl
West End Avenue
Amsterdam Avenue
Lincoln Center
Columbus Avenue
Broadway
Central Park West
Central Park
Columbus Circle
W 66th St
W 60th St
W 59th St
W 58th St
W 57th St
W 56th St
W 55th St
W 54th St
W 53rd St
W 52nd St
W 51st St
W 50th St
W 49th St
W 48th St
W 47th St
W 46th St
W 45th St
W 44th St
W 43rd St
W 42nd St
W 34th St
W 28th St
Pier 99
Pier 98
Pier 97
Pier 96
Pier 95
Pier 94
Pier 92
Pier 90
Pier 88
Pier 86
Pier 84
Pier 83
Pier 81
De Witt Clinton Park
Midtown West
Twelfth Avenue
Eleventh Avenue
Tenth Avenue
Ninth Avenue
Eighth Avenue
Seventh Avenue
Dyer Avenue
Lincoln Tunnel
Garment District
Madison Square Garden
Penn Station

CHAPTER 9

TIMES SQUARE

1 Barbetta
2 Joe Allen's
3 Becco
4 Lattanzi
5 FireBird
6 Frankie & Johnnie's
7 Edison Hotel
8 I. Miller Building
9 Church of St. Mary
10 St. Malachy's Church

MIDTOWN WEST

11 Russian Samovar
12 Gallagher's Steakhouse
13 Museum of Arts & Design
14 Henri Bendel
15 Museum of Modern Art (see p. 194)
16 St. Thomas Church
17 CBS Building (see p. 194, 199)
18 The Paley Center for Media
19 Former Tishman Building (see p. 194)
20 Rockefeller Center
21 Minamoto Kitchoan
22 Pier 96 (see p. 39)
23 Hudson River Powerhouse

Times Square & Midtown West

TIMES SQUARE

Restaurant Row

9.1 **Barbetta**
321 West 46th Street between Eighth and Ninth Avenues
212 246 9171; www.barbettarestaurant.com

9.2 **Joe Allen's**
326 West 46th Street between Eighth and Ninth Avenues
212 581 6464; www.joeallenrestaurant.com

9.3 **Becco**
335 West 46th Street between Eighth and Ninth Avenues
212 397 7597; www.becco-nyc.com

9.4 **Lattanzi**
361 West 46th Street between Eighth and Ninth Avenues
212 315 0980; www.lattanzinyc.com

9.5 **FireBird Russian Restaurant**
365 West 46th Street between Eighth and Ninth Avenues
212 586 0244; www.firebirdrestaurant.com

Before or after the theater, "Restaurant Row," West 46th Street between Eighth and Ninth Avenues, with almost every building occupied by a restaurant, offers a wide choice of cuisines—American, French, Italian, Spanish, Russian, kosher—at a wide range of prices. My favorites: Becco for pasta; Joe Allen's for atmosphere; FireBird for decor; Barbetta for old-fashioned elegant service; and Lattanzi for the delicacies of the Roman ghetto.

KENNETH SEEMAN GINIGER
Publisher, editor, and author

9.6 Frankie & Johnnie's Steakhouse

269 West 45th Street between Seventh and Eighth Avenues
212 997 9494; www.frankieandjohnnies.com

For a living glimpse of Damon Runyon's Manhattan, that gin-drinking, hat-wearing, Lucky-smoking town, get yourself seated at the table next to the first full window on the left as you enter Frankie & Johnnie's, which since 1926 has been feeding Broadway types and theatergoers. The steak house is on the second floor, and you will be looking past the ironwork of an artfully placed fire escape down to a slice of Eighth Avenue that encompasses the half-century-old neon signage proclaiming the presence of Smith's Bar, while above the saloon's roof rises the superb 1931 Art Moderne tower of Raymond Hood's original McGraw-Hill Building, over on 42nd Street. The view is good at twilight, wonderful in rainy twilight, and the steak you must have while taking it in won't disappoint you either.

RICHARD SNOW
Historian and author

9.7 Edison Hotel

228 West 47th Street between Broadway and Eighth Avenue

Cafe Edison

In the Edison Hotel
212 354 0368; www.edisonhotelnyc.com

This Midtown restaurant is nicknamed "the Polish Tea Room" (to distinguish it from its infinitely snootier Russian cousin) by the Broadway producers, directors, and actors who often lunch there. While you eat the classic deli food, served by that New York rarity, a waitstaff that isn't comprised of actors, you may well overhear what's in the works for next year's Broadway season.

GREGORY MOSHER
Theater director and producer

9.8 I. Miller Building

1929, Louis H. Friedland
167 West 46th Street at Seventh Avenue

As you stroll down Broadway after your matinee, stop and glance at the inscription on the façade of 167 West 46th Street (close to the northeast corner of Seventh Avenue and 46th Street), the site of the I. Miller shoe shop that served New Yorkers from 1929 into the 1970s. The words "The Show Folks Shoe Shop Dedicated to Beauty in Footwear" describe I. Miller's two passions—shoes and stars. As an added attraction, four statues by Alexander Stirling Calder (father of Alexander Calder of mobile fame) appear in niches below the inscription. Miller invited the public to vote for their favorite actresses as models. The winners were Ethel Barrymore as Ophelia, Mary Pickford as Little Lord Fauntleroy, Marilyn Miller as Sunny, and Rosa Ponselle as Norma.

THERESA CRAIG
Writer

9.9 Church of St. Mary the Virgin

1895, Napoleon Le Brun & Sons
145 West 46th Street between Sixth and Seventh Avenues
212 869 5830; www.stmvirgin.org

Established in 1868 as the first Episcopalian church in America to combine the Roman Catholic liturgical tradition with the Protestant tenets of the Anglican church, St. Mary's is a bastion of the "high church" ceremonial tradition in America. The church is famous for its use of incense, which hangs particularly heavy on humid days, and enjoys the nickname "Smoky Mary's." The second and current building has the distinction of being the first church façade in New York City to be adorned with religious statues, counter to the prevailing Puritan tradition eschewing religious iconography. Fewer than forty years later the climate had changed dramatically. The "new" building completed in 1895 is one of the surprises of New York's grid of streets, which hides some of the city's best assets. Located mid-block on 46th Street between Sixth and Seventh Avenues, just steps from Times Square, the building, with its eighty-foot nave, was once the tallest and most prominent structure in the neighborhood. Now the church lies virtually buried in the skyscrapers of the last century. Ironically, it was the skyscraper technology that allowed this impressive complex of church, mission house, and rectory to be constructed in fewer than two years. New visitors and the many pilgrims who find their way here each day are agape at the splendid interior, decorated in the French Gothic taste with a sky-blue ceiling and gold stars. This combination is steep competition to the nexus of neon and bright lights less than a block away. No single work of art dominates the space; instead it is the sum of its parts: the four marble altars, probably a hundred statues, and the exceptional late-Victorian metal, glass, and woodwork. The Aeolian-Skinner organ is one of the most famous church organs in the world and is particularly well suited to the building. These elements combine to enhance the most ceremonious celebration of the Mass. The services, especially High Mass at 11 a.m. on Sunday, have particular style and dignity. While the social tradition of the church has progressed (there are women priests, and gays and lesbians are welcomed), the service has a decidedly old-fashioned air. After the 11 a.m. service there is coffee hour where a great cross section of the city is present. Over homemade cakes and cookies, you are just as likely to meet a visiting bishop, a homeless person, or a Park Avenue matron.

THOMAS JAYNE
Interior designer

Cherished Churches

9.16 St. Thomas Church
1914, Cram, Goodhue & Ferguson
1 West 53rd Street at Fifth Avenue
212 757 7013, www.saintthomaschurch.org

12.27 Christ and St. Stephen's Church
1880, William H. Day
120 West 69th Street between Broadway and Columbus Avenue
212 787 2755; www.csschurch.org

9.10 St. Malachy's Roman Catholic Church
1903, Joseph H. McGuire
239 West 49th Street between Broadway and Eighth Avenue
212 489 1340; www.actorschapel.org

5.3 Church of the Ascension
1841, Richard Upjohn; 1889, interior renovated by McKim, Mead & White
36–38 Fifth Avenue at West 10th Street
212 254 8620; www.ascensionnyc.org

New York, unlike European capitals, is not too faithful to her treasures. Paris wouldn't have let the wrecking ball get anywhere near the Empire Theatre (see p. 136), that elegant little jewel box, or the marvelous, stately Metropolitan Opera House (the old one, not the Lincoln Center World's Fair-ish one).

But God and the Chamber of Commerce willing, some of my favorite icons are still around. To start with, I'm a church junkie—not so much for the grandiose cathedrals like St. John the Divine and St. Pat's. But I love St. Thomas; its stained-glass rose window is hard to beat.

Christ and St. Stephen's Church has wonderful windows, too. They were designed by Sir Edward Burne-Jones, a nineteenth-century painter.

The actors' chapel in St. Malachy's Roman Catholic Church is beloved, of course, by all us showbiz types who appreciate their staying open late so that those who work in Broadway shows can worship after the curtains come down.

I have a sentimental spot in my heart for Church of the Ascension. It's not at all grand, but in the halcyon days of the 1930s when I first attempted to storm Manhattan's bastions, it was open all night. I shed many a tear on its altar as I asked God please to let me find work so I could stay in this glittering, improbable city and not have to retreat in defeat to Alabama.

HUGH MARTIN

The late Hugh Martin was a songwriter. He wrote the score for Meet Me in St. Louis, in which Judy Garland sings "The Trolley Song" and "Have Yourself a Merry Little Christmas."

MIDTOWN WEST

9.11 The Russian Samovar

256 West 52nd Street between Broadway and Eighth Avenue
212 757 0168; www.russiansamovar.com

When Joseph Brodsky was alive, he and I would often go to the Russian Samovar to drink and talk about poetry. It was always vodka—many flavors of it. Joseph would usually have cilantro. I would have cranberry. We talked and talked, stopping now and then to take large bites of smoked salmon, smoked sturgeon, and pickled herring, usually with black bread. And the caviar we consumed! The food, like the vodka, was excellent. But what made the Russian Samovar special was its owner, Roman Kaplan, who knew Joseph before he came to this country. He is one of the warmest and most generous men that I have ever known. Whenever I go to New York, I go to the Russian Samovar, sit down, have some vodka, and talk with

Roman. A gifted pianist plays sad Russian songs. Almost everyone in the restaurant is speaking Russian. Mikhail Baryshnikov, who is a part owner, is a frequent patron. Joseph hovers nearby.

MARK STRAND
Poet

9.12 Gallagher's Steak House

228 West 52nd Street between Broadway and Eighth Avenue
☎ 212 245 5336; www.gallaghersnysteakhouse.com

This sprawling speakeasy-turned-restaurant has been here since 1927 when Helen Gallagher (a former Ziegfeld girl) and Jack Solomon opened the place. Take a peek at the meat from the street—the front window offers a prime view of the walk-in locker loaded with aging marbleized beef at this classic steak house just off the Great White Way. The wood-paneled walls are covered with portraits of celebrities, sports heroes, and legendary racehorses—from Jackie O to Joe DiMaggio to Man o' War. Sit "under the bull" (one of the best seats in the house) or perhaps at Marilyn Monroe's table (Number 83), where one night she was thrilled when the mutually starstruck Myrna Loy, and then Henry Fonda, paid calls to her corner banquette. Joe DiMaggio (Number 84) was a regular, too. When a young boy requested his autograph, "Broadway" Joe Namath responded by grabbing a roll from the bread basket and telling the kid he'd sign only if he ran deep for a pass. Liza Minelli and her mom, Judy Garland, considered Gallagher's a real New York joint. The red-and-white checkered tablecloths attest to its zero-pretension, comfortable comfort-food attitude.

Gallagher's legendary late owner, Jerome Brody, was the founder of Restaurant Associates and at one time also owned the Four Seasons, the Oyster Bar, and the Rainbow Room. The friendly waiters and bartenders have been here for years and treat everyone like a celebrity. The oval

9.14 Henri Bendel (former Coty Building)

1909, façade by Woodruff Leeming
714 Fifth Avenue between 55th and 56th Streets

Lalique windows

1912, René Lalique

While you're window-shopping at Henri Bendel, look up to the top three floors to see René Lalique's lead-crystal Art Nouveau windows, the only example of his architectural glass in New York, and one of few examples in the United States.

Go to the back of the store and up the winding staircase to each mezzanine, where you can see the etchings up close. Merchandise sometimes obscures the view, but you can still get a good look at the tulips and vines crisscrossing gracefully through the panes. Lalique also designed the original interior, commissioned by the French perfumer Coty, for whom the building was built. Messieurs Coty and Lalique had neighboring businesses on Place Vendôme in Paris and, as a designer for the perfume labels and bottles, Lalique was the natural choice for Coty's flagship store in the United States. Though the Lalique interior no longer exists—the entire store was renovated in the 1990s—the windows (also recently restored) are a sparkling piece of Belle Epoque Paris in Midtown Manhattan.

LANA BORTOLOT
Writer

9.16 St. Thomas Church

1 West 53rd Street at Fifth Avenue
212 757 7013; www.saintthomaschurch.org
Check the website for a schedule of choral services.

The St. Thomas Choir of Men and Boys is recognized as the premiere choral ensemble of the Anglican musical tradition in the United States today, and as one of the world's finest choral groups. Patterned after the Continental and English cathedral and collegiate chapel choir models, and comprised of men and boys, it consists of twelve professionals from the New York City metropolitan region singing countertenor, tenor, and bass parts, while eighteen boys from the St. Thomas Choir School provide the soprano section. The school is the only church-related residential choir school in the country, and one of only four schools of this type remaining worldwide.

Go for Handel's *Messiah* just before Christmas, one of three major concerts yearly with accompanying orchestra. On a wintry evening, New Yorkers can pretend they are climbing the steps of the Imperial Chapel in Vienna. Or go for one of the numerous occasions between mid-September and May, on which you can hear this choir's large and beautiful repertory of mass settings, canticles, anthems, cantatas, and oratorios at services. The combination of voice, music, and magical Gothic setting is uplifting.

JANE FISHER
Marketing consultant

9.18 The Paley Center for Media

1991, John Burgee and Philip Johnson
25 West 52nd Street between Fifth and Sixth Avenues
212 621 6600; www.paleycenter.org

John Burgee and Philip Johnson's building attempts to discipline the twentieth century's unruly mass media inside a tight little tower of respectability and historic allusion, exemplified by a grand country house window above a Romanesque doorway. Fat chance.

Everyone has a favorite treasure in this seductive archive of history and entertainment (formerly the Museum of Television and Media)—Roosevelt, HUAC, Bankhead, Benny, *I Love Lucy*, *The War of the Worlds*—but respectability has little to do with it. More like a need to connect with the lost anarchies of showbiz and the compulsiveness of the filmed past.

My first choice is always Imogene Coca, sublime clown and stooge to Sid Caesar in *Your Show of Shows* (1950–1954), the benchmark series from America's heroic age of television comedy, when programs went out live and scary. Pop-eyed, toothy, and built like a collapsible bird, Coca is the token girl in a Manhattan boys' town—the gagsters joining Caesar in the famous room above City Center included Carl Reiner, Mel Brooks, Neil Simon, and Woody Allen—and when she is on screen you don't even look at the star. Caesar is brilliant but very aggressive; Coca distills an air of eagerness, gentility, and incompetence that would be funny with no script at all. I never tire of "The Clock," in which C and C run amok as malign, desynchronized figures on a Mittel-European timepiece; or "The Lorelei," in which our heroine acquires a tutu and falls over the scenery while trying to stay out of sight. *Swan Lake* was never the same after that.

Reserve your viewings from the catalog in the lobby as you arrive; you will then be allotted a booth in a viewing room. There are also public showings from the collection of more than fifty thousand items every day. One drawback: no café, but here in Midtown you'll hardly go short, and MoMA is on the next block.

MICHAEL RATCLIFFE
Former literary editor and chief book critic, The Times (London)

9.20 Rockefeller Center

1932–1940, The Associated Architects: Reinhard & Hofmeister, Corbett, Harrison & MacMurray; Raymond Hood, Godley & Fouilhoux

West 48th Street to West 51st Street between Fifth and Sixth Avenues

212 632 3975; www.rockefellercenter.com

New York State has many architecturally notable venues. Given the variety of scale, use, and context, it is extremely difficult to single out just a few projects. Some of the indigenous styles, like the rhythmical Manhattan brownstones, the rich expressions of the cast-iron district, the glorious skyscrapers, the parks, and many cultural centers, are wonderments in themselves. But on the basis of enrichment to the human experience, I would have to rank Rockefeller Center at the top. This complex of buildings, larger than some cities, is a marvel of urban design, enduring architecture, and integrated art.

The composition of massing and open space has made Rockefeller Center the most powerful and dramatic man-made environment in the world. Upon entering the complex from Fifth Avenue between 49th and 50th Streets, one is immediately struck by the intimacy of the axial allée with its refined low-scaled flanking buildings, central gardens, and restrained storefronts. As the gardens gently slope toward the delightful, oasis-like central plaza with its sunken courtyard, they form a perfectly proportioned forecourt for the soaring sixty-story RCA Building (now the G.E. Building). Beyond the face of this multiple-slab tower, form immediately draws the eye up and marks the focal point of the center.

Each building in the ensemble is beautifully scaled and balanced to support the overall composition. While the components forming the central axis are symmetrical, the remainder of the buildings vary in height and bulk, thereby blending naturally into the surrounding urban fabric. Remarkably, there is no clear demarcation of Rockefeller Center. Except for the sunken plaza area and an unusual sense of visual order with a consistently high quality of architectural expression in a similar vocabulary, the streetscape does not dramatically change from adjoining neighborhoods.

The architectural vocabulary, a unique blend of Art Deco and vertical modern, consists primarily of naturally cleft limestone, refined bronze storefronts, and metal spandrel panels. The lower elevations are solid stone with elegantly balanced combinations of ribbon glass and punched retail windows. As the buildings rise, the façades turn to exquisitely composed vertical bands of limestone, alternating with windows and recessed limestone or rippled cast-aluminum spandrels that create a dramatic soaring effect. These vertical elements continue to the top of each wall plane, building energy as they rise and meet the sky.

Each building has a unique entry that creates visual interest and identity at the pedestrian level. The Fifth Avenue buildings have nicely scaled, recessed courtyards that appropriately relieve the congestion on the crowded sidewalk and create dramatic settings for the huge bronze sculptures. Most entries are marked by polychrome reliefs above the openings, each with its own theme relating to the original tenancy of the respective buildings. The lobbies—all different—have their own ambience, with large wall murals, black granite Deco motifs, terrazzo floors, and wainscot. Some are more successful than others, but all are executed with an artistic flair and sense of permanence. The underground network of shopping concourses, subway access, and service corridors, linking the buildings to the sunken plaza as well as to each other, is a marvel in itself.

No aspect was overlooked in the design of this remarkable complex, and it works just as well today as it did when it opened seventy years ago! This is urban design at its finest—holistic, timeless, futuristic, culturally enriching, uplifting, pedestrian-oriented, and economically viable. It may never be matched.

BRUCE S. FOWLE
Architect

Rock's Paper, Scissors

7.14 **Books Kinokuniya**
1073 Sixth Avenue between 40th and 41st Streets
212 869 1700; www.kinokuniya.com

9.21 **Minamoto Kitchoan**
608 Fifth Avenue between West 48th and West 49th Streets
212 489-3747; www.kitchoan.com

A visit to the Japanese bookstore Kinokuniya makes an exhilarating field trip for those interested in books, graphics, and the visual refreshment of the Eastern aesthetic. The store specializes in Japanese books, magazines, and English books on Japan (check out the collection of Japanese cookbooks in English). Although those not fluent in Japanese can only appreciate the graphics, anyone should be able to follow the diagrams in the sophisticated and specialized assortment of origami manuals. For a lovely inventory of origami paper, walk upstairs to the mezzanine level—and if you are someone who has been known to lust after a beautifully engineered and designed notebook, buckle your seat belt. You will find a sublime assortment here, along with an irresistible array of stationery, paper goods, and all manner of related items. Several of the binders here can be customized by choosing from a wide array of inserts: dividers, clear envelopes, paper with different colors, lines, and grids, and more. Even the staple removers are a delight, as are many of the pens, clips, drawing pads, notebooks, and blank books. The discriminating calligrapher will appreciate the wide selection of paints, inks, and brushes. There are clipboards, erasers, and pencil cases for the design-forward student. Stickers for kids. Chic aluminum containers as well as cardboard drawers and nesting boxes.

This is the place to find the gift you won't find elsewhere: sachets wrapped in printed silk and tucked in a beautiful wooden box; or metal, ceramic, and lacquer paperweights and desk accessories, which will be appreciated by an executive or an aesthete. Wrap it up in one of the decorative papers, available by the sheet, printed with traditional Japanese designs.

There is a small snack counter on the main floor of Kinokuniya that serves teas, coffees, soft drinks, sandwiches, and cakes. For more elaborate fare, walk down the block to Minamoto Kitchoan, a Japanese confectionery filled with exotic sweet delicacies artfully displayed.

ANGELA HEDERMAN
Publisher

9.23 Hudson River Powerhouse

1900–1904, McKim, Mead & White
12th Avenue between West 58th and West 59th Streets
646 918 7917; www.hudsonriverpowerhouse.com

The IRT powerhouse is one of the most unusual architectural monuments in America. Designed by McKim, Mead & White in 1900 to power the very first section of the New York City subway system, it was the largest powerhouse in the world, and used the most sophisticated technology in the production of electrical power at that time. The delicately adorned exterior of the powerhouse was designed in the Beaux-Arts style, reflecting the civic-minded ideals of the City Beautiful movement. In 1904, *The New York Times* described it as " . . . an ornament to the west side that enhances rather than diminishes the value of the surrounding property. But for its stacks, it might suggest an art museum or public library rather than a powerhouse."

In 1959, the building was sold to Con Edison for use as a power station for the New York City steam system. The utility promptly built a flat brick addition to the building, covering its western façade. As the demand for steam waned over the last twenty years, Con Edison has decommissioned most of the building and recently demolished the last of the original five smokestacks. The once majestic turbine hall stands largely empty. Decades of neglect have left other scars: steel loading doors have damaged the finely carved terra-cotta friezes and the original building cornice is entirely gone.

Efforts to designate the building a historic landmark, in 1979 and 1990, failed in the face of the powerful public utility. In 2007, The Hudson River Powerhouse Group was formed to lobby the city to designate the powerhouse a landmark, raise funds to restore the building, and re-purpose this once grand powerhouse as a public space. It remains to be seen if this gem will be preserved or demolished.

BASIL WALTER
Architect

10
The Mall
Sheep Meadow
W 66th St
E 66th St
E 65th St
Central Park
Wollman Rink
The Zoo
The Pond
Columbus Avenue
Broadway
Central Park West
Fifth Avenue
Madison Avenue
Park Avenue
Lexington Avenue
W 60th St
E 60th St
Columbus Circle
Central Park South
E 59th St
E 58th St
W 57th St
E 57th St
Midtown West
E 56th St
E 55th St
E 54th St
E 53rd St
E 52nd St
E 51st St
E 50th St
E 49th St
Rockefeller Center
W 48th St
E 48th St
W 47th St
E 47th St
W 46th St
E 46th St
W 45th St
E 45th St
W 44th St
E 44th St
W 43rd St
E 43rd St
Times Square
Vanderbilt Avenue
Grand Central Terminal
W 42nd St
E 42nd St
Bryant Park
New York Public Library
E 41st St
E 40th St
Murray
Garment District
Eighth Avenue
Seventh Avenue
Sixth Avenue (Avenue of the Americas)
W 34th St
E 34th St
Madison Square Garden
Penn Station
Midtown South
W 28th St
E 28th St

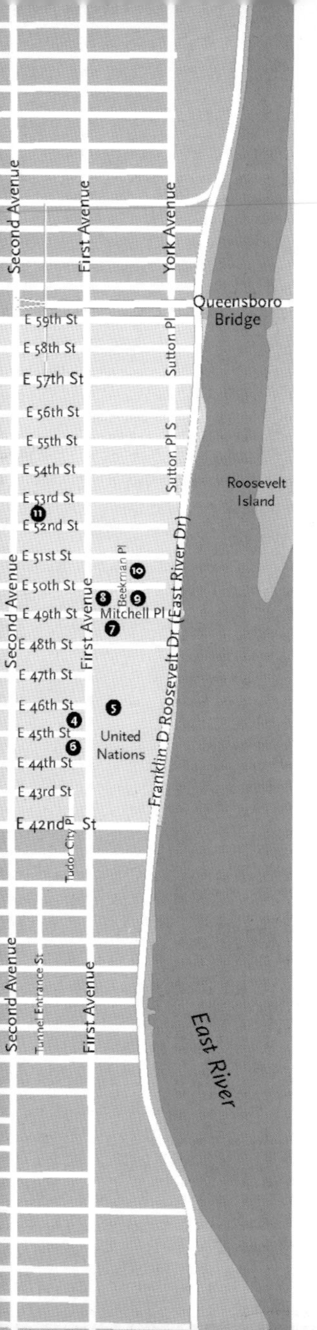

CHAPTER 10

MIDTOWN

1 New York Yacht Club
2 Grand Central Terminal
3 Sakagura
4 Kaufmann Conference Room
5 United Nations Headquarters
6 United Nations Plaza Apartments
7 Mitchell Place
8 Beekman Tower
8 Top of the Tower Restaurant
9 Luxembourg Mission
10 Home of Paul Rudolph
11 Wood Frame Houses
12 St. Peter's Lutheran Church
13 Seagram Building
13 The Four Seasons
13 Brasserie
14 Villard Houses
15 Lever House
16 Racquet and Tennis Club
17 St. Regis-Sheraton Hotel
18 Segment of Berlin Wall
19 Samuel Paley Plaza
20 Cartier
21 Fifth Avenue Presbyterian Church
22 Tiffany & Co.
23 Sherry Netherland Clock
24 Pepsi-Cola Building

Midtown

10.1 The New York Yacht Club

1900, Warren & Wetmore
37 West 44th Street between Fifth and Sixth Avenues
212 382 1000; www.nyyc.org
Not open to the public.

The architects of Grand Central Terminal, Warren & Wetmore, humored their seafaring Gilded Age clients with this outrageous 1900 Beaux Arts façade. Among the building's stately columns and arches are fantastic nautical motifs pirated from the designs of High Renaissance galleons and grottoes. Into each tall clubhouse window, an old ship appears to have just sailed, trailing sea foam in its wake which pretends to pour over the stone ledges and into the street.

COLTA IVES
Curator of drawings and prints, The Metropolitan Museum of Art

10.2 Grand Central Terminal

1913, Reed & Stem and Warren & Wetmore
East 42nd Street at Park Avenue

As Sun Tzu, author of *The Art of War*, might have put it, "Never stand between a commuter and his train." The vast marble floor of Grand Central Terminal is the prime vantage point for observing the remarkable sight of New Yorkers walking. Unlike out-of-towners, who walk four abreast, arms swinging widely, or who stand stolidly unmoving when you try to get past, New Yorkers walk sleekly, rapidly as surgeons on rounds. They dodge and shift, adjusting shoulders and briefcases to allow one another to pass with minute precision. You can see them on any New York street, their shoulders drawn in, arms barely swinging, advancing with long strides. You can see them inching into traffic, jockeying on corners, waiting for their moment of opportunity. They juggle coffee cups, cigarettes, briefcases, groceries, and gym bags, and still manage to have a hand free to hail a cab or gesticulate to their companion. But the newly scrubbed Grand Central is the best place to watch New Yorkers walk. Stand on the steps leading to Vanderbilt Avenue and look down at the wonderful ballet. Each person is on an urgent mission, each must take the shortest path to their train or office or shrink; they cannot yield, but none collide. It is the essence of New York's grace.

DAVID HELLERSTEIN
Psychiatrist, author, journalist, and professor

The Whispering Gallery

In Grand Central Terminal, East 42nd Street and Vanderbilt Avenue entrance

When I was a boy, it seemed to me that this acoustical oddity was pretty well known, but in recent years nobody I've mentioned it to has heard of it. The Whispering Gallery offers another reason (not that one is needed) to visit the magnificently restored Grand Central Terminal. Once in the station, go to the Oyster Bar and at the main entrance, which is on the ramp to the lower level, turn your back to the restaurant, look up, and you'll see a tawny, supple Guastavino tile dome riding on four piers. Go to one of these piers and stand with your face close into the corner; send a companion to the one diagonally across the way. Then speak softly; your voices will sound in each other's ears, as close, intimate, and audible as if you were sitting together in a small car rather than murmuring across a broad concourse full of urgent clatter.

RICHARD SNOW
Historian and author

In the bowels of the bustling terminal, not far from the Oyster Bar, is a remarkable corner best visited in the dead of night. A crossing pair of vaulted arches creates an acoustically perfect spot. Two lovers may stand at opposite ends of the cavern, whisper sweet nothings, and be heard only by each other.

JOHN JILER
Playwright and author

Oyster Bar
In Grand Central Terminal
East 42nd Street and Vanderbilt Avenue
212 490 6650; www.oysterbarny.com

A pearl, a treasure, this vast, bustling eighty-eight-year old classic is tucked under Guastavino's vaulted tiled ceilings at the foot of Grand Central Terminal's great ramps. Not exactly a secret, this New York institution serves the freshest and widest range of seafood in the city. Choose from more than two dozen different types of oysters and more than two dozen types of fish. A real New Yorker will skip the dining room, sit at the lunch counter and ask Charlotte for a half-dozen briny, luscious cherrystones, followed by the creamy, plump oyster pan roast. You'll be back tomorrow for more.

TRACEY HUMMER AND FREDERIC SCHWARTZ
Writer and Architect

10.3 Sakagura

211 East 43rd Street, B1F, between Second and Third Avenues
212 953 7253; www.sakagura.com

You'll find the best sushi in New York at Sakagura, an elegant sake bar improbably located in the basement of a Midtown office building.

ALEXANDER DUFF
Restaurateur

10.4 Edward J. Kaufmann Conference Rooms

1965, Alvar Aalto

In the Institute of International Education

809 United Nations Plaza (First Avenue) between East 45th and East 46th Streets

For tours: ☎ 212 963 8687; www.un.org/tours

Alvar Aalto (1898–1976) was one of the most important and influential Modernist masters of the twentieth century. Frank Lloyd Wright briefly put his ego in the backseat to praise him as a genius and, with this endorsement, architectural historian Edgar J. Kaufmann Jr. (of Fallingwater family fame) commissioned Aalto to design the twelfth-floor conference room in 1965. Located in the Institute of International Education, the space overlooks the United Nations and the East River. The only place in New York where one can experience the Finnish architect's work, his convertible, blond-on-blond interior seamlessly combines fluidity and sensuousness with practical and functional details. The undulating walls include Aalto's signature hockey-stick-like birchwood slat sculpture and sedate ash panels. For a splash of color, Aalto framed openings in the entry hall with cobalt blue tiles. Jump at the chance to see this somewhat secret spot, recently "saved" by the Municipal Art Society.

TRACEY HUMMER AND FREDERIC SCHWARTZ
Writer and Architect

10.5 United Nations Headquarters

1953, International Committee of Architects

United Nations Plaza (First Avenue) between East 42nd and East 48th Streets

Guided tours only: ☎ 212 963 8687; www.un.org/tours

A world unto itself stretching six blocks, from 42nd to 48th Streets along First Avenue and the East River, the

U.N. Headquarters complex is the architectural apotheosis of modern functionalism and the embodiment of post-World War II optimism. On land given to the U.N. by John D. Rockefeller, the buildings we see today include the Secretariat, a thirty-nine-story glass-and-aluminum curtain-wall skyscraper, the low-slung profile of the General Assembly with its awkward dome, the Conference Building overlooking the river, and a library. Given the geopolitical structure of the U.N., perhaps it is not surprising that the buildings are the result of design by committee. In 1947, New York architect Wallace Harrison chaired an international board of design comprised of ten architects from various member countries, including Le Corbusier from France and Oscar Niemeyer from Brazil, whose ideas were seminal to the final outcome. Harrison hoped that the "workshop for peace," an economical, functional, and efficient modern design, would symbolize the rational ideals of the member nations. The unfortunate addition of the dome over the Assembly chamber had been requested by the American Representative to the U.N., Senator Warren Austin, because he believed this traditional architectural element was a necessary symbol for a new world capitol.

The interior is well worth a tour, as much to observe the ambitious, complex work of the organization as to enjoy the art (such as the Fernand Léger murals in the Assembly chamber), interior design, and views from the dining room overlooking the river, from which one sees the southern tip of Roosevelt Island (which still awaits its presidential memorial), and the giant, decades-old Pepsi sign in Queens. Near the visitors' entrance, one can also mail cards and letters with unique U.N. stamps from the post office on the lower level. Take note of the three council chambers, each designed by a Scandinavian at the time when the concept of "Scandinavian design" was born. Finn Juhl (Denmark) designed the Trusteeship Council, Sven Markelius (Sweden) designed the Economic and Social Council, and Arnstein Arneberg (Norway) the Security Council. As any student of modern architecture must realize, the renowned Alvar Aalto of Finland, who was at the peak of his career, is absent from this architectural constellation—this, for the simple and unfortunate reason that Finland was not yet a member country of the U.N. Interestingly, some years later, in 1965, this omission was corrected when Aalto was given an opportunity to design his surrogate council chamber across from the U.N. atop the former Institute of International Education. Believing that New York deserved a work by the Finnish master, Edgar Kaufmann Jr. commissioned Aalto to design the Edgar J. Kaufmann Conference Rooms, to be named after his father. The elder Kaufmann was a Pittsburgh merchant who also had a strong design sensibility: he commissioned Frank Lloyd Wright for his home, Fallingwater. The Kaufmann Conference Rooms are one of only three works by Aalto in the United States.

PETER REED
Senior deputy director for cultural affairs, MoMA

Peace Bell

1952, Chiyoji Nakagawa

In the Garden of Peace, northwest of the Secretariat

212 963 8687; www.un.org/tours

A grand Shinto bell gong of two hundred and fifty six pounds is sheltered in a shrine on the grounds of the United Nations. Cast in Japan of tinkling coins from more than sixty countries, its history is magical.

In 1952, sixty United Nations officials at a Paris conference table dreamed aloud, searching for a symbol whose language people of the world would understand. Discussion led to each tossing coins from his pocket onto the table. An observer delegate from Japan offered to have an esteemed bell foundry cast them into a giant bell, adding pennies from the children of Japan. Famous throughout history, Asian bells have been forged of molten metal, often including donated coins to add to the sentiment and tone of the bells. This one is inscribed "Long Live Absolute World Peace" in Japanese.

Each September, there is a celebrated ringing of the bell to open the General Assembly of the U.N. It also rings for Earth Day in the spring and other special occasions.

TERRY MAYER
Jewelery designer and bellologist

53rd Street Stroll

10.6 **United Nations Plaza Apartments**
First Avenue at 44th Street

10.7 **Mitchell Place**
East 49th Street between First Avenue and Beekman Place

10.8 **Beekman Tower**
1928, John Mead Howells
3 Mitchell Place, 49th Street east of First Avenue

10.8 **Top of the Tower Restaurant**
3 Mitchell Place, 26th floor
212 980 4796; www.thetopofthetower.com

10.9 **Luxembourg Mission to the United Nations**
17 Beekman Place at East 50th Street
212 935 3589; www.un.int/luxembourg

10.10 **Former Home of Paul Rudolph**
1987, Paul Rudolph
23 Beekman Place at East 50th Street

10.11 **Wood Frame Houses**

312 and 314 East 53rd Street between First and Second Avenues

10.13 **Seagram Building**

1958, Ludwig Mies van der Rohe (with Philip Johnson; also Kahn & Jacobs)

375 Park Avenue between East 52nd and East 53rd Streets
www.nyc-architecture.com

10.13 **Brasserie**

2002, Diller and Scofidio

100 East 53rd Street between Park and Lexington Avenues
☎ 212 751 4840; www.patinagroup.com

10.13 **The Four Seasons**

1959, Philip Johnson & Associates

In the Seagram Building
99 East 52nd Street
☎ 212 754 9494; www.fourseasonsrestaurant.com

10.15 **Lever House**

1952, Gordon Bunshaft of Skidmore, Owings & Merrill

390 Park Avenue between East 53rd and East 54th Streets

10.16 **Racquet and Tennis Club**

1918, McKim, Mead & White

370 Park Avenue between East 52nd and East 53rd Streets
☎ 212 753 9700
Not open to the public.

10.18 **Segment of Berlin Wall**

On East 53rd Street between Fifth and Madison Avenues, east of Samuel Paley Plaza

10.19 **Samuel Paley Plaza**

1967, Robert Zion and Harold Breen in association with Albert Preston Moore

3 East 53rd Street between Fifth and Madison Avenues

9.16 **St. Thomas Church and Parish House**
1914, Cram, Goodhue & Ferguson
1 West 53rd Street at Fifth Avenue
☎ 212 757 7013; www.saintthomaschurch.org

9.19 **Former Tishman Building**
666 Fifth Avenue between 52nd and 53rd Streets

9.15 **The Museum of Modern Art**
11 West 53rd Street between Fifth and Sixth Avenues
☎ 212 7089400; www.moma.org

9.17 **CBS Building**
1965, Eero Saarinen & Associates
51 West 52nd Street at Sixth Avenue
www.nyc-architecture.com

A walk west across 53rd Street from Beekman Place to Sixth Avenue offers an unrivaled concentration of architectural gems.

Start at the monolithic United Nations Plaza Apartments at 44th Street and First Avenue, home to Truman Capote in the last years of his life, and the residence Robert Kennedy established when he ran for the U.S. Senate in 1964.

Walk north to 49th Street and cross the avenue to a little one-block street, Mitchell Place, named for a distinguished nineteenth-century jurist. The major structure on this small, inclined street (corner of First and Mitchell) is Beekman Tower. Originally the Panhellenic Hotel, built as a proper residence for college alumnae who were sorority members, some of the bricks in this 1930s modern building bear the Greek letters of prominent college sororities. Occupying the crown of the twenty-six-story suite hotel is the aggressively Art Moderne Top of the Tower Restaurant and cocktail lounge. Its architectural furniture, wrought-iron and obsidian-glass tabletops, and grand piano allow me to close my eyes and see William Powell and Myrna Loy bobbing for olives, or Ginger Rogers dancing backward with Fred Astaire.

Continue up the street to the understated luxury of Beekman Place. The toponymic street was part of the Beekman family farm during the Colonial and Revolutionary War eras. Young Nathan Hale, Yale graduate, schoolteacher, and America's first spy, was allegedly hanged on the "north forty" of Beekman's farm.

On the east side of this cul-de-sac (corner of 50th Street, No. 17), is an elegant townhouse that now bears the coat of arms of the Grand Duchy of Luxembourg, a relatively new tenant in the large limestone structure with its splendid East River view. This newly minted consulate was the home of American composer and lyricist Irving Berlin for the last forty-two years of his life.

Born in Russia as Izzy Ballin, Berlin died at age one-hundred-and-one (1888–1989), outliving the copyrights on a number of his songs. He wrote "White Christmas" and "God Bless America," as well as the music and lyrics to such Broadway classics as *Annie Get Your Gun*. After his death, his daughters sold the house to the Grand Duchy. It was fitting, since Berlin's last major Broadway hit, *Call Me Madam*, was set in that tiny nation.

After this medley of memories and an envious look at the late architect Paul Rudolph's house on the northeast corner of 50th Street and Beekman Place and the wrought-iron balconies on the adjoining town houses, briskly make your way to 53rd Street. Find there an anachronistic pair—the last two wood frame houses in Midtown Manhattan. These well-maintained Federal-era dwellings are on the south side of 53rd Street between First and Second Avenues (Nos. 314 and 312).

On the left side of 53rd Street as we approach Park Avenue is New York's only Mies van der Rohe—the Seagram Building. This bronze and bronze-glass tower brought the plaza back to New York. Its two reflecting pools are coolly inviting in the warm weather, and when the illuminated Christmas trees are set afloat on them during the holiday season, who the hell needs tickets to *The Nutcracker*? If this monument to the International School and the geniuses of the Bauhaus wasn't enough as an edifice, it also houses two unique restaurants, the Brasserie on the 53rd Street side of the building, and on the 52nd Street side the remarkably consistent and glorious forty-three-year-old Four Seasons (see p. 200). The latter has a liberal sprinkling of Van der Rohe's Barcelona chairs, a well-placed Picasso or two, and interiors so striking that the restaurant has its own designation as an official landmark.

Catercorner to the Seagram Building is another icon of the International Style, Lever House. Designed by Gordon Bunshaft of Skidmore, Owings & Merrill, it has been designated a landmark by the New York City Landmarks Preservation Commission. Lever House was the first glass-and-steel curtain-wall building erected on Park Avenue (1952). The Anglo-Dutch firm sacrificed certain economies of scale by letting Mr. Bunshaft open up the site as much as possible. The office tower itself is offset to the right on top of a windowed and landscaped one-story pavilion. Between the columns of the pavilion sits a plaza area and interior spaces fit for art exhibitions and, at Christmastime, the joyful Lever House carousel.

In 1952, Lever House was a jolt of emerald glass and stainless steel on neo-Renaissance Park Avenue. This L-shaped new resident was particularly striking as it reflected the heavy stonework of that bastion of the Brahmins, the Racquet and Tennis Club, designed by McKim, Mead & White. The Racquet and Tennis Club sold its air rights and, in 1981, a dense application of the floor-area ratio was used with brutal effectiveness by Skidmore, Owings & Merrill in its design of that forty-four-story giant that runs from 52nd to 53rd Streets.

At 520 Madison Avenue, a segment of the Berlin Wall is mounted by a fountain in a well-hidden plaza at the south-west end of the building between Madison and Fifth. The side of the wall that faced West Berlin is filled with graffiti in an Abstract Expressionist mode, while the side that faced east is pristine concrete, with the exception of some pock-marks approximately nine millimeters in diameter.

It is time for an island of elegant tranquility—Samuel Paley Plaza, also known as Paley Park, just west of 520 Madison. The gentle cascades of the waterfall running down the back wall of New York's first vest-pocket park are not only visually relaxing, but also provide a baffle against the cacophony of a busy crosstown street. Conveniently placed Bertoia chairs and a discreet snack bar make Paley Park a perfect urban oasis.

Refreshed in a literal sense at Paley Park, cross Fifth Avenue and gratify your spiritual sense at Cram, Goodhue & Ferguson's superb French Gothic St. Thomas Church and Parish House. Although its exterior and interior designs are of the French style, St. Thomas keeps its Anglican connection with windows by Whitefriars of London. St. Thomas is noted for its superb male choir (see p. 176), and it is fitting that a magnificent choir should have a majestic reredos (choir screen). Bertram Goodhue designed the reredos with sculptures by Lee Lawrie.

The one-million-square-foot embossed aluminum-clad siding on the southwest corner of 53rd and Fifth, 666 Fifth Avenue, formerly known as the Tishman Building, has its own hidden treasure—a lobby waterfall by the late Isamu Noguchi (enter from 53rd Street).

Press onward to view the Museum of Modern Art. Its original structure, plus its expansions and additions, were done by an all-star team of architects: Edward Durell Stone, Philip Johnson, Philip Goodwin, and Cesar Pelli.

Your walk ends on the southeast corner of 53rd Street and Sixth Avenue, at the only high-rise building designed by Eero Saarinen. Its honed and beveled columns of gray granite have earned it the sobriquet "Black Rock." The CBS Building (see p. 194), commissioned by company founder, the late William Paley, has been designated an official New York City landmark.

Saarinen designed the building inside and out, with a lot of input from art connoisseur Paley and the vice president for corporate design, Louis Dorfsman (Dorfsman's signature typeface, CBS News, abounds throughout the building). The Finnish-American master even specified the ashtrays in the reception areas on each floor. True to his Northern European roots, Saarinen chose the late lamented Scandinavian retailer Bonniers to supply the ashtrays. This masterpiece of creativity and entrepreneurship stands in its recessed plaza like an elegant maître d'hotel in a classic temple of haute cuisine.

LEE GELBER
Urban historian and tour guide

10.12 St. Peter's Lutheran Church

1977, Hugh Stubbins & Associates
619 Lexington Avenue at East 54th Street, in the Citicorp Center
☎ 212 935 2200; www.saintpeters.org/art

Environmental Sculpture

1977, Louise Nevelson
Erol Beker Chapel of the Good Shepherd

Enter the still space of St. Peter's Church. Concerts are given here; art exhibits change. But I come to seek out a permanent installation—the painted-wood sculpted environmental mystery by Louise Nevelson. It is designed to be entered, wandered into, stayed with. The structure waits like a building with an address, yet you must come upon its door by accident. Passageways are walled by constructions of boxes, dowels, some recognizable as drawer handles or newel posts, perhaps, but no part is any longer an object apart, with any name or function separate from the whole. Inner spaces contain opposites, as though shadow and light were equal and the same; surfaces simultaneously invite touch and warn against probe. I go back to this space as to a recurrent dream of a place familiar and fascinating.

CHARLOTTE MANDEL
Poet

Black and White

10.13 **Seagram Building**
1958, Ludwig Mies van der Rohe, with Philip Johnson; Kahn & Jacobs
375 Park Avenue between East 52nd and East 53rd Streets

9.17 **CBS Building**
1965, Eero Saarinen & Associates
51 West 52nd Street at Sixth Avenue

1.12 **Marine Midland Bank**
1967, Skidmore, Owings & Merrill
140 Broadway between Liberty and Cedar Streets

I used to think that, with the exception of Frank Lloyd Wright's Guggenheim Museum, the best works of architecture built in New York City during the last half of the twentieth century were the black buildings: the Seagram Building designed by Mies van der Rohe, the CBS ("Black Rock") building designed by Eero Saarinen, and the Marine

Midland Bank designed by Skidmore, Owings & Merrill.

But as the world we live in has grown more ominous, I think it will be the white buildings that will stand out, adding their much-needed light to the third millennium.

RICHARD MEIER
Architect

10.13 Seagram Building

1958, Ludwig Mies van der Rohe, with Philip Johnson; Kahn & Jacobs

375 Park Avenue between East 52nd and East 53rd Streets

It happens that this great building contributed to my becoming an art historian. While it was under construction, the Museum of Modern Art installed in one of their regular galleries a full-size mockup of a stretch of the bronze facing, with I-beam moldings between the bays. How vividly I remember the amazing way this was mirrored on floor and ceiling. I was still in school, but looking back, this and Mondrian really did it for me.

Pay attention to certain, perhaps underappreciated, features: the unfussy disposition and lofty but unintimidating proportions of the lobby as a space of transition from the terrace, and the relation of the tower to the shorter block behind. My single favorite view is looking up from the south side entrance on 52nd Street at the asymmetrical, rectilinear composition framing the sky.

JOSEPH MASHECK
Art historian

10.13 The Four Seasons

1959, Philip Johnson & Associates

In the Seagram Building

99 East 52nd Street

212 754 9494; www.fourseasonsrestaurant.com

I still love the Four Seasons restaurant in the Seagram Building. At first, Mies and I weren't sure what would go in those spaces. At one point we considered a car showroom. Fortunately, the final decision was for a restaurant. I got to do the interiors since Mies was eager to get back to Chicago.

The Grill Room and the Pool Room are different in feel, but they are two of the prettiest rooms in New York. More than forty years later, these designs still please me greatly. One of the more amusing elements is the chain window coverings. Have you seen how they move with the air currents? I can't take credit for that effect; it's just the way it turned out. Those types of things often just happen in architecture. The entire project was an architect's dream—I was working with not only Mies van der Rohe, but Phyllis Bronfman Lambert.

PHILIP JOHNSON
Architect

For only a fraction of the cost of a trip to one of the two main dining rooms, I recommend a drink at the bar of the Four Seasons restaurant, the quintessential New York power scene for more than forty years. From Marie Nichols's fluttering, gold-anodized aluminum curtains (a happy accident of the ventilation system) to Richard Lippold's perilously perched sculpture over the bar, this Philip Johnson-designed space is an appropriate counterpart to the building in which it sits, Ludwig Mies van der Rohe's bronze masterpiece, the Seagram Building.

DAVID FISHMAN
Architectural historian

You are walking down the street in Midtown Manhattan when you realize you need a bathroom. This is not a problem. Head directly to the Seagram Building and the Four Seasons restaurant. Go to the bar on the second floor of this wondrous example of Modernist architecture, order a drink and the crab cakes, sit back for thirty seconds and take in the real magic of Mies van der Rohe and Philip Johnson's brilliance, then walk briskly down the stairs to the men's room. There you will encounter the most lush, extravagant, and completely perfect combination of marble and wood man has ever envisioned.

After this Zen-like experience, return to the bar, sip your drink, and marvel at the golden beaded window treatment, pulsing at something roughly equivalent to your new, reduced heart rate. (That Mies and Johnson did not know warm air currents would facilitate this visual effect when they designed the space only proves there is an architectural god out there somewhere.) Finish your crab cakes, have another drink—or not—and now, more slowly than you entered, walk out the middle door leading to the Grill Room and toward Park Avenue.

As you exit, directly in front of and around and above you is Roy Lichtenstein's thirty-two-foot-high black-and-white *Brush Stroke*. Humorous, huge, wonderful, it's a big sculpture—as good as sculpture gets—by a painter. For me, it's the sweetest dessert.

And so there you have it. A Midtown imperative turned into an aesthetic, spiritual, and culinary vacation—all in about thirty minutes.

DENNIS ASHBAUGH
Artist

10.14 Villard Houses

1884, Joseph Wells, façades; Stanford White, interiors; 1981, restored by James Rhodes

451–455 Madison Avenue between East 50th and 51st Streets

The architectural historian Henry-Russell Hitchcock applauded the Renaissance detailing of the houses. For me, however, they are much more, both urbanistically and architecturally. The entry court is New York's first, and perhaps finest, vest-pocket park. The use of brownstone is at once majestic and recalls common row houses. Careful scaling can be seen in the entrance porches, in the conglomeration of six houses—two of which are not entered off the courtyard—in the deflection of the main house to the sunny south, and in the bisection of the main axis into two houses (now lost). All this brings to mind precedents much more varied than the detailing of a simple Renaissance palazzo. Pay no attention to the Palace Hotel except to note that it pretty much leaves the original façades intact.

ROBERT LIVESEY
Architect

10.17 St. Regis-Sheraton Hotel

2 East 55th Street at Fifth Avenue

King Cole Bar and Lounge

1906, Maxfield Parrish

212 753 4500; www.stregisnewyork.com

Stop for a drink at the King Cole Bar and Lounge and admire the magnificent twenty-eight-foot mural by Maxfield Parrish (1870–1966), whose studio was not far away at 49 East 63rd Street. This spectacular painting illustrates the eponymous nursery rhyme. Commissioned in 1905 by Nicholas Biddle for Colonel Astor, it was originally installed in the Hotel Knickerbocker on Times Square. Astor also owned the St. Regis, and the mural was moved to its present site in the 1930s.

MARGARET A. BRUCIA
Latin teacher and scholar

10.19 Samuel Paley Plaza

1967, Robert Zion and Harold Breen in association with Albert Preston Moore

3 East 53rd Street between Fifth and Madison Avenues

This little vest-pocket park is a lovely spot that easily takes one away from the surrounding bustle of Midtown Manhattan. Replete with waterfall, this park offers a

🍴🍷 bonus during summer months by serving from its tiny food stand the best hot dog in New York. Grilled and served on a buttered bun, it is made even better by the surroundings.
JIM CODDINGTON
Chief conservator, MoMA

A civilized oasis in one of the most congested parts of the city, landscape architects Robert Zion and Harold Breen's Samuel Paley Plaza was the first and by far the best of the city's vest-pocket parks. Located on a tight, forty-two-by-one-hundred-foot site, Zion & Breen expertly manipulated just a few key ingredients—twelve honey locust trees, roughly hewn granite pavers, ivy-covered gray brick side walls, chairs by Harry Bertoia, tables by Eero Saarinen, and a rear wall of cascading water tumbling over stone that fortuitously whites out just enough of Midtown's din—to create a remarkably restrained and sophisticated outdoor room suitable for contemplation, conversation, a quick snack (there's a discreet kiosk just to the side of the entrance), or simply a refreshing rest. Built and maintained with private 🍴🍷 funds, Paley Park is the prototype that has unfortunately either been ignored or poorly imitated. The good news is that the original one-tenth-of-an-acre parklet looks—and works—just like new.
DAVID FISHMAN
Architectural historian

Paley Park has been a favorite spot of mine since I was a child. It is an utterly urban landscape that cannot help but suit New York. The space is serene, elegant, and modern. The water wall is a particularly welcome element in Midtown. The architect, Robert Zion, worked on landscapes with Philip Johnson, which may explain why I feel such an affinity for the design. How wonderful that a private source, in this case William Paley, could create such a gem of public space.
HILARY LEWIS
Urban planner and architectural historian

Horological Stroll

10.20 Cartier
653 Fifth Avenue at 52nd Street

10.21 Fifth Avenue Presbyterian Church
7 West 55th Street at Fifth Avenue

10.22 Tiffany & Co.
727 Fifth Avenue at 57th Street

10.23 Sherry Netherland Clock
Fifth Avenue at 59th Street
www.nyc-architecture.com

12.3 Delacorte Clock
1965, Andrea Spadini
Above the arcade between the Wildlife Center and the Children's Zoo
www.nycgovparks.org

Watch the clock as you take a leisurely stroll up Fifth Avenue to the southern end of Central Park. Begin at 653 Fifth Avenue (the southeast corner of 52nd Street) and note the time on the ornate clock between the windows of Cartier's second and third floors. As you proceed uptown, notice the golden hands and numerals of the clock on the Fifth Avenue Presbyterian Church at 55th Street. Continue north for two blocks and admire the Tiffany clock, supported by a nine-foot-tall Atlas. At 59th Street, take a moment to look at the elegant Sherry Netherland street clock, one of seven clocks designated as landmarks by the city's Landmarks Preservation Commission. Cross the street and enter Central Park at the corner of 60th Street and head north on the walkway to the zoo. Located above the walkway at 64th Street near the Arsenal is one of my favorite clocks—the musical Delacorte Clock. Its clocktower houses two clockfaces on its north and south sides. Sitting on top of the tower are two bronze monkeys with hammers who appear to strike a large bell to sound the hours of the day, while six musical animals revolve around the tower to nursery rhyme tunes. The animals give a shorter performance on the half-hour. The best show, of course, is at noon.

BETTY KEIM

Editor, writer, and musicologist

10.24 Former Pepsi-Cola Building, now ABN AMRO Bank Building

1960, Gordon Bunshaft and Natalie DuBois of Skidmore, Owings & Merrill

500 Park Avenue at East 59th Street

Anybody who doubts that a simple Modernist grid of aluminum and glass can amount to a composition that is somehow more than just a grid of aluminum and glass, should get a load of this. Superbly proportioned, the building is at once earthbound and light. Each single window unit consists of a broad, horizontal rectangle of plate glass above a narrower aluminum parapet-like panel, with two elements together comprising, to the eye, an approximate square. And these "horizontals-and-a-half" in turn stack up vertically in regular bays. Between are vertical mullions of an astute slenderness, on the scale not of a skyscraper but of an urbane mansion. Here is perhaps a hint of Russian avant-garde suprematism, as well as of the Italian Renaissance.

JOSEPH MASHECK

Art historian

Art Underground

To obtain a free copy of *Art en Route*, send an email to artsfortransit@mtahq.org, or write to MTA Arts for Transit, 347 Madison Avenue, New York, NY 10017.
www.mta.info/mta/aft

Take the MTA self-guided tour by using *Art en Route: Your Guide to Art in the MTA Network*. The guide will lead you to over a hundred works of art in the transit system, including works in the subway, Grand Central Terminal, and Penn Station. The tour includes mosaics, sculptures, and faceted glass installations by such internationally known artists as Elizabeth Murray, Maya Lin, and Donald Lipski, as well as works by other well-known and emerging artists. *Art en Route* is organized according to rail and subway lines.
SANDRA BLOODWORTH
Artist, and director of Metropolitan Transportation Authority Arts for Transit program

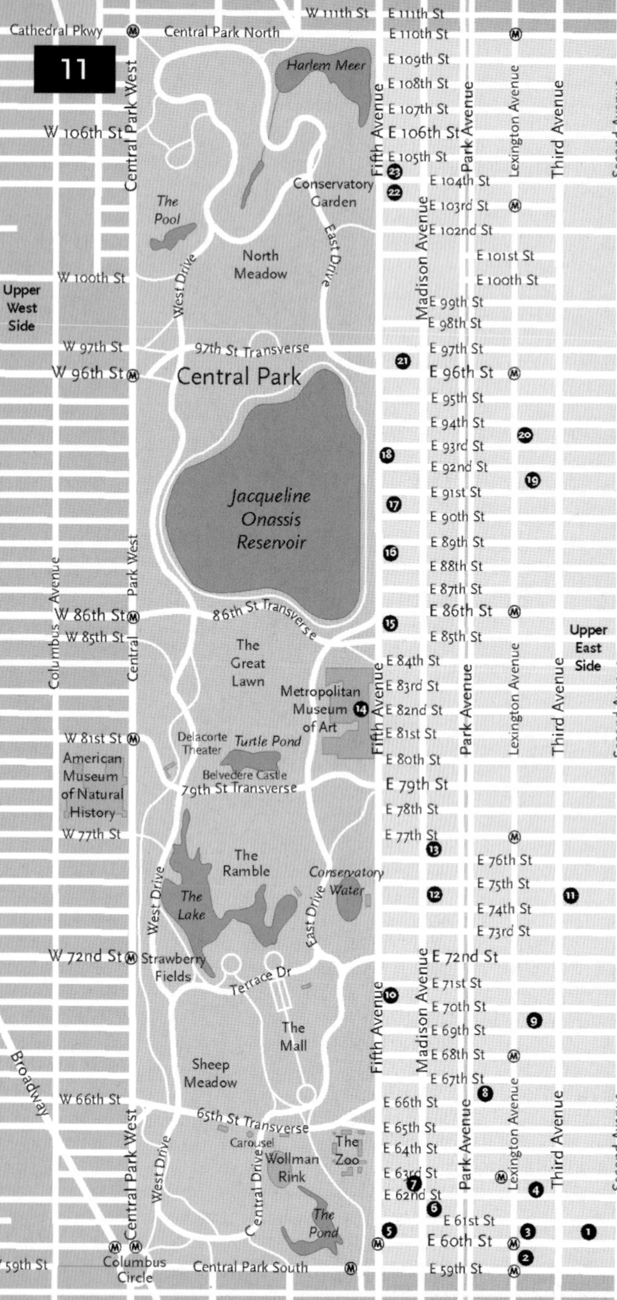
11
Cathedral Pkwy
Central Park North
W 111th St
E 111th St
E 110th St
Harlem Meer
E 109th St
E 108th St
E 107th St
W 106th St
E 106th St
E 105th St
Central Park West
Fifth Avenue
Park Avenue
Lexington Avenue
Third Avenue
Second Avenue
E 104th St
Conservatory Garden
E 103rd St
E 102nd St
The Pool
North Meadow
East Drive
West Drive
Madison Avenue
E 101st St
E 100th St
W 100th St
Upper West Side
E 99th St
E 98th St
W 97th St
97th St Transverse
E 97th St
W 96th St
Central Park
E 96th St
E 95th St
E 94th St
E 93rd St
E 92nd St
Jacqueline Onassis Reservoir
E 91st St
E 90th St
E 89th St
E 88th St
E 87th St
Columbus Avenue
W 86th St
86th St Transverse
E 86th St
W 85th St
E 85th St
Upper East Side
The Great Lawn
E 84th St
E 83rd St
Metropolitan Museum of Art
E 82nd St
E 81st St
W 81st St
Delacorte Theater
Turtle Pond
American Museum of Natural History
E 80th St
Belvedere Castle
79th St Transverse
E 79th St
E 78th St
W 77th St
E 77th St
The Ramble
E 76th St
Conservatory Water
E 75th St
The Lake
E 74th St
E 73rd St
W 72nd St
Strawberry Fields
E 72nd St
Terrace Dr
E 71st St
E 70th St
The Mall
E 69th St
E 68th St
Broadway
Sheep Meadow
E 67th St
W 66th St
E 66th St
65th St Transverse
E 65th St
Carousel
The Zoo
E 64th St
Wollman Rink
Central Drive
E 63rd St
E 62nd St
The Pond
E 61st St
E 60th St
W 59th St
Columbus Circle
Central Park South
E 59th St
1
2
3
4
5
6
7
8
9
10
11
12
13
14
15
16
17
18
19
20
21
22
23

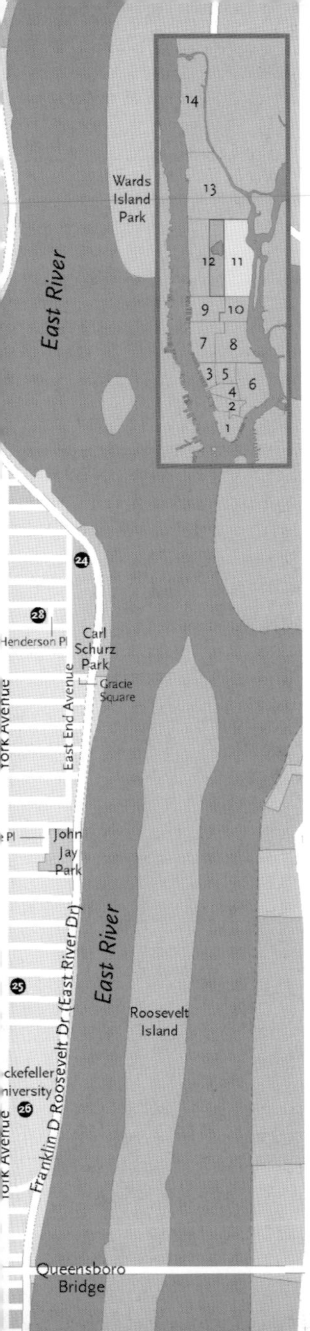

CHAPTER 11

UPPER EAST SIDE

1 Serendipity 3
2 Arts for Transit
3 Subway Inn
4 Tender Buttons
5 The Metropolitan Club
6 Viand
7 Ursus Rare Books
8 Seventh Regiment Armory
9 Urasenke Chanoyu Center
10 The Frick Collection
11 Candle Cafe
12 Whitney Museum
13 Bemelmans Bar
14 Metropolitan Museum
15 Neue Galerie New York
16 Guggenheim Museum
17 Carnegie Mansion
18 The Jewish Museum
19 Clapboard House
20 Kitchen Arts & Letters
21 St. Nicholas
22 Museum of the City of NY
23 El Museo del Barrio
24 Gracie Mansion
25 Sotheby's
26 Rockefeller University
27 Mount Vernon Hotel Museum
28 Henderson Place (see p. 290)

Upper East Side

11.1 Serendipity 3

225 East 60th Street between Second and Third Avenues
212 838 3531; www.serendipity3.com

While Holly Golightly was eating breakfast at Tiffany's, all the cool kids in New York City were having frozen hot chocolates at Serendipity. The sandwiches and sodas, which are quite good, are mere obstacles to amazing desserts. The ambience is cozy and fun. Children's treasures, miniature tea sets, stuffed animals, and marbles are sold at the front of the shop. While hectic city life persists on just the other side of the door, this little haven promises nourishment and fun. My particular favorite—grilled cheese and a Coke and a caramel sundae for dessert.
DEBORAH SKELLY
Attorney and author

If you have kids, bring them here and let them gorge on the giant sundaes. Then take them to Central Park so they can run around for eight hours 'til they come down.
ERIC STOLTZ
Actor

11.2 Arts for Transit: *Blooming*

1996, Elizabeth Murray
In the subway station at 59th Street and Lexington Avenue
www.mta.info/mta/aft

The best way to experience artist Elizabeth Murray's surreal metropolitan masterpiece is to stumble upon it (or rather, into it) by accident—preferably when half asleep. Change subway trains at 59th Street, and you will pass through a work of contemporary art that is also a playful visual pun. In *Blooming*, Murray has conjured a subterranean world of dreamy, evocative images. Gigantic trees with serpentine branches form a blooming dale—a witty allusion to the department store above. Along one wall towers a fantastic high-heeled slipper trailing long golden laces—a lost Manolo Blahnik, possibly? In ribbons of steam, fat yellow coffee cups spill poetic aphorisms: "In dreams begin responsibility," by Delmore Schwartz, and "Conduct your blooming in the noise and whip of the whirlwind," by Gwendolyn Brooks.

A longtime subway rider herself, Elizabeth Murray has said that she created her monumental mosaic for workers on their daily commute from Queens into Manhattan. For the price of a subway token and the willingness to climb a few stairs, you can see it, too. Take the trip. It will wake you up. It will make you smile.

ANN BANKS
Journalist

11.3 Subway Inn

143 East 60th Street between Lexington and Third Avenues
212 223 8929

This is the end of the line and the last great dive in Midtown. Up and running since 1933, its great neon "Subway Inn" sign has survived outside, as has its original Art Moderne glass-block storefront. Between takes of *The Seven Year Itch*, Marilyn Monroe stepped off the grate and dropped in to throw a few back with fellow straphangers. Photos and paintings of the blonde bombshell line the smoky walls. Once through the doors, you realize that this grimy broken-down joint is for the serious rider and regulars board at noon. When you're down and out, pop some quarters into the great jukebox and down a double Johnnie Walker on the rocks.

TRACEY HUMMER AND FREDERIC SCHWARTZ
Writer and Architect

Go to the Subway Inn on 60th Street and Lexington Avenue, and order a whiskey and a draft beer to back it up, then sit there and soak up one of the last authentic bars in New York. If you have two rounds the tab won't surpass ten bucks.

When you're done, walk outside and look diagonally across Lexington Avenue at the tiny brownstone that seems to be stuck into the enormous skyscraper that surrounds it. The story goes that an old Italian woman lived in the top-floor apartment for decades. When developers wanted to build the skyscraper, they offered her a buyout of her lease—and she refused. They doubled their offer, she still refused. After she turned down a million dollars, they decided to build it around her, which they figured would drive her out. It didn't. When I think about the beautiful stubbornness of New Yorkers, I think about this woman. For years she lived there, keeping her window boxes filled with fresh flowers through the spring, summer, and fall.

DAN ALGRANT
Filmmaker

11.4 Tender Buttons

143 East 62nd Street between Lexington and Third Avenues
212 758 7004; www.tenderbuttons-nyc.com

Whether you're trying to replace a missing button, looking for the perfect buttons for a homemade sweater, or just in a browsing mood, come to this little button boutique. You may not have thought of buttons as interesting or note-worthy, but step inside this quaint shop (here since 1967) and you'll marvel at the selection. Organized in small self-serve boxes, you can find buttons in every style made from horn, vegetable ivory, silver, leather, crystal, wood, Bakelite, and ranging in price from fifty cents to a few hundred dollars. Framed on the wall and just for show are rare, antique buttons that give the store more of a museum feel. The friendly staff can help you find a particular button or make inspired suggestions.

SARAH CAPLAN
Designer, graphic artist, and writer

11.5 The Metropolitan Club

1894, McKim, Mead & White

1 East 60th Street at Fifth Avenue

212 838 7400; www.metropolitanclubnyc.org

Not open to the public.

My vote for the prettiest room in the city just might be the main room of the Metropolitan Club; you might have trouble getting in, but just go up the stairs and gaze in at a McKim, Mead & White marble, soaring-ceilinged treasure.

JOHN GUARE
Playwright

11.6 Viand

673 Madison Avenue between East 61st and 62nd Streets

212 751 6622

If you are looking for a quick bite in Midtown, pop into Viand for a classic New York coffee shop experience. Established in 1976, this miracle of Manhattan real estate caters to a wide cross section of New Yorkers—from the Upper East Side matron dripping in furs to the neighborhood cop on the beat.

Waiters call out orders like "jack with tommy" (grilled cheese with tomato), "full house" (grilled cheese with tomato and bacon), "short stack bac" (two pancakes with bacon), and "42 whiskey down" (four eggs, two plates, rye toast). Viand is famous for its fresh turkey sandwiches, delicious cheeseburgers, and a great tuna salad. The hospitable owner oversees his galleyesque eatery like a captain on his ship in a storm.

ROBERT KAHN
Architect

11.7 Ursus Books and Prints

699 Madison Avenue, third floor, between East 62nd and East 63rd Streets

212 772 8787; www.ursusbooks.com

🎁 Ursus offers a vast selection of rare books, fine bindings, and first editions covering a broad range of subjects. Here, you will find manifestos from Marx to Marx, literature from Shakespeare to Joyce, and illustrated books by artists Dürer to Picasso. In the Bs alone, Ursus has had the elusive first edition of *En attendant Godot*, the Complutensian Polyglot Bible, and a twelve-volume first-edition Babar collection. To experience perfect symmetry, locate a first edition of Bemelmans's *Madeline*, then head down to the lobby for a drink in Bemelmans Bar to celebrate your good fortune. Book-loving tourists and book-reading former presidents can be found browsing through the shelves. Ursus also offers a superior selection of art books and a room of decorative prints from the seventeenth through the nineteenth centuries.
ROBERT KAHN
Architect

Nathan Hale Was Here

While Nathan Hale may have said he had "but one life to lose" for his country, there are four places in Manhattan that claim to be where he lost it.

The most visible site is his statue in City Hall Park, placed there on the probably mistaken presumption that that's where the British hanged him as a spy in 1776.

The most invisible site was marked by a plaque in a slaughterhouse on First Avenue in the East 40s, since razed to make way for the United Nations. The plaque was saved and reproduced at the Yale Club at the corner of Vanderbilt Avenue and East 44th Street, across from Grand Central Terminal. It must have seemed logical since Hale was a Yale man (class of 1773). No matter that the plaque says he was hanged "near this site" and the Yale Club is nowhere near any of the alleged sites.

The slaughterhouse claim was nearer, because most

historians now seem to agree that the heroic twenty-one-year-old was hanged from a tree in the British encampment at what is now the intersection of Third Avenue and East 66th Street. A new plaque at the entrance to the Banana Republic at Third and 65th indicates that the dastardly deed was probably done near the 66th Street corner. The Dove Tavern stood there in 1776. It's a Starbucks now.
RICHARD MOONEY
Journalist

11.8 Seventh Regiment Armory

1879, Charles W. Clinton
643 Park Avenue between East 66th and East 67th Streets
212 616 3930; www.armoryonpark.org

The Park Avenue Armory (Seventh Regiment Armory), host to numerous art fairs throughout the year, is a fascinating building to explore. At one end of the ground floor is the Tiffany Room, covered top to bottom with decoration—stained glass, mosaic, and metalwork.
NADINE ORENSTEIN
Curator, Prints and Drawings Department, The Metropolitan Museum of Art

11.9 Urasenke Chanoyu Center

153 East 69th Street between Third and Lexington Avenues
212 988 6161; www.urasenkeny.org

Housed in Mark Rothko's old studio is the Urasenke Chanoyu Center, a nonprofit society that cultivates an appreciation of the Japanese tea ceremony. Membership is not required to attend one of the monthly classes, presided over by a kindly older gentleman. The transformation of the space is quite incredible, and the devotion of the staff is touching as they set about educating you about the ceremony, emphasizing the role of the guest as well as that of the host.

Certainly the experience depends on the group you attend with, but the force with which it demands you stop your day and experience the beauty of the ceremony itself, both deliberate and simple, is great. Before and after the actual ceremony there are short lessons about the aesthetics as well as general philosophy of tea and life. While it sometimes stays on a less-than-profound level, it is always pleasant. *Wabi-sabi*, the Japanese aesthetic of imperfect and impermanent beauty, is among the discussions, and guests are encouraged to participate.

LAURIE MCLENDON

The late Laurie McLendon was the owner of Shi and Papivor on Elizabeth Street in Nolita.

11.10 The Frick Collection

1914, Carrère & Hastings; 1935, renovated as a museum by John Russell Pope

1 East 70th Street at Fifth Avenue

212 288 0700; www.frick.org

Closed Mondays.

It's easy to love the Frick, not only because of its great works of art and sumptuous rooms, gardens, and fountains, but because it is relatively small and intimate for a museum. One can go there for half an hour or forty-five minutes and see the entire collection briefly. The Frick very seldom loans art and rarely moves pictures; and it is this consistency that allows one to retain its artworks so indelibly in one's mind.

AGNES GUND

President Emerita, MoMA; Chairman, Mayor's Cultural Affairs Advisory Commission of New York City

The price of bliss in New York City is eighteen dollars. This is the admission fee to the Frick Collection, a once-private house just steps off Fifth Avenue, where you may enter the enchanted interior garden court. Beneath the vaulted glass ceiling, supported by paired columns, is a

grand Roman atrium with year-round plantings of exotic palms, orchids, and ferns. You may want to sit awhile among the carved stone benches and listen to the water-music of the enormous fountain with its squatting frogs. You would certainly want to experience the incredible sense of serenity by gazing at Jean Barbet's *Angel* (1475), whose beautiful face and gently closed wings seem to whisper, "Rest, rest." And when you have recovered your ability to see with fresh eyes, you are ready to stroll along the outer corridors and into the great room to view some of the best-known paintings by the greatest European artists.
JEAN RATHER
Artist

For an exceptional afternoon in New York City, visit the Frick. With its few rooms, this is an incredibly manageable experience. The collection mirrors the weight, substance, and gravitas of Frick himself and contains remarkable paintings by Hans Holbein the Younger (*Sir Thomas More*), Bellini (*Saint Francis in the Desert*), Ingres (*The Comtesse d'Hausonville*), as well as beauties by Vermeer, Rembrandt, and Georges de la Tour. As I tell my students, the only reason Frick is remembered (despite his power, wealth, and "robber baron" status) is because of this magnificent art collection.
SIMON DINNERSTEIN
Artist

The Frick is exquisite, especially the Whistlers.
HUGH MARTIN
Songwriter

Saint Francis in the Desert
c. 1480, Giovanni Bellini
In the Living Hall

One of the more unusual masterpieces of Venetian art from the late fifteenth century, Giovanni Bellini's *Saint Francis in the Desert* is a celebration of God through landscape. Standing on an outcropping of rock outside his cave, Saint Francis curves his spine backwards toward the makeshift study behind him, greeting warm sunlight as it falls over his body. Barefoot, lips parted, and with his palms exposed (perhaps a reference to his receiving the stigmata, although his wounds are already visible), Francis' thin body is dwarfed and humbled by the beauty of his natural surroundings. An olive tree bends toward him, grapevines fall over his study, water spills from a spout in the rock, and a shepherd tends his flock (all details that carry Christian symbolism). With painstaking attention to detail, Bellini has infused his composition with brilliant color, enticing us to feel the same spiritual ecstasy that Francis found in his own backyard.

KATEY BROWN
Art historian

11.11 Candle Cafe

1307 Third Avenue between East 74th and East 75th Streets
212 472 0970; www.candlecafe.com

The best vegan restaurant in the city, in a neighborhood where you'd never expect to find such a thing. The staff is wonderful and the dishes are tasty as well as inventive.

KATHARINE RISTICH
Editor, Theheart.org and Femina.com

Three Paintings

9.15 Broadway Boogie Woogie

1943, Piet Mondrian
The Museum of Modern Art
11 West 53rd Street
212 708 9400, www.moma.org

11.10 Saint Francis in the Desert

c. 1480, Giovanni Bellini
The Frick Collection
1 East 70th Street at Fifth Avenue
212 288 0700; www.frick.org

11.14 Juan de Pareja

1650, Diego Velázquez
The Metropolitan Museum of Art
1000 Fifth Avenue at 82nd Street
Second floor, Gallery 16, The Old Masters Gallery
212 535 7710; www.metmuseum.org

May I present a walk comprised of paintings, which, at points in my life, were destinations of sustenance and in which I identified various New York City aspects. Go straight to the mentioned paintings, and try not to be distracted by the other beauties calling for attention. Keep the enterprise clean.

At the Museum of Modern Art, go to Piet Mondrian's great *Broadway Boogie Woogie*, painted in homage to his adopted city in reverence for its ongoing energies, movements, sounds, rhythms, and intensities. Give the painting at least five minutes of concentration. Leave.

Go to the Frick Collection and straight to its Bellini, *Saint Francis in the Desert*. New York City is a teeming place (remember *Boogie Woogie*), but it is made up of millions of pure individuals. Here is Saint Francis, surrounded by beings, a golden light, his town, but he is alone in communion with an energy directed only to him (see the wind in the olive tree) in an otherwise still environment. He is alone, inspired, and fully conscious of his greater self.

It's on up to the Met for a visit with Diego Velázquez's *Juan de Pareja*. Stand in awe of Velázquez's total mastery of the illusion achieved through the workings of the eye, the hand, and the paint. Be reminded by Pareja, an obviously

proud man of color, of our own city's ethnic diversity and how much that adds to our power and beauty.
BRICE MARDEN
Painter

11.12 Whitney Museum of American Art

1966, Marcel Breuer & Associates; 1998, addition by Gluckman Mayner
945 Madison Avenue at East 75th Street
212 570 3600; www.whitney.org

Dwellings

1981, Charles Simonds
In the stairwell between the second and third floors

The mysterious ruins of a lost nomadic civilization can be seen on a second-floor window ledge of a palatial neo-Classical building at 940 Madison Avenue, across the street from the Whitney Museum. Seldom noticed by passersby, the diminutive clay dwellings and ritual towers are the abandoned habitations of the Little People, a vanished urban tribe that has been fully imagined, chronicled, mythologized, and architecturally contextualized by the artist Charles Simonds. *Dwellings*, a three-part site-specific piece, was commissioned by the Whitney Museum and installed in 1981. A second part of *Dwellings* is perched on a chimney at the right back corner of the building and is also visible to pedestrians from across the avenue (field glasses helpful here). The principal component of the work is permanently installed inside the Whitney, above a window in the airshaft of the main stairwell, between the second and third floors. From that window, all three parts of *Dwellings* are visible, although the label describing the piece in the museum fails to mention that there are two more parts of the work. If you don't know about the outdoor pieces and don't, by chance, spot the one on the far right window ledge, you will miss seeing these extraordinary and beguiling works of art.

Starting in the early 1970s, Simonds constructed nearly three hundred outdoor pieces representing the abandoned settlements that marked the passage of the Little People. They were deliberately impermanent works, made of unfired clay, sand, twigs, bits of cloth, and other materials that would eventually decay outdoors. Simonds sited the pieces chiefly in the slums of the Lower East Side, half-hidden in the earth and litter of vacant lots, or tucked into crevices of crumbling brick walls. He expected these street pieces would be stolen, destroyed by neglect and weather, or otherwise lost to sight. And they were. The physical traces of these tiny primitivistic villages are gone now, though recorded on film and in photographs. Simonds made similar works on wooden platforms, for indoor viewing, and for keeping. The only outdoor ruins that remain are on pricey Madison Avenue on a building used as a bank until mid-1999, an irony most likely intended by Simonds.

Simonds's constructions strongly evoke the archaeological ruins of the cliff-dwelling Anasazi, who lived in the Four Corners region of the American Southwest from roughly 600 C.E. to 1300 C.E. The Anasazi, precursors of the Pueblo culture, vanished as enigmatically as Simonds's mythical Little People. His invented civilization and its vestigial settlements hint at a nostalgia for a simpler child-like past, but there is nothing sentimental about Simonds's art. His work challenges conventional perceptions of scale, of artwork as precious collectible, of historical record as reliable. What's more, it has powerful narrative appeal. Looking at *Dwellings*, we can't help wondering about the daily lives and dreams and social realities of the Little People, can't help thinking about how and if they differ from us, ordinary folks wandering the canyons of vast and difficult cities. These provocative ruins are small in size only, and certainly worth seeing.

LUCIENNE S. BLOCH
Writer

The Stair at the Whitney

Of all the museums in the city, the Whitney captures the vibe of the local and national art scene the best. The collection is sophisticated yet accessible, raw but accomplished. And Breuer's 1966 building, an idiosyncratic landmark, well reflects the strength, fluidity, and independence of the art inside, even as it complements the staid brownstone fabric of the surrounding neighborhood.

As a visitor moves between floors, the stair becomes a showcase for the structure's finessed tectonics. The massive elements of the museum's construction are delicately assembled and organized in a way that communicates eloquently the various scales at work within the building. In a very confined area, the stair combines poured-in-place concrete walls (with the aggregate carefully exposed), stone slab stair treads suspended from those walls, oversized, elegant bronze balustrades, and wooden handrails and benches, and sets them off with a stepped pane of glass that recalls the inverted ziggurat form of the structure and brings in the light of the city.

Take a break between floors, sit on a bench at one of the landings and talk about the art, feel the building, and watch the crazy cross section of people walking up and down the stairs.

SCOTT GLASS
Architect

11.13 Bemelmans Bar

1947, murals by Ludwig Bemelmans
Madison Avenue between East 75th and East 76th Streets
In the Carlyle Hotel
212 744 1600; www.thecarlyle.com

Legend has it Bemelmans Bar in the Carlyle Hotel was one of the late Jackie O's favorite haunts, and that her protests, along with cries from others, helped save this landmark from being remodeled into just another Madison Avenue piano lounge ordinaire. Classy, but not fussy, Bemelmans is so elegantly dim that the most shimmering celebrity can be rendered inconspicuous in the shadows of the deep leather booths. Fine, since sighting the rich and famous isn't the appeal here—people come to see the walls. Four walls of murals, once vibrant and now perfectly subdued by half a century of nicotine fumes, teem with characters you will immediately recognize unless you spent your childhood in a culvert. Ludwig Bemelmans, author, artist, and restaurateur, was best remembered as the creator of the *Madeline* books. In 1947 Bemelmans brought his characters in out of the rain and painted them to life among seasonal views of Central Park. Ever since, twelve little girls in two straight lines, and tweed-clad, shotgun-packing rabbits welcome regulars famous and not.

For a half-century a self-portrait of Bemelmans near the bar has overseen the preparation of countless thousands of perfect martinis by the white-tuxed, black-tied batenders. The bartenders are no-nonsense veterans, and while only a few could possibly remember Bemelmans himself, they speak of him as if this good friend has just stepped from the room.

I try to visit whenever I'm in New York. One afternoon when I was either dressed well enough or the lights were low enough that I might be mistaken for an Upper Eastsider, the barman headed to my booth with a phone in his hand, just like the movies, bowing from the waist—I swear he clicked his heels—and offered me the receiver, inquiring, "Miss Colgate?"

I was tempted by the mischievous Madeline perched just over my shoulder: Take the call, take the call!

"Miss Colgate?"

But gumption failed and I could only reply, "I wish."

The barkeep and I had a good laugh, and a few moments later I was delivered a potent something on the house, which is exactly the type of hospitality Bemelmans himself was loved for.

SARAH STONICH
Writer

For me, an evening at Bemelmans Bar has always been both fanciful and familiar. When I was a young editor just getting started in New York, a visit to Bemelmans meant slowly savored martinis and a meal of homemade chips, rosemary-marinated olives, and divine mixed nuts. I would float through the front door, past the tastefully dressed giraffe with the yellow handbag that graces the wall near the entry, and casually settle in for a cocktail and conversation. Tommy, the friendly Irishman who has been tending the bar for more than forty years, made me feel right at home. I would slip into a tufted leather banquette and slip back in time. By the end of the evening, I felt as though I had stepped out of a Noël Coward play. Today, the experience of turning back the elegant clock at Bemelmans is every bit as transporting. The refined service and urbane pianist, along with the warm glow of the room and Ludwig Bemelmans' amazing wall murals, have endured and I expect always will.

KATE SPADE
Co-founder, Kate Spade New York

11.14 The Metropolitan Museum of Art

1000 Fifth Avenue at 82nd Street
212 535 7710; www.metmuseum.org

For me, the best expenditure of two hours' recreation in New York City is a visit to the Metropolitan Museum of Art. In fact, I enjoy my trips to the museum so much that

I go about every two weeks. There is always a new exhibition to be seen or an old collection to be revisited in order to learn even more about it. The permanent collections that draw me to visit again and again are the Egyptian Art collection and Arms and Armor.

I have been a frequent visitor to the museum for many years. When I became a Member of Congress in 1969, I compared life in New York City to Washington, D.C. New York came out way ahead for a host of reasons, of which the museum is only one.

EDWARD I. KOCH
Former Mayor of New York City

Greek and Roman Art

First floor

Cubiculum from Boscoreale

40–30 B.C.E.

Walking along the sidewalks of New York we sometimes want to know what lies behind the anonymous walls of urban structures. Where are the brilliant salons of Cole Porter where beautiful people chat wittily over cocktails? The period rooms at the Metropolitan Museum of Art allow us to enter elite environments from different periods in history. My favorite is the richly painted *cubiculum* (small bedroom) excavated from the villa of P. Fannius Synister at Boscoreale (just north of Pompeii), now installed in the Greek and Roman Galleries.

It is decorated in what art historians term the Second Style of Roman painting, a system of complex perspectives that may derive from architectural stage backdrops (*frontes scaenarum*). These views appear to open behind the actual wall plane, which is reinforced by painted columns and piers. The ancient viewer would move about the room and imaginatively escape into three different worlds: the courts of urban sanctuaries, cityscapes of jostling buildings, and a rocky landscape. Modern visitors can also suspend belief and project themselves back into the middle of the first century B.C.E. Elsewhere in the galleries are other paintings from the same villa. These feature near-life-size figured scenes (megalography) that derive from the decorations found in Hellenistic royal courts. The paintings, together with some of the statuary and luxury items displayed in the galleries, provide an *Architectural Digest*-like glimpse into the opulent private lives of wealthy Romans.

PETER J. HOLLIDAY
Professor, History of Art and Classical Archaeology, California State University, Long Beach

Metropolitan Museum Figure Tour

The most omnipresent image in the history of art is the figure. At the Metropolitan Museum, you can follow the figure through thousands of years. Unique in this part of the world in offering such a sweeping reach in a single location, the museum provides visitors a view of this entire arc in one of the finest collections anywhere. The striking similarity between the "beginning" and the "present"—between the Cycladic and Brancusi—is a marvelous paradox, which we have the good fortune to witness here.

Third millennium B.C.E.:

Cycladic art
Greek and Roman Art Galleries
First floor

With only crude tools at hand, our forebears created splendid frontal images of themselves in kind. They would have a lasting effect on the making of sculpture into the twentieth century.

Fourteenth century B.C.E.:

Fragment of the Face of a Queen
1353–1336 B.C.E.
Egyptian Art Galleries
First floor

In a glass case near the entrance to the Temple of Dendur, find this piece composed from yellow jasper, the second hardest stone known to man after the diamond. Note the little stand with the metal pin, required when this piece came to the Met in 1926 because there was no drill strong enough to pierce the jasper. Ponder, then, how the contour line of the lip was carved in 1350 B.C.E.

Fourteenth century B.C.E.:

Haremhab as a Scribe of the King
1336–1323 B.C.E.
Egyptian Art Galleries
First floor

Find it, also, near the entrance to the Temple of Dendur. This king worked his way up to sovereign without the usual bloodline requirement. This portrayal of him seems to keep that crucial fact in mind, juxtaposing refined elegance and mass, and seeming to say that power can be achieved only through intelligence. It is one of the museum's finest works.

Sixth century B.C.E.:

Kouros (Statue of a Youth)
590–580 B.C.E.
Greek and Roman Art Galleries
First floor

We've returned to the Greeks and Romans. The only tool in Attica at this time was the bull-nose chisel, which limited the ability to achieve a rounded naturalism. Still, look at the way the artist handled the hair, and pushed the chisel to create lifelike anatomy. This is a work of amazing intelligence and liveliness.

Fifth century B.C.E.:

Statue of Diadoumenos

69–96 C.E., Roman copy of a statue by Polykleitos c. 430 B.C.E.
Greek and Roman Art Galleries
First floor

This youth tying a fillet around his head is attributed to Polykleitos, the man who put the class in classical. Polykleitos invented the Classical canon: seven and one-half heads. This canon measures anatomical length in the following fashion: Squint with one eye closed and extend your arm. Using the thumb and index finger of the extended hand, measure the height of the head of the youth. This measurement equals one head. It is then one head again to the nipples. One head to the belly button. Half a head to the pelvic bone. Two heads to the knee. Two heads to the plinth. Total? Seven and one-half. Try it. This method of rendering the figure has lasted until the present day.

Third-Second century B.C.E.:

Veiled and Masked Dancer

Greek and Roman Art Galleries
First floor

Look at this little miracle—so miraculous in fact, so modern, the detailing so perfect, that some believe it is a phony. It's impossible to stay in one place when viewing it; one is forced to walk around it.

First century:

Old Market Woman

Greek and Roman Art Galleries
First floor

Here, genre and type supersede ideal beauty. The result is a startling, lifelike presence. Now leave the ancients and head for the roots of modern Europe.

Twelfth century:

Dancing Celestial
Irving Galleries for the Arts of South and Southeast Asia
Second floor

The apotheosis of figure as decoration. Near the Jain Temple, find this jewel wearing jewels in a pose of unabashed sexuality.

Thirteenth century:

Golden Boy
Charlotte C. Weber Galleries for the Arts of Ancient China
Second floor

This wooden masterpiece hovers between stasis and movement and stands in charmed vibration between the two.

Fifteenth century:

Virgin and Child
c.1420, attributed to Claus de Werve
Medieval Art Galleries
First floor

Take note of the rear view. Compare and contrast it with *Haremhab as a Scribe of the King.*

Fifteenth century:

Adam
1490–1495, Tullio Lombardo
Vélez Blanco Patio
First floor

A masterpiece of sexual sublimation. Here is a startling union: Modern Man's fig leaf on an ancient monumental sculpture, for the first time. Compare with Polykleitos's *Diadoumenos*.

Seventeenth century:

Bacchanal: A Faun Teased by Children
1616–1617, Gian Lorenzo Bernini
European Sculpture and Decorative Arts Galleries, first floor

The prodigy at work, at age nineteen. This piece shows you the master who will soon emerge.

Eighteenth century:

Jack and Belle Linsky Galleries
European Sculpture and Decorative Arts Galleries
First floor

Now you are at the Rococo. Despite the leap of two thousand years, you can find the *Old Market Woman* in these porcelains, on a different scale.

Nineteenth century:

New Hebrides Slit-Gongs
Arts of Africa, Oceania, and the Americas Galleries
First floor

These amazing structures are part functional—serving as drums—and part fertility figures; both male and female gender in one giddy form. Spiritual, too.

Nineteenth century:

Perseus with the Head of Medusa
1804–1806, Antonio Canova
Balcony above the Great Hall
Second floor

We're neo-Classical now and you have two precedents to consider: Polykleitos's *Diadoumenos* and Tullio Lombardo's *Adam*.

Nineteenth century:

Ugolino and His Sons
1865–1867, Jean-Baptiste Carpeaux

Burghers of Calais
1884–1895, Auguste Rodin (*cast in 1985*)
European Sculpture and Decorative Arts Galleries
Sculpture Court
First floor

Back downstairs to the Carroll & Milton Petrie Sculpture Court. Carpeaux gives us Dante's most harrowing canto brought to life. Rodin's sculpture of the doomed burghers as they make their way to the gallows, hints at Modernism's dialectic between collective suffering and personal growth.

Twentieth century:

Sleeping Muse
1920, Constantin Brancusi
Modern Art Galleries
First floor

Brancusi's polished simplicity completes the arc. You've not only journeyed some five-thousand years, you have, in significant ways, traveled full circle back to the Cycladic. One can quibble with this mix of work, but you'll see that the startling parallels overwhelm the inherent differences. It's the most convincing case under one roof for the notion of progress as inconsequential to art-making. Brancusi may have been a happy man when the electric sander was invented, but it didn't make him a better artist.

PIER CONSAGRA
Artist

Arts of Africa, Oceania, and the Americas

Michael C. Rockefeller Wing
First floor

The most internationally renowned collection of non-Western art on display is a series of treasures that includes a sixteenth-century ivory pendant mask depicting a queen mother from the kingdom of Benin, a primordial couple by a Dogon master, and a majestic series of monumental Bamana allegorical figures from present-day Mali.

ALISA LAGAMMA
Curator, Department of the Arts of Africa, Oceania, and the Americas, The Metropolitan Museum of Art

European Sculpture and Decorative Arts

First floor

The Studiolo from the Palace of Duke Federico da Montefeltro at Gubbio

c.1478–1483, Francesco di Giorgio Martini

Among the many treasures in the Metropolitan Museum, one worth spending some time with is the Gubbio *studiolo*. Created in Gubbio, central Italy, for the fifteenth-century humanist scholar and soldier Federico da Montefeltro, Duke of Urbino, this small private study embodies the diverse interests of a true Renaissance man. Federico was renowned for his love of books, art, and learning—he employed forty scribes in his library and five men to read him the classics during meals. His *studiolo* is an irregularly shaped room decorated entirely in perspective intarsia—wood inlay. The benches jutting into the room, the shelves and cabinets overflowing with artifacts symbolizing learning, art, and power, the half-opened cabinets, the organ, the birdcage—all are created with astonishing realism from thousands of minute slivers of different colored woods. The room repays careful study, as it is full of delightful tiny details. You can discover distinct strings on the musical instruments, legible text from Virgil's *Aeneid* on an open book, convincingly rendered shadows, a pair of eyeglasses neatly folded in their case, an hourglass full of sand. All the views are calculated for a person about five feet tall. If you crouch, you can see how the perspective works, particularly by watching as the circular headdress casually laid on the bench becomes, from the wrong point of view, a distorted ring with shadows in the wrong places, and then falls back into place as you stand up again. The Met completed its meticulous renovation of this friendly little room in 1996. The museum trustingly put up no barriers in front of the walls, and the light streaming in through the small window convincingly simulates sunlight. Although the *studiolo* was opened with great fanfare, it is now often empty for long stretches. You can easily spend a quarter of an hour there without seeing anyone except the guard, who checks periodically to make sure you don't touch anything.

JANET B. PASCAL
Writer and production editor, Viking Children's Books

One of the gems of the Medieval Department is the *studiolo* (or private study) of Federico da Montefeltro, Duke of Urbino, formerly located in his palace at Gubbio (a hilltown in the Umbria region of Italy). A masterwork of fifteenth-century craftsmanship, this intimate room—approximately sixteen feet by twelve feet—exhibits the illusionistic qualities of intarsia, or wood-inlay technique. Thousands of tiny pieces of wood act like a painter's palette: the multiple varieties, cuts, and grains of wood create the trompe l'oeil appearance of cabinet doors slightly ajar, revealing inside objects dear to a humanist's intellect and curiosity. Books are casually stacked or left open, as if someone has just thumbed through their pages. A parrot sits patiently on a perch in a cage. Lutes, candles, scientific instruments, a portable pipe organ, lectern, sand hourglass, convex mirror, hunting horn, and helmet are all displayed as cherished belongings of perhaps the most renowned *condottiere* (soldier of fortune) of his time. Among the visual rewards for feasting one's eyes in this room are the latticework designs that incorporate the effects of natural light from the window, as well as the use of perspective that invites our eyes to question the two-dimensionality of the flat wall.

KATEY BROWN
Art historian

Sienese Paintings

The Creation of the World and the Expulsion from Paradise
1445, Giovanni di Paolo
The Robert Lehman Collection
First floor

St. Anthony the Abbot in the Wilderness
c.1435, The Osservanza Master
The Robert Lehman Collection
First floor

The Journey of the Magi
c.1420, Sassetta
European Paintings Galleries
Second floor

Sienese painting has always been overshadowed by its more famous cousin, Florentine painting, which broke through to the full-on science of rational representation. By contrast, Sienese paintings are illogical and medieval—but that's exactly what modern viewers love about them. These paintings have spaces more absurd than Cézanne, colors right out of the comics, and images that tamp down academic space and accentuate the expressive. Candy-colored castles! Giant people walking through miniature worlds! Mystical experiences in improbable architectures! If you want to make a little pilgrimage to this uncanny world, there are some great Sienese paintings that you can visit at the Met. They are not presented with much fanfare and can be missed easily.

Go directly to the back of the ground floor of the museum to the Robert Lehman Collection, walk through the glass doors and along the wall on the left with paintings by Degas, Renoir, Cézanne, and Vuillard (some of the Vuillards alone make this worth the trip). Go back around the wall to the left to find the Sienese room, the first of a suite of semi-hidden rooms containing Lehman's collection of older paintings, all fitted out in red velvet and gilded wood to imply a fifteenth-century Italian environment. Hanging here are two outstanding examples of Sienese painting: *Saint Anthony the Abbot in the Wilderness* by the Osservanza Master, and *The Creation of the World and the Expulsion from Paradise* by Giovanni di Paolo. Both artists were active in the second quarter of the fifteenth century in Siena. You will probably find the di Paolo first because it is marked for the Museum's headphone audio tour. This heavily cracked painting shows Adam and Eve's expulsion from the garden set against a chart-like mini-universe that includes the prime mover himself presiding over everything from the circles of hell to the four great drainage ditches of the world.

Across the room is the extraordinary *Saint Anthony the Abbot in the Wilderness* by the Osservanza Master, a small tempera-and-gold painting hanging modestly amidst a wall of more conventional Madonna paintings. In it, a startled-looking Saint Anthony gestures toward a little gray bunny crouching at the base of a bare tree. There is an almost minimalist space and silence between the man and the animal, as though some phantom thing between them has been painted out. What's going on in the background is even weirder. The Osservanza Master seems to have had a background man who was either new at the job or a brilliant pre-Van Gogh hallucinator, four hundred years before his time. Saint Anthony and the mute bunny live in a wild and crazy pink-and-green world inhabited only by listing and hunkering animals. The action twists back along a pebbled path to a variety of green Mister Softee hills, some stuck with what look like cloves. The earth is orange, the castles are hot pink, the sea is bright green with a thrift-store-looking boat in it and, above it all, crows fly in a flaming sky lit up with crimson clouds.

For a comparison, visit the more polished Sassetta in the Met's regular Italian painting collection. Take the main staircase to the second floor, through the doorway straight ahead of you on the right side, into the first room of the corridor of fourteenth- to sixteenth-century Italian paintings. On the right side and behind glass, you will find the truly amazing *Journey of the Magi* by Sassetta, painted in tempera and gold on wood, c.1420. Here's the ubiquitous speckled path, but in this tiny painting all the townspeople march down a hill in a frieze-like procession, which disappears out of the painting as though it were stage left, leaving a lone horse's leg in view as it exits. As the people walk off, swallows pose, storks graze on mottled hills, stars bleed gold, trees lose their branches, and leaves and buildings glow in the distance, all in a painting the size of a piece of typing paper.

AMY SILLMAN
Artist

Islamic Art

Second floor

Deep inside the labyrinthine corridors of the Metropolitan Museum of Art are a series of galleries devoted to the museum's superb collection of Islamic art. These galleries are among the most serene and pleasant spaces within the museum—oases of repose and contemplation where you can see and enjoy works of art of incomparable beauty and power. Located in the southeast corner of the second floor, the galleries were designed in 1975 and they remain among the most intelligent and compelling displays of Islamic art anywhere in the world. They're home to more than twelve thousand works of art from almost every corner of the Islamic world—from Spain to India—that date from the eighth to the eighteenth century. Among my favorite objects, which have fascinated me since I was a graduate student and first encountered them, are the reconstruction of Núr ad-Dín's room from a wealthy Syrian home of the early eighteenth century; the great twelfth-century Seljuk incense burner in the shape of a lion; the dazzling tile mihrab (or prayer niche) from the mid-fourteenth century madrassa (school) of Imami in Isfahan; the majestic early sixteenth-century "Simonetti" carpet from Mamluk, Egypt; and the illustrated pages from the *Shahnama* or *Book of Kings* commissioned by the Safavid ruler Shah Tahmasp (1514–1576), one of the Islamic world's most ardent bibliophiles.

What distinguishes all these works is a precision of line, complexity of design, and a level of craftsmanship and detail that is not only breathtaking, but awe-inspiring. The weave of the "Simonetti" carpet, for instance, is a staggering hundred asymmetrical knots per square inch. Many of the colors used in the painting of the *Shahnama* are made from semi-precious ground minerals such as lapis lazuli and malachite. The lustrous gold backgrounds are, in fact, a thinly applied layer of gold leaf.

GLENN LOWRY

Director, The Museum of Modern Art

European Paintings

Second floor

The View of Toledo

c.1597, El Greco

After you have viewed the city, climb the steps at the Metropolitan Museum, head to the second floor (European Paintings), and be transported by El Greco's *The View of Toledo*.

This is not a painting of the state of grace already fully realized, like Bellini's wondrous *Saint Francis in the Desert* at the Frick Museum. Instead, we are in the middle of a hallucination, in the anxious peripheries of revelation. The sky is doubt, the landscape ambiguity, and the source of light a riddle.

As you travel through the painting, sweeping past the architecture, you are at once pulled by the weight of weather, human events, botany, history, a familiar world—time-bound, color-bound, language-bound—up to the prospect of the skyline that is Toledo. Here the painting abruptly stops. The skyline is a horizon. There is no beyond. There is only the above, leading the eye by way of the church spire to the light that creates the scene. Is it nighttime or day, twilight or dawn? All you really know is that a supernatural illumination is eclipsing the scene.

In this spot of time, the world of weather and human events stops. You have reached the terminus of earthly experience. There is no beyond, even though there is a potential for beyond. El Greco takes the scene, arrests it, holds it. Then, through a series of silvery gleams of light, he abstracts you from real time to the realm of timelessness. The entire painting unfolds within a shadow—which confesses to the mystery of spiritual illumination—toward the opening in the sky, an oculus in the celestial dome. You are in the exact spot where the ordinary is about to reach beyond itself to immanence.

This hallucination in light and dark releases the gradations of secular time and distance into a supernatural hilltop and sublimity, heaving upward and pointing, sky beyond sky, to receive God in an instant. As Thoreau would say, it is a light to behold but to dwell not in.
JACK BARTH
Artist

Madonna and Child
c.1480, Carlo Crivelli

Hidden among the many blockbusters in the Metropolitan Museum of Art are some wonderful little jewels that are, unfortunately, often overlooked by the average visitor. Carlo Crivelli's *Madonna and Child* is one of these.

Crivelli originally lived in Venice but left the city after serving a short prison term in 1457 for seducing a married woman. From that time forward he painted in the Provincia di Ancona. While Giovanni Bellini painted with oils in the new Renaissance manner, Crivelli, using egg tempera, created masterpieces more visually aligned with the Gothic painting tradition. The word best used to describe his paintings is sumptuous. His pensive Madonnas are cloaked in fabrics that are gilded and tooled so as to reflect, almost kinetically, a warm golden glow back to the viewer. During the early Renaissance this sheen was believed to be heavenly light.

This particular painting has the Virgin surrounded by a beautiful garland similar to those Andrea Mantegna used to adorn his Madonnas. However, unlike Mantegna, who used exotic assortments of fruits and flowers to construct his garlands, Crivelli preferred everyday fruits and mundane vegetables.

The Madonna has long, elegant, and slightly spidery fingers, a characteristic often found in Crivelli's paintings. She stands before a hanging drapery in Bellini-esque fashion while slivers of the local landscape appear on either side of the cloth. The baby Jesus sits on a bumpy lavender cushion that looks as if it could have been tailored from a hunk of dyed ostrich skin and ponders a housefly (a symbol of evil) the size of his foot. He simultaneously clutches a goldfinch, which, like the giant cuke, symbolizes redemption.

The juxtaposition of these wonderfully strange objects, the impact of the tooled gold, the peaceful, meditative Virgin, and the magnificent use of color, make this a jewel of a painting not to be missed.

FRED WESSEL
Artist and Professor Emeritus, Hartford Art School, University of Hartford

The Triumph of Marius
1729, Giovanni Battista Tiepolo

Elizabeth Farren, Later Countess of Derby
1790, Sir Thomas Lawrence

A brimstone-yellow banner flutters against a hot Italian sky and compels the eye and mind up the great staircase of the Metropolitan and into the collection of European paintings. The dazzling half-smile of an actress out for a walk on a breezy spring day makes further exploration of the English rooms hard to resist. Both these superb paintings display the particular genius of the Metropolitan for leading us effortlessly from one room of the enormous building into the next. Their appeal is immediate and obvious, but they are also about aspirations, both extinct and alive. Tiepolo's rich, shadowed procession of a Roman victory over the Moors reminded Venetians of their claimed—if phony—descent from ancient Rome, and of the political power they had just relinquished. There's a vintage, sulky-lipped Tiepolo matron in the bottom right-hand corner, but basically this is a great painting of a brimstone-yellow banner.

Known as "The Queen of Comedy" at London's Haymarket and Drury Lane theaters, Elizabeth Farren was so furious when Lawrence first catalogued her portrait as

An Actress that she demanded (and received) an apology. He claimed his original title had been *Portrait of a Lady*. Farren also wanted him to make her look fatter—Regency times were just around the corner and gentlemen's tastes were running to the zaftig. Happily, he declined, and gave us the best of everything: Portrait of an Actress Classy Enough to be a Lady. Dressed in oyster satin and furs, her face turning just long enough for the painter to capture its candour, she's gorgeous. The Earl of Derby had been potty about her for years and, Reader, she married him.

MICHAEL RATCLIFFE
Former literary editor and chief book critic, The Times (London)

Asian Art

Second floor

The Astor Court

1981

You don't know serenity until you visit the Chinese Scholar's Garden in the Metropolitan Museum. Ask for the Astor Court, named for the philanthropic Mrs. Brooke Astor, whose foundation paid for it. Tucked among the Asian Galleries on the second floor, this island of tranquility is modeled on a Ming dynasty courtyard—in the "Garden of the Master of the Fishing Nets"—in Suzhou, China, a city near Shanghai once renowned for its culture and elegance.

In those ancient times, a learned man had a scrupulously sculptured garden to which he might repair for composing poetic thoughts, maybe for tea and conversation, or just for quiet contemplation. In the Met, you might go to the garden to wonder at the delicacy of its design, to take a break from the hubbub, or even to compose your own verse. Others may be resting there when you enter, never many and always hushed.

The principal entrance is a moon gate—a big round hole in the wall, flanked by lions, under a motto that reveals the garden's secret in archaic script: "In search of quietude." The space inside measures about sixty by forty feet. A sheltered walkway lines two sides, with low walls to sit on. A graceful pavilion stands opposite, beside a spring trickling through rocks into a goldfish pond. Windows, cut out in lattice patterns, frame living bamboo and Asian grasses, while a large skylight bathes the scene in sunshine (on a good day). Everything about this lovely space came from China: the tile from an old imperial kiln reactivated for just this purpose; eroded rock formations from the bottom of Lake Tai, near Suzhou; timber from gingko, camphor and fir trees, and the rare *nan* evergreen. The garden and the fine paneled room that opens onto it were installed by twenty-seven Chinese craftsmen in 1980. They created a secret gem.

RICHARD MOONEY
Journalist

Iris and B. Gerald Cantor Roof Garden

1987, Kevin Roche, John Dinkeloo & Associates
Rooftop of Lila Acheson Wallace Wing
Open May to October.

After living in New York and visiting for many years, I face the challenge—how to see all those old friends and professional contacts when I'm only in town for a few days? Answer: arrange a collective rendezvous at 6 p.m. on Friday on the rooftop terrace of the Metropolitan Museum (open until 9 p.m. on Fridays and Saturdays). Cocktails, superb sculpture, views over Central Park of the capital of capitalism—the apotheosis of civilization.

FENTON JOHNSON
Writer

🍴 Lunch on the roof of the Metropolitan Museum—the fourth-floor Sculpture Garden—great view of Central Park and Midtown and Central Park West skylines.

JEAN PARKER PHIFER
Architect

11.15 Neue Galerie New York

1914, Carrère & Hastings
1048 Fifth Avenue at East 86th Street
212 628 6200; www.neuegalerie.org
Closed Tuesdays and Wednesdays.

If you ever wished for an art museum with an excellent collection that you could survey in its entirety in one visit, the Neue Galerie is for you. This small museum is housed in an elegant former mansion, dating from 1914. Originally designed as a private residence by Carrère & Hastings (who also designed the New York Public Library), it was occupied at one time by Mrs. Cornelius Vanderbilt III. More recently, it was home to the YIVO Institute for Jewish Research.

The collection focuses on German and Austrian fine art and decorative art of the early twentieth century. It is derived from the holdings of Serge Sabarsky and Ronald Lauder, an art dealer and businessman respectively, who share an abiding interest in this field. They purchased the building in 1994. You may or may not be familiar with the several German schools represented, namely, Die Brücke, Der Blaue Reiter, Neue Sachlichkeit, Bauhaus, and Werkbund. You will, however, recognize many of the artists they included, such as Klee, Schiele, Kandinsky, Klimt, Hoffmann, Van der Rohe, and many others who are shown at their very best.

LAWRENCE KAHN
Professor Emeritus of Pediatrics, Washington University

11.16 Solomon R. Guggenheim Museum

1959, Frank Lloyd Wright; 1992, addition by Gwathmey Siegel & Associates
1071 Fifth Avenue between East 88th and East 89th Streets
212 423 3500; www.guggenheim.org
Closed Thursdays.

Frank Lloyd Wright chose the location for the Guggenheim Museum for its proximity to Central Park, and his design encourages the visitor to communicate with nature, particularly from the vantage point of the small rotunda, or "Monitor Building," as he called it. Here, two glass-enclosed mini-rotundas are inscribed in wide terraces, one rectangular and one round. Although visitors are not allowed access onto these terraces, the new Gwathmey Siegel tower building, completed in 1992, includes a marvelous jewel of a sculpture terrace, which is open to the public. Access is through the fifth-level tower gallery. From this perch, the visitor has a superb view of Central Park and the Reservoir. An added bonus is a sculpture or group of sculptures from the Guggenheim's collection. Go at sunset and enjoy the silhouetted skyline of Central Park West. This is the view of only the privileged few who live on Fifth Avenue overlooking the park. An added attraction is reduced museum admission on Saturdays after 6 p.m.

After the Guggenheim, explore the charming residential neighborhood of Carnegie Hill and the Guggenheim's neighboring museums, including the Smithsonian's Cooper-Hewitt National Design Museum and the Jewish Museum (see p. 246). Pick up a picnic lunch from the museum café or any of the take-out shops on Madison and dine in the park. The most beautiful spot is the Conservatory Garden on Fifth Avenue and 104th Street (see p. 270).

LISA DENNISON
Executive, Sotheby's

11.17 Carnegie Mansion, now Smithsonian's Cooper-Hewitt, National Design Museum

1903, Babb, Cook & Willard

2 East 91st Street at Fifth Avenue

212 849 8400; www.cooperhewitt.org

Arthur Ross Terrace and Garden

Andrew Carnegie left us a legacy of public libraries across the country, but one of the best places to read is the garden in what was his own backyard. Now the Arthur Ross Terrace and Garden behind the Cooper-Hewitt, this plot of land is a well-kept oasis at the highest elevation on Fifth Avenue, located between 90th and 91st Streets. Descending the steps from Carnegie's former home, one enters a central lawn set among lovely plantings, with the original wisteria still flowering. Along a picturesque path winding around the circumference are welcoming benches, ideal for spending a bucolic afternoon outside while in the city. Looking through the enclosing wrought-iron fence (the only flaw in the view), west to Central Park and south to apartment buildings and the Church of the Heavenly Rest, it is hard to imagine that for the first fifteen years the Carnegies were in residence, the plot across the street held a decrepit wooden shack that sold lemonade, peanuts, ginger cakes, and other snacks. Now, the perfect afternoon in the garden includes a treat from one of Carnegie Hill's nearby gourmet food shops and an absorbing book—Mr. Carnegie no doubt would approve.

While neighbors used to be privileged with private keys, now all visitors access the garden through the Carnegie mansion, which Andrew and his wife, Louise, built for his retirement, intended as "the most modest, plainest and most roomy house in New York." (Along the way, take time to look for the charming period details adorning the interior of the house or view the exhibitions featuring objects from the extraordinary collections amassed by the Hewitt sisters.) Daydreaming in the garden, while looking at the southwest corner of the back limestone-and-brick façade, one can imagine Carnegie in his office within his private suite of rooms. Visitors would come seeking donations from Carnegie, who devoted the end of his life to dispensing his wealth for the benefit of society. To get to the philanthropist, supplicants had to pass through a small vestibule with a dropped ceiling then duck through a low doorway (Carnegie was only 5'2") to enter a library dominated by a painted frieze of inspirational quotations, where they would await the small but powerful man.

LISA PODOS
Arts educator

11.18 The Jewish Museum

1908, C. P. H. Gilbert; 1993, addition by Kevin Roche
1109 Fifth Avenue at 92nd Street
212 423 3200; www.thejewishmuseum.org
Closed Wednesdays.

In the heart of New York City there is a piece of ancient Jerusalem—a foundation stone from a wall that protected the city in the first century that tells a story of desperation, disaster, and transformation. In 66 C.E., the Jews of ancient Israel rebelled against their Roman overlords and hastily completed the city wall as a part of their defense system. The wall did not hold, however; the Roman army breached it, going on to destroy Jerusalem and the Temple, the focus of ancient sacrificial worship. The Jews were exiled from the city and were forced to devise an alternative form of worship, based on prayer in the synagogue and the study of the sacred texts. This new form of worship became the mainstay of Judaism thereafter. All this can be read from a single stone!

The foundation stone is one of more than eight hundred works of art and artifacts on view in the Jewish Museum's permanent exhibition, "Culture and Continuity: The Jewish Journey." Each tells a part of the dramatic story of the Jewish people's artistic and cultural creativity in response to the challenges of preserving and defining their identity over four millennia. I have many favorite objects in the show in addition to the foundation stone. One is a nineteenth-century Hanukkah lamp from Australia, decorated with kangaroos and emus. It started out as a souvenir from Down Under, with an emu egg hanging in the center. When the egg eventually broke, someone decided to convert it into a

Hanukkah lamp. Another favorite, also from the nineteenth century, is a painting by the German artist Moritz Oppenheim titled *The Return of the Jewish Volunteer*. It reflects both the opportunities and conflicts Jews experienced after the Emancipation, when they were allowed for the first time to participate as citizens in the activities of their adopted homeland. In the painting, the soldier has just arrived home from his unit, interrupting his family's Sabbath observance. While he is now free to serve his country, he has broken with his religious tradition by traveling on the Sabbath.

After viewing the permanent exhibition, the visitor might take a rest by examining the museum building itself, which is a gem. It was designed by Charles Prendergast H. Gilbert in the style of a François er French Gothic château. The second floor of the museum retains many of the original details of the rooms from the first half of the twentieth century, when the mansion was occupied by Felix and Frieda Schiff Warburg. In 1993, an addition was made to the building and the interior of the original mansion renovated. Architect Kevin Roche chose to extend the French Gothic façade and interior decoration, and the visitor will be hard-pressed to distinguish the original parts of the mansion from the more recent addition.

SUSAN L. BRAUNSTEIN
Curator of Archaeology and Judaica, The Jewish Museum

11.19 Clapboard House

1852, attributed to Albro Howell
160 East 92nd Street between Lexington and Third Avenues
Not open to the public.

This 1852 two-and-a-half-story residence is one of only a handful of wood frame houses remaining on the Upper East Side. In 1915, it was purchased by Willard Straight and his wife to serve as servants's quarters for their Fifth Avenue mansion on the corner of 94th Street.

The charming house has classical fluted columns on the

first-floor porch and the upper stories have wooden shutters at their windows. Although it's a designated New York City Landmark, this romantic and evocative orphan has received too little loving care in recent years.

MARGOT GAYLE

The late Margot Gayle was a preservationist, and co-founder of the Victorian Society of America.

11.20 Kitchen Arts & Letters

1435 Lexington Avenue between East 93rd and East 94th Streets
212 876 5550; www.kitchenartsandletters.com
Closed Sundays. (Closed Saturdays and Sundays in July and August.)

Proprietor Nach Waxman carries a marvelous assortment of books on food and wine, culinary history, and food ephemera. It's absolutely top drawer. He sells one food product, which happens to be my favorite olive oil—Alziari, in the beautiful blue can with stars on it. It's from Nice and is suave and full-flavored.

JANE DANIELS LEAR

Food and travel writer

11.21 St. Nicholas Russian Orthodox Cathedral

1902, John Bergesen
15 East 97th Street between Fifth and Madison Avenues
212 996 6638; www.russianchurchusa.org

St. Nicholas Russian Orthodox Cathedral of New York is the only example of Moscow Baroque in the United States, and a particularly splendid one. It is reminiscent of the world-famous Church of Protection in the historic Russian village of Fili (constructed in 1693), St. Nicholas-the-Great-Cross in Moscow, and several others. The cathedral is decorated with frescoes by the renowned Russian artist Sokolov, and in 1973 was declared a landmark by the City of New York. Few are aware, however, that this building is something of a monument to entirely different Russian-American relations that are today difficult to imagine. These could be characterized as the relations, if not between friends, then between close acquaintances, and span from the cultural to the military. The initial contributions toward the construction of the cathedral were made by the sailors of the Russian warship *Retvizan*, on which could be seen the mark "Made in Philadelphia." The *Retvizan* was sunk in the Russo-Japanese war and a cross from the ship's chapel was saved. Today this cross hangs in the cathedral.

The construction of the cathedral is connected with the then head of the mission of the Russian Church in the United States, Bishop Tikhon (Belavin). Bishop Tikhon was fluent in English and was able to establish strong and useful contacts in New York when he moved his headquarters here from San Francisco. He was to be the famous Moscow Patriarch, elected after Russia's February Revolution, who died in 1925, most likely with the participation of the Bolshevik administration. From 1924 to 1960, St. Nicholas Russian Orthodox Cathedral, in the heart of Manhattan, was the subject of a protracted legal battle over ownership of this remarkable example of Moscow Baroque.

YURI MILOSLAVSKY
Writer

11.22 Museum of the City of New York

1930, Joseph H. Freedlander
1220 Fifth Avenue at East 103rd Street
212 534 1672; www.mcny.org
Closed Mondays.

On Fifth Avenue, a stone's throw away from the magnificent Conservatory Garden in Central Park, is the Museum of the City of New York, home to a wonderful toy collection that tells the story of growing up in New York over the last three centuries. Particularly thrilling is a quiet room filled with antique doll houses dating back to 1769. As you contemplate these miniature universes filled with dolls dressed by long-forgotten children, a lost world begins to shimmer in your mind's eye. The crown jewel of the collection is the Stettheimer Doll House, created in the 1920s by Carrie Walter Stettheimer, hostess to New York City's avant-garde artists and writers. This extraordinarily detailed evocation of the Stettheimer's home and life has its own art gallery, which houses such works as Marcel Duchamp's miniature version of his *Nude Descending a Staircase*, an alabaster *Venus* by Gaston Lachaise, and other works of art by Albert Gleizes, and Marguerite and William Zorach.

Before you leave, take a look at Elizabeth Yandell's treasure box, circa 1885. Elizabeth, orphaned when she was six years old, kept this special box throughout her life, bringing it out on occasion to amuse her own children when they were ill. It's filled with mementos—a piece of rope from a trip to Europe, an autograph album, a favorite wax doll resplendent in a red-tasseled hat and gold-buttoned jacket, an assortment of shells and stones, a stuffed cat and dog, their fur rubbed smooth. Elizabeth's sadnesses and joys come vividly to life, although the child has

. . . grown up and gone away,
And it is but a child of air
That lingers in the garden there.
—R. L. Stevenson, "To Any Reader."

ANNE LANDSMAN
Novelist

11.23 El Museo del Barrio

1230 Fifth Avenue at East 104th Street
212 831 7272; www.elmuseo.org
Closed Mondays.

At El Museo del Barrio you will find a permanent exhibit of works by the Taino, a pre-Colombian Caribbean culture, as well as temporary exhibitions that might include such renowned Hispano-American artists as Frida Kahlo and

Diego Rivera (Mexico), Francisco Oller (Puerto Rico), Fernando Botero (Colombia), Amelia Paez (Cuba), and other Latin-American masters of the arts. Through their paintings one gets to know the passions, the imagination, the originality, the devotion, and the fascinating sense of style that has propelled these artists to become international figures in the art world.

ANITA VELEZ-MITCHELL
Writer

11.24 Gracie Mansion

1804, attributed to Ezra Weeks
In Carl Schurz Park, enter at East 88th Street and East End Avenue
212 570 4751; www.nyc.gov/html/artcom
Check website for information about tours.

Most Gracie Mansion visitors are drawn by the prospect of seeing the Federal-period house and its collection of fine and decorative art, or by the possibility of catching a glimpse of New York's mayor. However, three lesser-known features reveal traces of previous residents.

Elegant floor-to-ceiling windows in the Mayor's Library overlook the East River. On one windowpane is etched in script, "Millie, 1875," and beneath in a bold scrawl "Margie, 1965." Amalia Hermione Wheaton (Millie) was born at the mansion, and as a young girl scratched her name and birthdate on the window. Almost a century later, the young daughter of newly elected Mayor John Lindsay spotted the window. Her mother, pleased to have Margie bond with her new home, permitted her to write her own name on the glass.

The mansion's front door is framed by a finely carved Adam-style surround. Sharp-eyed guests note an odd, angled notch cut into the right side of the doorjamb. During the mayoralty of Edward I. Koch, the notch held a traditional Jewish mezuzah, a small case containing a piece of parchment. Written on the parchment is the Shema prayer, which reminds Jews of their obligations toward God. It is customary to kiss the mezuzah in passing. The mezuzah was removed at the end of Mr. Koch's term.

During early-twentieth-century construction projects, workers unearthed remains of narrow stone-lined tunnels leading from the mansion's basement to the riverbank. Historians identified the tunnels either as an escape route built during the American Revolution or as a stop on the Underground Railroad during the Civil War period. Visitors ask about the rumor that Mayor William O'Dwyer stashed money missing from city coffers in the tunnels before abruptly departing for Mexico in 1950. These stories are not true; modern archaeology has revealed instead that the tunnels, of the same vintage as the 1799 house, provided drainage for the basement, which tended to flood. The real secret is that the basement still floods.

DAVID L. REESE
Director, Gunster Hall, Virginia

11.25 Sotheby's

1334 York Avenue at East 72nd Street

Sotheby's Terrace Cafe

Tenth floor

212 606 7070; www.sothebys.com

Closes at 4 p.m.

Bid

In the lobby

212 988 7730; www.sothebys.com

Enter the new Sotheby's building, proceed directly to the tenth floor, grab a hot *panino* or a salad in the café, and head outside to the terrace. Linger and enjoy the great city feel. When you've had enough, walk back inside to the best new gallery space in New York City... some say in America. Or wander among French furniture, antiques, fab jewels, or very affordable prints, all on view on the approximately seventy-five-thousand square feet of exhibition space.

As a more serious alternative to the café, try Bid on the ground floor of Sotheby's: a wonderful "multi-starred" new American restaurant.

GERALDINE NAGER-GRIFFIN
Senior vice president, Sotheby's

11.26 Rockefeller University

1910, York & Sawyer
1230 York Avenue between East 63rd and East 68th Streets

Caspary Auditorium

1957, Harrison & Abramovitz
212 327 8000; www.rockefeller.edu
Open to the public for events only.

11

Harrison & Abramovitz's dreamy, hemispherical dome could have floated over from a World's Fair. This colossal sunken sphere, a forty-foot-high, ninety-foot-diameter bubble, was once covered with beautiful blue tiles. Slide into an aisle seat to gaze at the convex circles bulging everywhere. Imagine being inside a giant golf ball.

TRACEY HUMMER AND FREDERIC SCHWARTZ
Writer and Architect

11.27 Mount Vernon Hotel Museum & Garden, formerly the Abigail Adams Smith Museum

421 East 61st Street between First and York Avenues
212 838 6878; www.mvhm.org
Closed Mondays.

This is great fun—an eighteenth-century carriage house hidden in the middle of the city.

In 1796, William Stephens Smith and his wife Abigail Adams Smith, daughter of President John Adams, began construction of an estate on twenty-three acres of Manhattan's Upper East Side, at the time a rural area and a refuge from the congested city to the south. They named it Mount Vernon in honor of George Washington's Virginia home. Unfortunately, beset by financial troubles, the couple had to sell their unfinished property just a year later. By the turn of the century, under a different owner, the main house and stone carriage house (now housing the museum) were completed. In 1826, the main house was destroyed by fire and the carriage house was converted into a posh day resort called the Mount Vernon Hotel. The hotel operated there until 1833 and today is New York City's only surviving day hotel—one of only a handful of sites in the United States affording a window on hotel life in the early nineteenth century. It also contains a beautiful decorative arts collection, along with furniture, costumes, quilts and textiles, and historical documents.

LAURA LINNEY
Actor

Museum Evenings

www.iheartnymuseums.com

A city's best-kept secrets are often in plain sight. As any tour book will tell you in its listing of hours, most of the major museums in New York are open late on Friday and Saturday evenings. As many longtime aficionados of art in the city know, this is the time when tourists head downtown for dinner and the theater, and you can view the art undisturbed.

ELIZABETH WINTHROP
Writer

Museum Evening Hours

Admission is often waived, or discounted, during evening hours. Check websites for times, as they may vary.

Museum of Jewish Heritage (see p. 28)
Wednesdays until 8 p.m.; www.mjhnyc.org

El Museo del Barrio (see p. 250)
Wednesdays until 9 p.m.; www.elmuseo.org

National Museum of the American Indian (see p. 17)
Thursdays until 8 p.m.; www.nmai.si.edu

Paley Centre for Media (see p. 177)
Thursdays until 8 p.m.; www.paleycenter.org

The Jewish Museum (see p. 246)
Thursdays until 8 p.m.; www.thejewishmuseum.org

Museum of Arts & Design (see p. 175)
Thursdays from 6 p.m. to 9 p.m.; www.madmuseum.org

The Museum of Modern Art (see p. 194)
Fridays until 8 p.m.; www.moma.org

Whitney Museum of American Art (see p. 220)
Fridays until 9 p.m.; www.whitney.org

The Studio Museum in Harlem (see p. 307)
Thursdays and Fridays until 9 p.m.; www.studiomuseum.org

Solomon R. Guggenheim Museum (see p. 243)
Saturdays until 7:45 p.m.; www.guggenheim.org

The Metropolitan Museum of Art (see p. 224)
Fridays and Saturdays until 9 p.m.; www.metmuseum.org

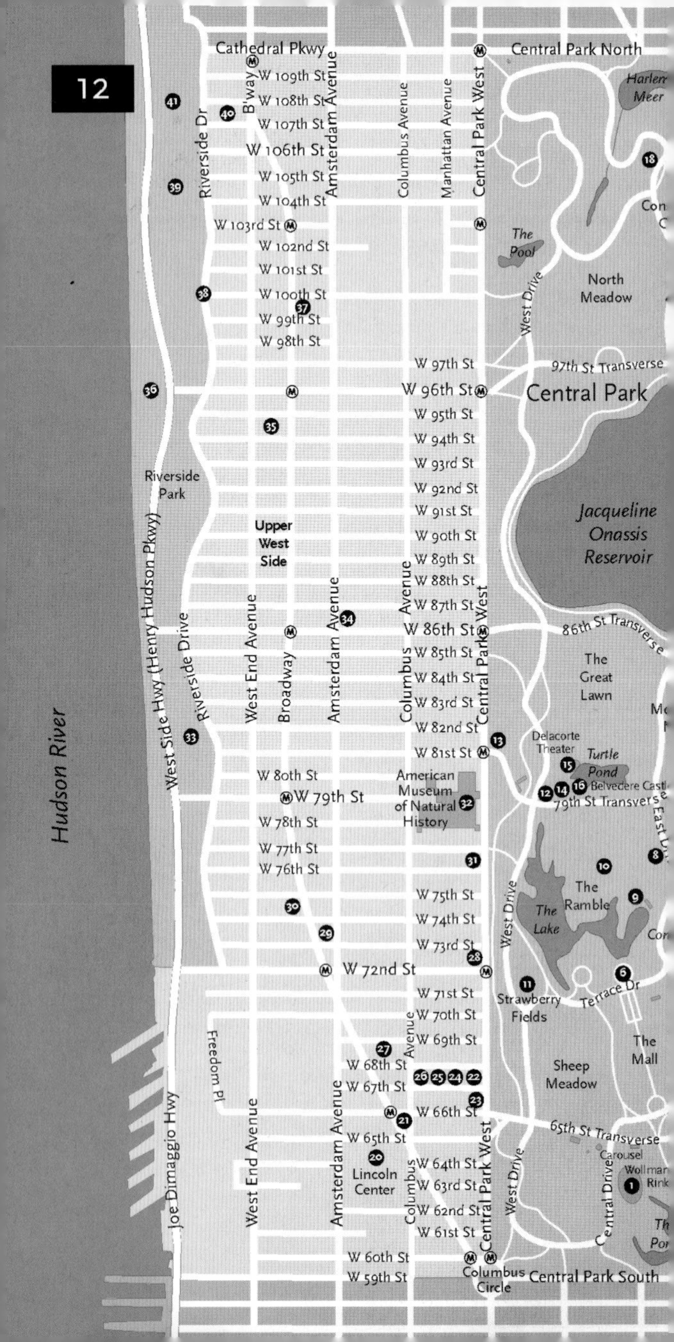

12

Cathedral Pkwy
Central Park North
W 109th St
W 108th St
W 107th St
W 106th St
W 105th St
W 104th St
W 103rd St
W 102nd St
W 101st St
W 100th St
W 99th St
W 98th St
W 97th St
W 96th St
W 95th St
W 94th St
W 93rd St
W 92nd St
W 91st St
W 90th St
W 89th St
W 88th St
W 87th St
W 86th St
W 85th St
W 84th St
W 83rd St
W 82nd St
W 81st St
W 80th St
W 79th St
W 78th St
W 77th St
W 76th St
W 75th St
W 74th St
W 73rd St
W 72nd St
W 71st St
W 70th St
W 69th St
W 68th St
W 67th St
W 66th St
W 65th St
W 64th St
W 63rd St
W 62nd St
W 61st St
W 60th St
W 59th St
Central Park South
Columbus Circle
B'way
Broadway
Riverside Dr
Riverside Drive
West End Avenue
Amsterdam Avenue
Columbus Avenue
Manhattan Avenue
Central Park West
West Side Hwy (Henry Hudson Pkwy)
Joe Dimaggio Hwy
Freedom Pl
Hudson River
Riverside Park
Upper West Side
American Museum of Natural History
Lincoln Center
Central Park
Harlem Meer
The Pool
North Meadow
97th St Transverse
Jacqueline Onassis Reservoir
86th St Transverse
The Great Lawn
Delacorte Theater
Turtle Pond
Belvedere Castle
79th St Transverse
West Drive
East Dr
The Ramble
The Lake
Strawberry Fields
Terrace Dr
The Mall
Sheep Meadow
65th St Transverse
Carousel
Wollman Rink
Central Drive

1 6 8 9 10 11 12 13 14 15 16 18 20 21 22 23 24 25 26 27 28 29 30 31 32 33 34 35 36 37 38 39 40 41

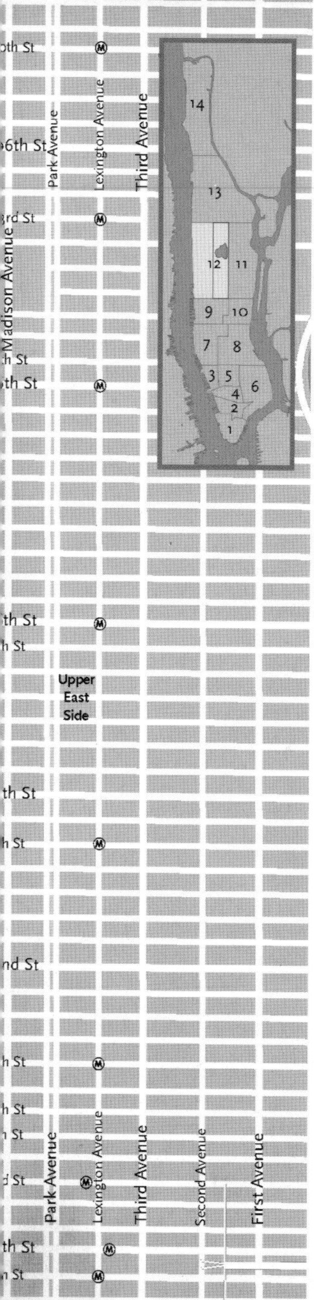

CHAPTER 12

CENTRAL PARK

1 Wollman Memorial Rink
2 Central Park Zoo
3 Delacorte Clock (see p. 205)
4 Balto
5 Central Park Tour
6 Bethesda Terrace
7 Conservatory Water
8 The Still Hunt
9 The Butterfly Habitat
10 The Ramble
11 Strawberry Fields
12 Swedish Cottage
13 Bird-watching in Central Park
14 The Shakespeare Garden
15 Delacorte Theater
16 Belvedere Castle (see p. 17)
17 Conservatory Garden
18 Andrew H. Green Bench
19 The Pumpkin Float

UPPER WEST SIDE

20 Lincoln Center
21 Arts for Transit
22 Hotel des Artistes
23 2 West 67th Street
24 Central Park Studios
25 Atelier Building
26 39 West 67th Street
27 Christ and St. Stephen's Church (see p. 172)
28 Dakota Apartments
29 Central Savings Bank (see p. 164)
30 Steps on Broadway
31 New-York Historical Society
32 Museum of Natural History
33 Riverside Park
34 Barney Greengrass
35 Pomander Walk
36 Riverside Park Tennis Courts
37 Wang Chen's Table Tennis Club
38 Firemen's Memorial
39 Hudson Beach Cafe
40 Nicholas Roerich Museum
41 Riverside Park

Central Park & Upper West Side

CENTRAL PARK

1876, Frederick Law Olmsted & Calvert Vaux
Central Park South (59th Street) to Central Park North (110th Street) between Fifth Avenue and Central Park West

12.1 Wollman Memorial Rink

1950, rebuilt early 1980s
Southeast corner of park, enter at Fifth Avenue and East 60th Street
212 439 6900; www.wollmanskatingrink.com
Open from late October to early April.

New York City has several outdoor ice skating rinks, but skating at the Wollman Rink in Central Park, especially at night, is a transcendent experience. I always think of the opening sequence of Woody Allen's *Manhattan*—you can almost hear Gershwin playing as you stare at the illuminated skyline of Central Park South. In the early evening when the kids go home, you can skate to Sinatra, Ella Fitzgerald, Fred Astaire, and Duke Ellington. There's a sense of continuity as you imagine the New Yorkers who skated on this spot a hundred years ago, when this part of New York was so far uptown it was considered "the country." They were dressed more formally—long skirts, bonnets, and fur muffs for the women, suits and overcoats for the gentlemen. But the delightful feeling of gliding, the shared silliness, the thrill of being outdoors on a cold night—these things don't change with the times. Go on "Cheap Skate" nights, when the admission fee is discounted and there's usually enough room to fall without taking anyone down with you. Bring your own skates if you can—the hard green plastic rental skates with frayed laces do not inspire gracefulness. Every hour or so the ice is cleared and it's time for a cup of the most delicious hot chocolate in the city. I don't know if it's really tastier than any other, but it seems that way when you are warming your frigid fingers with the heat from the paper cup and watching the Zamboni machine sweep the ice to a glassy smoothness. As the hot liquid travels through you, and the smell of chocolate fills you up, everything seems right with the world.

GINA ROGAK
Director of special events, Whitney Museum of American Art

12.2 Central Park Zoo

Redesigned 1988, Kevin Roche, John Dinkeloo & Associates
Enter at Fifth Avenue and East 64th Street
212 439 6500; www.centralparkzoo.com
Check the website for hours.

Go to the Central Park Zoo and pay tribute to the seals, then check in with the penguins, and then the polar bears, and your head will be screwed back on properly.

12

JOHN GUARE
Playwright

Madagascar Giant Day Gecko

Tropic Zone

In this city of egos where everyone's clamoring, "Look at me! Look at me!" there is one exquisite creature that makes a point of invisibility. Its beauty is so shocking that people cry out in surprise when they see it. That is, if they can see it.

It's displayed behind a floodlit window like a priceless piece of jewelry, but finding it amidst the tangle of ferns can take a good twenty minutes. It's not only a master of camouflage, but like the silver mime who works the subway, it rarely moves, clinging to the wall like a wad of chewed gum. Parents tend to spot it first—the electric-green Madagascar giant day gecko that lives in the Tropic Zone of the Central Park Zoo, along with two motionless tomato frogs.

Waiting for this shy and dainty soul to reveal itself takes time. A lot of time. Many don't have the patience and move on to the frolicking penguins and polar bears. But for those who adjust their vision to this miniature stage set, the rewards are exhilarating.

Suddenly, there it is! Glued to the wall beneath a fern! An intensely green lizard with a sprinkling of orange spots on its head and back. It's about a foot long with four hilarious cartoon toes on each foot. Its shiny black eyes are lidless and never flicker. Its only sign of life is a slight pulsing of the stomach. Avert your gaze for a moment, and it's gone. All you see are ferns and the two orange tomato frogs miserably trying to conceal themselves on the leafy green floor.

So there you stand, waiting for just one more glimpse. Now you see it, now you don't—the most ravishing peep show in all of New York City.

TINA HOWE
Playwright

12.4 Balto

1925, Frederick G. R. Roth
West of East Drive and 67th Street and north of the Zoo
www.centralpark.com

One of the statues in Central Park is a bronze of an Alaskan sled dog, a husky named Balto. The big dog seems a little out of place in New York, and his story involves a largely forgotten event in a faraway place.

In January 1925, in the depths of an exceptionally bitter winter, an epidemic of diphtheria broke out in Nome, on Alaska's west coast. The supply of antitoxin serum was soon used up, and with the coast ice-bound and no planes available, it was decided that the best way to get more serum was by dogsled. Twenty teams would be used in a relay that would start from the nearest point reachable by rail—almost seven hundred miles from Nome.

The serum was poured into a cylinder wrapped in a quilt. Each village along the route dispatched its best musher, teamed with the best dogs, to carry the cylinder through its territory. Along the way, temperatures dropped to more than sixty below, wind blew up to eighty miles per hour, and blizzard after blizzard rendered the crude trail invisible. One team was almost stranded on an ice floe. Two dogs froze to death.

The trip took seven days, and when the serum arrived safely in Nome, the story of "the great race of mercy" was widely reported. Nome's best-known dogsled racer, a man named Leonhard Seppala, had carried the serum more than ninety miles—twice as far as any other musher—and his daring wilderness exploits made him a hero to newspaper readers around the country.

In recent years, the success of the Iditarod race, which retraces much of the original route of the serum run, has revived the Seppala legend, and many people assume that Balto was Seppala's lead dog. In fact, Seppala passed over the black husky when he picked his team, preferring a faster dog named Togo. Balto, left behind, was then chosen by Gunnar Kaasen, the musher who wound up completing the final leg of the journey. Thus Balto, not Togo, was around for the photo op when Kassen handed the serum to Nome's doctor.

So visit Balto (in the winter, it's better that way), being sure to check for the ironic grin on his bronze mouth—and take your pooch.

SAM POSEY
Race-car driver, artist, and designer

12.5 Central Park Tour

Enter at Fifth Avenue at 67th Street
www.centralpark.com

Throughout Western civilization, public parks have been designed to provide an array of recreational opportunities, and Central Park may be viewed as the pinnacle of this achievement. My favorite walk through this park takes into account the use New Yorkers make of it, in addition to its finest views, its historical highlights, its natural charms, and some of its dramatic twists.

Enter the park from Fifth Avenue at 67th Street, and walk west to the statue of Balto (see p. 260). The statue honors the sled dog that saved Alaska from diphtheria and it has been sat upon by every kid passing by. Proceed westward through the tunnel until you come up onto Literary Walk. Pass Shakespeare and Burns, turn right and head north. This famous walk is lined with a spectacular collection of elm trees and is Frederick Law Olmsted's quintessential Victorian strolling promenade. Cross over 72nd Street, down the magnificent stairs, around Bethesda Fountain, and then bear slightly left to cross Bow Bridge, one of the two finest of the five original cast-iron bridges remaining in the park. Swans, boats, and lovers abound. Once across the bridge, head into the Ramble (see p. 265). Perhaps one of the greatest stopover points for migratory birds, the Ramble also plays host to meandering streams, Adirondack-style rustic benches, and all sorts of people.

Wend your way due north until you come out at Belvedere Castle with its medieval parapets and breathtaking views of the Great Lawn. Check out the Nature Center and ask the rangers some questions. Look carefully fifty yards to the east of the castle on the north side of the transverse: these secret stairs have taken many of the famous and notable—Paul Simon and a president or two—to and from great events. Stroll down around Turtle Pond and the Great Lawn if you have the time. Turn south now and find your way into and through the Shakespeare Garden (see p. 268) and past the Swedish Cottage (see p. 266). If you want to pop out of the park and visit the American Museum of Natural History (my favorite place in New York City), then do so here at 81st Street. Otherwise, stroll down along the west side of the lake, up into Yoko Ono's Strawberry Fields (see p. 265) and pause at the "Imagine" mosaic. Candles and hippies are always here. Continue down past the Sheep Meadow, where city residents get their tan and youngsters meet. Exit at Columbus Circle or head back east if you care to dally

at the Central Park Zoo, with its resplendent tropical birds, awesome penguin display, and idiosyncratic polar bears.
ALEXANDER R. BRASH
Chairman, Habitat Committee in the EPA's Harbor Estuary Program

12.6 Bethesda Terrace

1862, Calvert Vaux, designer; Jacob Wrey Mould, sculptor
Mid-park at 72nd Street
www.centralpark.com

The stonework at Bethesda Terrace at 72nd Street merits a close look. Moving east to west, the hand-carved sandstone piers and balustrades flanking the stairs both north and south of the road represent 1) spring, youth, dawn; 2) summer, adolescence, noon; 3) fall, adulthood, afternoon; 4) winter, old age, evening.
JEAN PARKER PHIFER
Architect

12.7 Conservatory Water

North of the Fifth Avenue and 72nd Street entrance
www.centralpark.com

Red-tailed hawks

In late spring and early summer, between May and July, the best show in town is at the Model Boat Pond. Along its west shore, facing Fifth Avenue, you'll find people with serious telescopes on tripods aimed up at the twelfth story of a building facing the park just north of 72nd Street. What's up there is a massive, sprawling nest of twigs that tops a long classical arch on the building's façade. The nest—huge and messy, and under the official protection of the National Fish and Wildlife Department—is the home of the red-tailed hawks who have made Central Park their unlikely home. Any of the telescope owners will let you have a look, and you can home in on this beautiful feral family, fierce-eyed, preening, and unbelievably wild. By June the chicks will be clearly visible in the nest, stalking stiffly back and forth, peering out across the park like sentries, waiting for dinner, leading their own unknowable lives before you. Suddenly, into your field of vision, a parent arrives; silent, a rush of reddish feathers, vast smothering wings beating backwards. The chicks make a swarming rush forward, there is a voracious flurry of attention, and dinner is over. The parent moves regally to the edge of the great nest, swivels its neck, gives a pitiless stare out into the park, and sails off again, gliding smoothly out into the upper air. The hawk-watchers cheer.

ROXANA ROBINSON
Author and biographer

12.8 The Still Hunt

1883, Edward Kemeys
East Drive at East 77th Street
www.centralpark.com

Walk down East Drive. On an overhang, find a bronze, life-size statue of a mountain lion, crouched ready to pounce. This Central Park reminder of the wilderness from which Manhattan was carved can have a startling effect on passersby who happen to glance up.

KASSY WILSON
Exhibitions coordinator, Museum of the City of New York

12.9 The Butterfly Habitat

Mid-park at 74th Street

To the left of the Boathouse Restaurant, near where bicycles are rented, is a fenced-in area with flowering wild plants. This is a butterfly habitat, a garden created specifically to attract the winged creatures. Beyond and to your left, up the pathway and then down, is "the point," a place where you can see Bethesda Fountain from the other side of the lake.

MARGOT ADLER
Correspondent, National Public Radio

12.10 The Ramble

Between 73rd and 78th Streets
www.centralpark.com

Shunned by many due to its reputation as a furtive and dangerous place by night, the Ramble is Frederick Law Olmsted's vision of primeval New York. Park thickets, untrimmed trees, and apparently unintended streams belie the skilled artfulness of this romantic pre-Gotham fantasy. Rustic stonework and a few ruins are the only hint that this place, like everything else in Manhattan, has been willfully shaped by man.

WALTER CHATHAM
Architect

12.11 Strawberry Fields

Near Central Park West between 71st and 74th Streets
www.centralpark.com

Enter the park at West 72nd Street and find Strawberry Fields, the oasis planted by Yoko Ono in memory of John Lennon. You can be one of the thousands who have stood for a meditative moment by the Italian mosaic circle inscribed with the word "Imagine." Every year on the night of the anniversary of John Lennon's death (December 8, 1980), several hundred people gather here, holding candles and flowers. They sing every Beatles song they can remember until about one o'clock in the morning, when the police insist that they leave. Strawberry Fields has lovely grass

to lie on, luxurious plantings of trees and foliage, and a sense of peace that is extraordinary in New York City.
MARGOT ADLER
Correspondent, National Public Radio

12.12 Swedish Cottage Marionette Theater

1876, Manneus Isaeus
Between Delacorte Theater and 79th Street Transverse
212 988 9093; www.centralpark.com
Reservations are required.

Central Park as a haven from the noise and the intensity of everyday city life, is no secret. However, the park does contain little-known features, one of which is the Swedish Cottage Marionette Theater. Just south of the Delacorte Theater, at the base of the Shakespeare Garden, one discovers a nineteenth-century Swedish cottage designed originally as a one-room schoolhouse exhibit by prominent Swedish architect Manneus Isaeus for the 1876 Centennial Exposition at Philadelphia. Frederick Law Olmsted was so taken with it that he paid fifteen hundred dollars to have it shipped and rebuilt in 1877 in the new park he co-designed in New York.

Subsequently utilized as public restrooms, a nature study, and civil-defense headquarters during World War II, in 1947 it became the headquarters and workshop of the Central Park Marionette Theater, which produced touring shows. Budget cuts eradicated funding for touring, and the interior was redesigned in in1973 to include a permanent theater.

Decades of neglect and disrepair threatened the building with demolition by the early 1990s. The long and distinguished history of delightful productions of children's classics, in conjunction with the City Parks Foundation, proved its saving grace. A coalition of private and public interests raised funds for a $1.5 million renovation in 1997.

Besides a beautiful and historically faithful restoration of the exterior details, a new proscenium stage and modern technical facilities now enable the talented staff and visiting artists to produce what is arguably the finest marionette theater for children in the United States.

In May 1998, the Swedish Cottage Marionette Theater reopened to the public with a glorious production of *Gulliver's Travels*, followed by equally magnificent presentations of *Jack and the Beanstalk* and *Sleeping Beauty*. At a ticket price of five dollars, it's one of the true bargains and secret treasures of New York.

KEVIN JOSEPH ROACH
Set designer

12.13 Bird-watching in Central Park

West 81st Street and Central Park West
For information about bird-watching:
NYC Audubon Society: ☎ 212 691 7483; www.nycaudubon.org
Linnaean Society: ☎ 212 252 2668; www.linnaeannewyork.org
Starr Saphir: ☎ 212 304 3808; 917 306 3808
Parks Department: www.nycgovparks.org

Birding is one of Central Park's best secrets. Indeed, it's considered one of the fifteen most extraordinary birding sites in the United States during spring and fall migrations. That's because birds—more than two hundred and seventy species—come to the park as they cross the Atlantic flyway. Most New Yorkers believe the park belongs only to people, pigeons, rats, and squirrels, but it turns out that suburbs do not provide migrating birds with enough cover from predatory hawks, so Central Park, with its seed-bearing trees and forested areas, has become a haven for hundreds of thousands of birds to rest and feed during their long migratory flights.

A host of organizations, including the Audubon Society,

the Linnaean Society, and the Parks Department, lead bird-walks, and this is the best way to get a feel for birding in the park, especially since the best birding site, the Ramble, is a maze of complex paths in which it is easy to get lost. My favorite guide is Starr Saphir, who has been doing these walks for years, and even the total amateur, armed with a pair of binoculars, will see miraculous things in a couple of hours. I've lived near the park for fifty-two years, yet before I met Saphir, I had never seen a scarlet tanager, or a green heron, or twenty species of warblers.

The birding log, a diary in which expert birders record what they've seen in the park that day, can be found at the Boathouse Restaurant (where you can also get your morning coffee). Other animals and flowers are often included as well, and if you read back through the year's entries, you'll be amazed at the exuberant life of the park.

MARGOT ADLER
Correspondent, National Public Radio

12.14 The Shakespeare Garden

c. 1915
West 79th Traverse near Belvedere Castle

Each flower of this literary maze is mentioned in one of Shakespeare's poems or plays. The medley of herbs and flowers brings the Bard's works into a very beautiful and amazing tangle of winding green and varicolored swirls. This small garden offers lovely benches to sit amidst the poetry of posies and read Shakespeare's sonnets.

KAREN MOODY TOMPKINS
Artist

12.15 Delacorte Theater

1962, Eldon Elder

Mid-park, enter at Central Park West and West 81st Street or Fifth Avenue and East 79th Street

☎ 212 539 8750; www.publictheater.org

In 1962, after a contentious dispute with Robert Moses —the undisputed czar of public construction in New York City for about thirty years—the enterprising theatrical producer Joseph Papp obtained permission to perform Shakespeare plays in the middle of Central Park. He set up a group of bleachers and established free "Shakespeare in the Park," which soon became a desirable summer attraction in New York (June through August). The unbeatable Mr. Papp secured the promise of a check from George Delacorte for the construction of a real amphitheater to be built in lieu of the bleacher arrangement.

Unfortunately, a new mayor, less prone to cultural fantasies than his predecessor, turned down the proposal for a structure that would have remained through the ages, though the design had already been approved by his own commissioner of parks. Joe Papp's persistence eventually forced the mayor to permit the creation of a two-thousand-seat amphitheater, provided its wood appearance and main platform construction marked it as a "temporary" structure. The amphitheater has now stood for twenty-four years, and though it requires yearly repairs, it is much enjoyed by the community.

If one is willing to queue for them, free tickets are available only on the day of performance at either the Delacorte Theater or the Public Theater (425 Lafayette Street). Senior citizens have a less crowded queue of their own in front of the Delacorte box office.

GIORGIO CAVAGLIERI

The late Giorgio Cavaglieri was an architect.

North End of Central Park

Above the 96th Street Transverse

Most people vaunt the pleasures of Central Park, but few have ventured to its northern end. Once feared as a haven of crime, now the only thrills that await visitors (during the daytime) are the mise-en-scène of raw rock, tight crevices, rushing water, and ruins of a fort that served in the War of 1812. Olmsted's attempts to make a veritable portrait of the natural world, running the gamut from the pastoral to the sublime, can only be fully savored by those who push into the undercrofts of the bridges and passages he created in the "wild" northern end above 100th Street. Calm your nerves afterwards in the refinements of the Conservatory Garden.

BARRY BERGDOLL
Philip Johnson Chief Curator of Architecture and Design, The Museum of Modern Art

12.17 Conservatory Garden

1936, Gilmore D. Clarke, Thomas D. Price & M. Betty Sprout; 1983, redesigned by Lyndon B. Miller
Enter at Fifth Avenue between East 104th and East 105th Streets
www.centralpark.com

Central Park offers many pleasures, but none so unexpectedly delightful as the Conservatory Garden. Perhaps because most visitors frequent the southern end of the park, it comes as a complete surprise to walk through the ornate iron gate that once guarded Cornelius Vanderbilt's mansion on Fifth Avenue and 58th Street, and find yourself in this elegant time warp. There are three gardens, each in a different style. The south garden (my favorite) is done in informal English, themed to Frances Hodgson Burnett's children's classic *The Secret Garden*. Narrow slate paths bordered by exquisite plantings draw you to the center, where a tree-shaded lily pond, watched over by a bronze pair of children, attracts many birds.

The center garden is classic Italian, with its long manicured lawn leading to a dramatic, unadorned fountain spouting its single, geyser-like spray. In the background, a terrace of yew and spiraea lead upward to an arbor covered in Chinese wisteria, most beautiful in spring when it is overrun by purple blossoms.

The North Garden, with its shallow pool featuring a trio of dancing nymphs in its center, is French. Enter from one of its four arbors, covered with white-and-pink-tinted roses. This garden offers dazzling displays of tulips in spring and chrysanthemums in the fall. Come on a beautiful day and be prepared to stay a while.

LORRAINE B. DIEHL
Writer

I treasure the formal, symmetrical walks of the Conservatory Garden at 105th Street in Central Park. The fountains and their quiet, enclosed surroundings are a sheer joy, especially the fountain in the North Garden, where nymphs combine innocence and hedonism in a perfect, idiosyncratic picture of happy youth in motion.

MARIA ARRILLAGA
Writer and professor

Amidst the magnitude of the city, you can sit in relative quiet, hearing only the drips of water from the garden's nymph fountain. For its breadth of flora and generous and strategically placed benches, the garden still feels like an undiscovered treasure. It is the perfect afternoon spot and a great gateway to the newly restored Harlem Meer.

CLARE BELL
Program manager, Roy Lichtenstein Foundation

Andrew Haswell Green

12.18 **Andrew H. Green Bench**
1929, John H. Van Pelt & Margaret Van Pelt
Near East Drive at 105th Street
www.centralpark.com

2.12 **The Consolidation of Greater New York Sculpture**
1906, Albert Weinert
In the Surrogate's Court Building
Chambers Street vestibule
31 Chambers Street

Andrew Haswell Green is a personal—and utterly forgotten—hero of mine. He's sometimes described as the Robert Moses of the nineteenth century, yet hardly anyone knows his name. He supervised the creation of Central Park, rescued the city from bankruptcy after the Boss Tweed scandals, and helped create the Metropolitan Museum of Art, the Bronx Zoo, the Museum of Natural History, Riverside Park, and the New York Public Library. But most importantly, he was the man who championed the 1898 consolidation of the five boroughs into the New York City that exists today. That triumph earned him the title "The Father of Greater New York." After nearly five decades of selfless public service, the eighty-three-year-old Green was shot dead on the front steps of his home in a case of mistaken identity.

All that exists in the city to honor his memory is a forlorn stone bench in Central Park that's not even listed on most park maps. The original five trees that surrounded the bench—each one representing a borough—succumbed to Dutch elm disease decades ago, so in 1998 the Parks Department rededicated the bench and planted new saplings.

Green's greatest accomplishment, the consolidation, is almost as forgotten as he is. But just inside the entranceway of the Surrogate's Court Building you'll find a monument that marks the event, a sculpture titled *The Consolidation of Greater New York*. Allegorical Ms. Brooklyn is shown reaching out to allegorical Ms. New York, a union that, I can assure you, was easier to render in marble than in real life.

MICHAEL MISCIONE
Manhattan Borough Historian

12.19 The Pumpkin Float at Harlem Meer

Northeast corner of park
www.centralparknyc.org

On most days at the Harlem Meer you can find children fishing with long poles and bread dough. But if you come on a Sunday shortly before Halloween, you can watch as hundreds of children bring carved pumpkins with candles inside and float them on wooden rafts on the Meer—a magical site as darkness falls.

MARGOT ADLER
Correspondent, National Public Radio

UPPER WEST SIDE

12.20 Lincoln Center for the Performing Arts

West 62nd to West 66th Street between Columbus and Amsterdam Avenues
www.lincolncenter.org

Sit on the rim of the plaza fountain and feast your eyes and mind on the monumental cluster of buildings devoted to the performing arts. Next, move to the North Plaza and contemplate the glorious Henry Moore in a reflecting pool.

GEORGE WEISSMAN

The late George Weissman was president of Phillip Morris Companies and board chairman of the Lincoln Center for the Performing Arts.

North Plaza

1965, Dan Kiley

One of the most restful places in the Upper West Side is the little park, designed by the legendary landscape architect Dan Kiley, in front of the Vivian Beaumont Theater at Lincoln Center. Shade trees and a large reflecting pool set off two Henry Moore sculptures, and the three huge glass walls that appear to support Eero Saarinen's simple and graceful theater building shimmer with the light off the pool. From early morning until the crowds pour out from the various Lincoln Center attractions, it's a fine place to bring a snack or just sit and collect your thoughts.

GREGORY MOSHER

Theater director and producer

12.21 Arts for Transit: *Artemis, Acrobats, Divas and Dancers*

1998, Nancy Spero
66th Street-Lincoln Center subway station
www.mta.info

My current favorite piece of subway art is Nancy Spero's *Artemis, Acrobats, Divas, and Dancers*, twenty-two multicolored glass mosaic panels on either side of the train tracks at Lincoln Center. All the figures are women—diving, dancing, running, playing musical instruments, performing acrobatic feats, rollerskating. They are culled from classical and contemporary sources and are the perfect introduction to the performing arts center directly above. On the downtown platform, the mythological figure Diva repeats, sometimes large, sometimes smaller, but always sheathed in royal golds and crimsons and attended by other, more delicate, goddesses and warriors. The mosaicist, Peter Colombo, who worked on this project for three years, possibly has cut the finest, most detailed smalti since ancient times. His mixes of tiny colored glass tesserae sparkle brilliantly among the surrounding stretches of larger, more solidly colored glazed ceramic mosaic tiles. Thin bands of Naples yellow, Etruscan red, and cobalt blue cleverly flow from section to section, uniting them while elucidating individual passages.

JOYCE KOZLOFF
Artist

West 67th Street Studios

12.22 Hotel des Artistes

1918, George Mort Pollard
1 West 67th Street between Columbus Avenue and Central Park West
Not open to the public.

12.23 2 West 67th Street

1919, Rich & Mathesius
2 West 67th Street between Columbus Avenue and Central Park West

12.24 Central Park Studios
1905, B.H. Simonson and Pollard & Steinam
15 West 67th Street between Columbus Avenue and Central Park West

12.25 Atelier Building
1905, B.H. Simonson and Pollard & Steinam
33 West 67th Street between Columbus Avenue and Central Park West

12.26 39 West 67th Street
1907, Pollard & Steinam
39–41 West 67th Street between Columbus Avenue and Central Park West

West 67th Street, just off Central Park West, harbors one of the most remarkable urban environments in Manhattan. The high façades lining the narrow street primarily belong to apartment buildings, many created as artists' studios. George Mort Pollard designed the finest of them, particularly the neo-Gothic Hotel des Artistes (No. 1). The windows of its façade, like No. 2 across the street, reveal the double-height spaces inside intended for painters. The Hotel des Artistes was built by a syndicate of artists as a studio and apartment building; the artists rented half the building to nonartists and realized enough of a profit that there was a rush to erect similar buildings. Among them were: the Central Park Studios (No. 15); the Atelier Building (No. 33), whose lobby features some of the finest period Gothic detailing; and 39–41 West 67th, which has a stack of bay windows on the street façade made of sheet metal, rather than masonry. Among the tenants of the lavish spaces above were Isadora Duncan, Norman Rockwell, Alexander Woolcott, Noël Coward, Fannie Hurst, and John V. Lindsay.

Fortunately, recent additions to the street, including two studios for ABC Television (149 Columbus Avenue)

designed by Kohn Pederson Fox in 1978, respect the scale of their neighbors and maintain the tight environment.
PETER J. HOLLIDAY
Historian of classical art and archaeology

12.28 Dakota Apartments

1884, Henry J. Hardenbergh
1 West 72nd Street at Central Park West
Not open to the public.

When I was a kid trying to escape the monotony of Flatbush, I'd take the D train across the bridge each Saturday to the place I really belonged: Manhattan. Despite all the mysteries and glories I discovered, I remember the rush I got walking up Central Park West and coming upon that behemoth of a building for the first time, that German Gothic/French Renaissance/English Victorian cacophony called the Dakota. Of course, I didn't know the architectural styles when I was fifteen. I only knew this wasn't Brooklyn. This wasn't Flatbush. This was glamour. This was sophistication. This was Manhattan. Although half-shutters mask the first-floor windows, you can still peer into an apartment or two, now as then; I was dazzled by the enormous rooms, and the spectacular architectural details. I remember wondering, "Who lives here? What kind of people can be surrounded by this luxury?"

Of course, this was before December 8, 1980, when John Lennon was killed outside the building. Now, tourists come by the score to pay their respects or gawk. But when I first discovered the building, its pop-culture claim to fame was that it was where *Rosemary's Baby* was filmed.

The Dakota was designed by Henry Hardenbergh, who also designed the Plaza Hotel. Legend has it that it was called the Dakota because it was so distant from the then-urban hub. About ten years ago the grime of New York City was sandblasted away and now, instead of the black sooty color I remember, it's a camel-hair tan. It seemed more gothic, more foreboding with the dirt, but I still can look at it for hours in amazement: the moldings, the terracotta panels, the corner pavilions, and the storybook gables and roofing.

Don't try to penetrate its courtyard. The ever-present guard knows exactly who should be there and who shouldn't. The apartments are for Yoko, Betty, Rex, and their friends. But we mortals can still marvel at the magnificence. I've lived on the Upper West Side for more than twenty-five years, but every time I walk down 72nd Street I become the fifteen-year-old from Brooklyn, gazing up in amazement at my favorite building in New York.

GLEN ROVEN
Composer

12.30 Steps on Broadway

2121 Broadway at West 74th Street
212 874 2410; www.stepsnyc.com

While most New Yorkers and visitors find the ballet at Lincoln Center the finest in spectator sports, I prefer to participate in this incredible art form. On any given day there are numerous marvelous classes to take at Steps, a dance studio fortuitously located upstairs from Fairway Market at 74th Street and Broadway. There is no more heavenly spot in New York; upstairs the sounds of *Don Q* or *Swan Lake* or *La Bayadère* treat your ears, and downstairs there is the heady symphonic perfume of basil and figs and olives. At Steps, anyone who is qualified and has training may pay for a ticket and take a class.

Classes are taught by seasoned ballet masters from all parts of the globe, and in many classes the positions, steps, and instructions are given in French, the universal language of ballet. On any given day, the higher-level classes might include visiting professionals and hopefuls. The reward after

an hour and a half of focused class is the last exercise, when the dancers leap across the floor to a selection of the pianist's choice. Afterwards, everyone runs down the stairs to Fairway to pick up dinner before going home or to the ballet or back out into the streets of the city.
JANE TUCKER VASILIOU
Vasiliou & Co.

12.31 New-York Historical Society

1908, York & Sawyer; 1938, addition of north and south wings by Walker & Gillette; 1990s, restoration by Beyer Blinder Belle
170 Central Park West between West 76th and West 77th Streets
☎ 212 873 3400; www.nyhistory.org
Closed Sundays and Mondays.

Henry Luce III Center for the Study of American Culture
2000, Beyer Blinder Belle
Fourth floor

This is an institution that has been overlooked and eclipsed by other New York institutions such as the Museum of the City of New York and the Met. It has recently been brought back to new life by former New York City Parks Commissioner Betsy Gotbaum. She has gone through their many collections of artworks related to old New York families and furnishings—including paintings, sculpture, furniture, household tools, and decorative objects, much of it stored and unseen for many years but now on display in the wonderful new Henry Luce III Center for the Study of American Culture—and also found the funding so that this great institution could be ready for the twenty-first century.
MARIO BUATTA
Interior decorator

Although many residents and visitors to New York City may be familiar with the New-York Historical Society and its various exhibitions, few seem to know about the Luce Center on the building's fourth floor. It's like the city's attic, with an amazing collection of Americana, including a piece of George Washington's coffin, a barrel used for the opening ceremonies of the Erie Canal in 1825, Duncan Phyfe's tool chest, a collection of a hundred and thirty-two Tiffany lamps, and thousands of other objects and artworks. While much of the material has little more than an accession number, there are wall displays with more information and computer stations set up throughout the gallery where visitors can search through a database of the museum's collection for greater detail. It is a pleasure just to walk around and look at the things that catch your eye and, best of all, you can pick up an engaging audio guide that is offered for free. Anyone interested in American history will find this a treasure trove.

THORIN TRITTER
Historian

Reading Room
Second floor

The Reading Room of the New-York Historical Society is the portal to one of the great institutional repositories for the city's secrets. The library's marvelous collections of broadsides, newspapers, sheet music, and documentation about the history of New York City hotels have been assembled over the course of nearly two hundred years, and capture the textures of everyday existence now hidden under the strata of New York's various past lives. These, too, are represented and preserved in the society's stacks and drawers: the turbulent geological prehistory, the Dutch, English, and Revolutionary periods, the great fires, the slave trade and brutal repression of African-American revolts, mercantile expansion and the Civil War, the influx of immigrants and the consolidation of Greater New York at the end of the nineteenth century, and the whole history of the twentieth. Little known to the general public—to which it is open—or even to those who tour the galleries on the first and second floors, or the Henry Luce III Study Center on the fourth, the library is a mecca, and a home away from home for scholars who return day after day to mine its archives of books, letters, manuscripts, maps, prints, drawings, and photographs.

BARNET SCHECTER
Historian and author

New York's Royal Governor

12.31 New-York Historical Society
170 Central Park West between West 76th and West 77th Streets
212 873 3400; www.nyhistory.org
Closed Sundays and Mondays.

1.3 Admiral's House
1708
Governors Island
www.govisland.com
Not open to the public.

1.10 Trinity Church
1846, Richard Upjohn
Broadway at Wall Street
212 602 0800; www.trinitywallstreet.org

Edward Hyde, Lord Cornbury, first cousin to England's Queen Anne, whom he "mightily resembled," was New

York's royal governor from 1702–1708. Although the occasional historian will dismiss this as vile anti-Royalist gossip, he was also fond of showing up—at work and at play—in women's clothing. Reputedly, after nights of drinking, he would stumble onto the wooden ramparts of the colony's fort and accost soldiers, who mistook him for a tipsy wench. He would give them a tug on the ear (apparently his favorite body part) and rush off shrieking. Among Cornbury's many achievements during his stay here was the introduction of horse racing to America. Here, for your amusement and instruction, are city landmarks trodden, in an elegant pair of pink slippers, by His Lordship.

The New-York Historical Society owns a portrait, reputedly of Cornbury, wearing a low-necked blue silk dress with a hoopskirt and fitted bodice. The canvas is in the style of itinerant painters of the day, who would bring "blanks"—ready-made portraits lacking only the head—to the homes of prospective customers.

Cornbury's arms and hands—swanlike and ivory—are an ill match to his face with its heavy jowls, protruding lower lip, and self-satisfied expression. The society also owns an agonized letter, on parchment, that Cornbury wrote to his father while still in England, begging him to liquidate his debts.

Governors Island, in New York Harbor, contains Lord Cornbury's second great achievement, after horse racing. He persuaded the colonial legislature to grant him the huge sum of fifteen hundred English pounds to fortify the harbor against "French privateers." Two years went by without the appearance of the proposed battlements. People did notice, however, that much of the primeval timber on the northeast end of Nutten's Island had been felled, and a grand mansion of imported brick—a fabulously expensive material in seventeenth-century America—was going up.

From its description in the annals of the New York legislature, one expects something the size of the New York Public Library's 42nd Street branch, but to our standards, the house is disappointingly small, and looks to have been resurfaced by Garden State brickface.

City Hall Park was the site of Debtor's Prison, an unheated plank structure in back of the tavern that then served as City Hall. Cornbury found his way into this accommodation in 1708 when, upon the death of Queen Anne, the colonial legislature and an army of other creditors descended upon him. He did not emerge until 1709 when his father's death simultaneously made him the Third Earl of Clarendon and economically solvent.

Trinity Church, on lower Broadway facing Wall Street, received its land (and the contiguous parcels on which many of the houses of commerce now rest) as a royal grant from Cornbury. Burned by the British during the Revolutionary War, it, too, has been rebuilt. Cornbury's wife, a wealthy Irish heiress named Katharine O'Brian (to whose funeral Lord Cornbury is reputed to have worn a dress), is still buried there, apparently forgotten.

KATHRYN NOCERINO
Poet and writer

12.32 American Museum of Natural History

Central Park West at 79th Street
212 769 5100; www.amnh.org
Open daily.

Holden Caulfield's Tour of the Museum of Natural History

Ask any child in New York City. Whether it's the girl with the skates in J. D. Salinger's 1945 novel *The Catcher in the Rye* or a contemporary kid whizzing by on Rollerblades, the answer will be the same: "the museum" means the American Museum of Natural History. Tracing the history of life and matter from the very beginning of time, the museum also contains the personal history of countless children, some of whose earliest memories have been formed in its shadowy halls.

One such child was Holden Caulfield himself. In Miss Aigletinger's fourth grade, he used to visit the museum "damn near every Saturday." "I knew that whole museum routine by heart," he tells us, recollecting with great nostalgia.

A teacher myself, I imitate Miss Aigletinger. Every year, when my seventh graders read *The Catcher in the Rye*, I take them to the Museum of Natural History to retrace Holden's path. We steer clear of the newer exhibits—the Hall of Biodiversity, the glassy new Rose Center—and explore the older, dustier recesses of the museum that seem never to change. As if on a treasure hunt, the kids try to find the same Indians, the same dioramas, the same "glass cases" that Holden describes in such vivid detail. Take this tour with us, guided by Holden's voice, and see how you score on the quiz that follows.

What to bring:

- J. D. Salinger, *The Catcher in the Rye.* (Remember, this is a literary pilgrimage and the book is our map.)
- A pen or pencil
- A handful of marbles
- Candy or gum for optional smuggling into the Imax theater. Just don't get caught.

Start at the main entrance on Central Park West, where the building sprawls like a fortress across from the trees. Passing the triumphal statue of Theodore Roosevelt, go up the stairs and into the rotunda, where the lofty ceiling echoes with the shouts and shrieks of school groups, tourists, and disgruntled babies. Read the four inscriptions on the walls.

Go down the stairs to the first floor, make a left and

walk through the museum shop to the Imax theater. Built in 1995, it is not the same auditorium that Holden remembers, but with its huge screen, squeaky chairs, and enveloping darkness, it still feels like you are in "the only nice, dry, cozy place in the world." If you like, you can chew on some squashed gumdrops you've kept hidden in your pocket.

Proceed to the Hall of Northwest Coast Indians that Holden remembers as "a long, long room and you were only supposed to whisper." No such rule is instituted today, but it doesn't need to be. Full of monstrous, huge-eyed totem poles, cruel spears, life-size dioramas of bear dances and shamans, the room is so vast with mystery and shadow that speaking aloud feels disrespectful. If you have dramatic flair, however, drop your handful of marbles on the stone-and-mosaic floor so that they "make a helluva racket."

Look carefully at the first display case on your left. Various members of the Kwakiutl tribe are performing domestic tasks, and near the corner is the source of one of Holden's earliest erotic memories. There was "this squaw weaving a blanket," he confides, who was "sort of bending over, and you could see her bosom and all. We used to sneak a good look at it. . . . " She is, in actuality, not weaving a blanket, but her bosom is indeed showing if you sneak a good look at it.

Exit the Northwest Coast Indians and you'll be confronted by the gigantic Haida Indian canoe. Holden is right when he says it's "about as long as three goddamn Cadillacs in a row, with about twenty Indians in it." Circle the canoe a couple of times to take in its size—the entire boat was carved out of a single red cedar—and to appreciate all the poses, masks, and weapons of the chief, oarsmen, and attending medicine men. At the center of the prow, find the "witch doctor," or shaman, in the wolf-headed mask; he is Holden's favorite.

Unfortunately, some of the exhibits have been removed since Salinger's time. The lone Eskimo that Holden describes fishing so intently at his ice hole no longer exists, nor do some of the dioramas with the birds flying south. But you can still find a few, painted in illusionistic perspective, as well as deer "with their pretty antlers and their pretty skinny legs." Spend some time in the great mammal exhibits on the first and second floors (just retrace your steps back to the staircase) and wander through the forests and veldts with their flora and fauna captured in place and time. "You could go there a hundred times and . . . nobody'd be different. The only thing that would be different would be you."

Quiz:

1. What are the titles of each of Teddy Roosevelt's inscriptions?
2. In which inscription does Roosevelt mention "game boys"?
3. In Miss Aigletinger's class, you were supposed to hold hands with your partner. What was the name of Holden's partner and why didn't he like holding hands with her?
4. What does Holden remember about candy and gum in the auditorium?
5. What was the Kwakiutl Indian really doing?
6. Holden calls the Haida Indian canoe a "war canoe," but the craft is actually built for a ceremonial feast. What is the feast called?
7. How many Indians are in the canoe exactly?
8. How many fish has the Eskimo caught?
9. What happens when you look upside down at the birds flying south?
10. After speaking to the little girl, what part of the museum does Holden visit?

Answer Key:

1. Youth, Manhood, Nature, and the State . . . . 5 points
2. Youth . . . . 5 points
3. Gertrude Levine. Her hands were sweaty or sticky . . . . 10 points
4. They made the auditorium smell nice, like it was raining outside . . . . 10 points
5. She is shaving cedar bark for a paddle . . . . 10 points
6. A potlatch . . . . 10 points
7. Seventeen . . . . 10 points
8. Two . . . . 10 points
9. They look like they're in an even bigger hurry to fly south . . . . 10 points
10. Trick question. He changes his mind and decides not to go in . . . . 20 points

Scoring Guide:

0–35 You are a worse student than Holden. Reread the book at once!

40–65 Mediocre at best. Go hang out with Ackley, or even worse, Stradlater.

70–85 Not bad. Take a break and listen to "Little Shirley Beans."

90–100 You are an expert! Treat yourself to Holden Caulfield's tour of the "toons" at the Metropolitan Museum of Art.

JANE AVRICH
Writer and teacher

12.33 Riverside Park

1873, original design by Frederick Law Olmsted
Riverside Drive to the Hudson River between West 72nd and West 158th Streets
www.nycgovparks.org

It is little recognized among tourists that Riverside Park is the gateway to one of the most spectacular views in New York City. Enter the park at 90th Street. Proceed down the hill, past the playground with the hippo. Straight ahead, down a seemingly neglected set of steps, through the tunnel (the traffic from the West Side Highway exit is on your right), and there you have an incredible Hudson River view. On your right stands the George Washington Bridge and on your left is downtown Manhattan, accessible now via a bicycle path that runs along the Hudson River. Before you stretches the river, and past that, New Jersey.

NADINE ORENSTEIN
Curator, Prints and Drawings Department, The Metropolitan Museum of Art

A good place to enter is at 72nd Street, which forms the southern end of the park. Standing sentry here is a statue of Eleanor Roosevelt, a patron saint of the liberal Upper West Side. Walk west through the arch that leads under the West Side Highway and you'll find yourself facing the majestic Hudson River. The walk along the river is one of the most bracing in the city, and the view north toward the George Washington Bridge is stunning. A short stroll will bring you to the 79th Street Boat Basin, home to an eccentric community of houseboats. During summer months, you can watch the sun set over a beer and burger at the Boat Basin Cafe (seasonal, 212 496 5542; www.boatbasincafe.com), though be warned that in the

evening the place becomes a singles zoo. Walking farther north, you'll find a path leading back under the highway and into the park proper, where joggers, dog walkers, parents with strollers, and other Upper West Side types abound.
MICHAEL MASSING
Journalist and writer

12.34 Barney Greengrass

541 Amsterdam Avenue between West 86th and West 87th Streets
212 724 4707; www.barneygreengrass.com
Closed Mondays.

An Upper West Side landmark, Barney Greengrass looks much as it did when it moved here from Harlem in 1929, and the Greengrass family still runs it. Here you can get oversized platters of bagels, cream cheese, lox, and whitefish; the specialty is eggs scrambled with nova and onions. At weekend brunch, the place is packed, so be prepared to wait, but it's worth it for a taste (literally) of the old Jewish Upper West Side. (The giant apartment building across the street, the Belnord, was once home to Isaac Bashevis Singer, the Yiddish writer.)
MICHAEL MASSING
Journalist and writer

A genuine New York fixture—three generations, ninty-plus years in business, more than seventy in the same location—Barney Greengrass is the place to experience one of New York's ur-cuisines: the salty-sweet-smooth salmon, sturgeon, and whitefish that are the product of the long Jewish love affair with smoked fish. Who eats at Barney's? Mavens. Old-timers. Upper West Side families, returnees from the huge New York diaspora, Philip Roth characters (see *Operation Shylock*), Philip Roth himself, and now, you. A good—and traditional—place to start is the scrambled eggs with lox and onions, but for my money, true perfection lies in the lox and kippered salmon with onion, tomato, and scallion cream cheese. I recommend having it on a toasted everything bagel, but no matter what bagel you choose, you'll be in smoked-fish heaven.

MARTHA SCHULMAN
Writer and teacher

London Mimicry

12.35 **Pomander Walk**
1921, King & Campbell
West 94th Street to West 95th Street between Broadway and West End Avenue

11.28 **Henderson Place**
1882, Lamb & Rich
East 86th Street between York and East End Avenues

New York's signature architectural style is the imaginative towers of the skyscrapers built during the first third of the twentieth century. At ground level, you have either the very plain brownstone Edith Wharton so detested, or buildings that echo the cities of Europe, most often London.

My favorite bit of this architectural mimicry is Pomander Walk, built in 1921 and named for a popular Broadway play of the time. This easy-to-miss thoroughfare, which runs parallel to Broadway and West End Avenue between 94th and 95th Streets, was, like the play, named for a tiny street in the London suburb of Chiswick.

Although the gates have been closed since 1986, on a recent sunny morning it took literally no more than two minutes before a resident, on her way back from shopping, let me in. Up a flight of a dozen steps is an enchanted streetlet, its scaled-down Tudor houses apparently modeled after the sets of the long-forgotten play. In front of each house is a well-tended garden in the English country style. Looking up, you see window boxes with hanging flowers that enhance the overall theatricality.

New York is a much more sociable city than it is given credit for being, but Pomander Walk seems incredibly like some small town where everybody knows everybody else.

Pomander Walk has an architectural cousin across town on East 86th Street, just around the corner from Gracie Mansion. Henderson Place, which runs only half a block, has a row of red brick townhouses in Queen Anne style. What distinguishes them from so many other imitations of London is the fact that they do not seem full size. The miniaturization gives them a sweet theatricality. (Not surprisingly, the Lunts lived here for many years.)

These elegant houses face an undistinguished modern apartment building, so they do not have the enveloping enchantment of Pomander Walk. But they are a reminder of the kind of imagination New York developers used before their only consideration was how high, and thus, how lucrative.

HOWARD KISSEL
Art and theater critic, and author

12.37 Wang Chen's Table Tennis Club

2628 Broadway between West 99th and West 100th Streets
212 864 7253; www.wangchenttc.com

Wang Chen proudly claims to be the only place in Manhattan where one can play the "official" version of table tennis. Walk in and the differences between the official version of the game and the Ping-Pong of your youth immediately become apparent. The official-sized tables are considerably smaller than the Ping-Pong tables in basements and frat houses across America. The players of the official game bend at the waist and hold their arms at seemingly painful, crooked angles in their quest for the perfect spin with which to launch the balls across the net. As a result, the best players look like extraordinarily well-muscled marionettes as they lurch forwards and back, hitting balls to each other.

Go during the day and you may see Nigerian businessmen conducting deals in the Yoruba language over games of table tennis, or the associates from a major New York investment bank on a corporate outing.

Go in the evening and you may be able to watch Renata Pulochova, who once played on the Czech national table tennis team, Wang Chen, once the No. 4 female table tennis player in the world, George Brathwaite, who was one of the "Ping-Pong diplomats" to China in 1971, or an up-and-coming table tennis star.

Or sign up for a lesson—my instructor spent much of my lesson asking me to "move, please move," praising me on those rare occasions when I actually did move with, "Thank you. Very good!" My friend, considerably more energetic than I on that particular evening, actually received instruction on how to spin the ball.

Or simply go and play a game or two, while steeping yourself in the table tennis subculture surrounding you. Or if you don't want to play, go to watch anyway.

KATE HARTNICK ELLIOTT
President, Hartnick Consulting

A Summer Evening in Riverside Park

12.36 **Riverside Park Tennis Courts**
Riverside Park at West 96th Street
212 978 0277; www.riversideparkfund.org
Open April to November.

12.39 **Hudson Beach Cafe**
Riverside Park at 105th Street
917 370 3448; pdohurleys.com
Closed in the winter. Check website for schedule.

Take a stroll along the promenade. Stop at the community gardens at 89th Street, and enjoy the Upper West Side's interpretation of an English country garden. Drop down to the river's edge at 95th Street, and continue to the public tennis courts on 96th Street. Play here at sunset, with a river breeze. When your game is finished, follow the sounds of salsa music to the Hudson Beach Cafe on 105th Street in Riverside Park, where Puerto Rican and American flags are displayed proudly above the bar. Dance, have a margarita, and toast the city for nights like this.

GEORGIA O'NEAL
Owner, Tree and Leaf Farm

12.38 Firemen's Memorial

1913, Attilio Piccirilli, sculptor; H. Van Buren Magonigle, architect
Riverside Drive at West 100th Street

At the funeral service for Deputy Chief Kruger in 1908 (he died at a fire on Canal Street), Episcopal Bishop Henry Potter called for the erection of a monument to honor the heroism of New York City firefighters. Newspapers throughout the city took up the bishop's plea, and a few years later the Firemen's Memorial was dedicated, high on top of Riverside Drive, in beautiful park-like surroundings: a quiet, somber setting amidst the hustle of Broadway and near Columbia University only a few blocks away. The inscription on the monument reads, "To the men of the Fire Department of the City of New York who died in the line of duty, soldiers in a war that never ends, this memorial is dedicated by the people of a grateful city." Each October, memorial services are held here by the department. Completely refurbished in 1991, this monument is for firefighters a sacred and honored place, and for New Yorkers, a reminder of the price paid for their safety.

THOMAS VON ESSEN
Former New York City Fire Commissioner

12.40 Nicholas Roerich Museum

1898, Clarence F. True

319 West 107th Street between Broadway and Riverside Drive

212 864 7752

This is a fabulous museum in a charming town house displaying the work of the rather mystical Russian artist Nicholas Roerich. Many of the paintings reflect his intense spirituality and deep passion for art.

KAREN MOODY TOMPKINS

Artist

12.41 Riverside Park Above West 96th Street

There is, of course, that pesky problem of the West Side Highway directly to one side, but the beauty of this particular unsung river path is that it maintains a distinctly nonlandscaped feel. There are no railings, no gardens, no restaurants—only a straight shot up the west side of Manhattan along the river, the George Washington Bridge ahead in the distance, and the rocky coastline of New Jersey to espy on the other side. If you're a serious runner—as, say, in training for the New York City Marathon (which is worth doing at least once)—you can run over the bridge for a truly magnificent view.

KATHLEEN DEMARCO VAN CLEVE

Author, screenwriter, and film producer

Olde New Yorkese

New York City's blend of immigrants, émigrés, transients, and natives has produced a lexicon that is pleasantly peculiar to New York City. From the beginning of this urban city-state, new and different languages were heard on the street; according to one historian, in 1626, eighteen different languages could be heard in the village of Nieuw Amsterdam.

However, with the changes wrought by assimilation, technology, economics, immigration patterns, politics, mores, and the city's own ever-changing atmosphere, some words and phrases are either disappearing or becoming as archaic and obscure as Shakespeare's "yclept." Here are some favorites that are fast disappearing from New York's vocabulary:

On Line: When the Internet was just a twinkle in Thomas Watson's eye, New Yorkers wanting to gain admission to Radio City Music Hall or buy tickets for the latest Broadway hit stood on line. The rest of the country stood "in line."

Egg Cream: This ambrosia-like beverage contains neither eggs nor cream. The traditional version of this drink, inhaled in candy stores and luncheonettes throughout the five boroughs, consisted of tooth-rattlingly cold milk, chocolate syrup, and soda water. With the disappearance of soda fountains—the seltzer of soda water spigots was critical to the true egg cream—the beverage and the name are rapidly slipping into memory.

Candy Store: Not to be confused with Godiva, Perugina, or even Fanny Farmer. A true candy store was a neighborhood institution, selling newspapers, cigarettes, and other tobacco products, candy bars, bulk penny candy, and school supplies. A good candy store also had a soda fountain where one could be refreshed with a two cents plain, an egg cream or, in season, a lime rickey, or a Mello Roll.

LEE GELBER
Urban historian and tour guide

13
W 158th St
W 157th St
W 156th St
Audubon Terrace
High Bridge Park
Macombs Dam Bridge
W 155th St
W 154th St
W 153rd St
W 152nd St
W 151st St
W 150th St
W 149th St
W 148th St
W 147th St
W 146th St
Sugar Hill
Macombs Pl
Harlem River
Harlem River Drive
Major Deegan Express
Riverside Park
Riverside Drive
Broadway
Amsterdam Avenue
Convent Avenue
St Nicholas Avenue
St Nicholas Pl
Edgecombe Avenue
Jackie Robinson (Colonial) Park
Bradhurst Avenue
Hamilton Heights
W 145th St
145th St Bridge
W 144th St
W 143rd St
W 142nd St
W 141st St
W 140th St
W 139th St
W 138th St
W 137th St
Hamilton Pl
Hamilton Terrace
Riverbank State Park
West Side Hwy (Henry Hudson Pkwy)
(Eighth Ave)
W 138th St (Odell Clark Pl)
Lenox Avenue (Malcolm X Blvd)
Manhattanville
W 136th St
W 135th St
W 134th St
W 133rd St
W 132nd St
W 131st St
W 130th St
W 129th St
W 128th St
W 127th St
W 126th St
W 125th St
St Nicholas Park
St Nicholas Terrace
Frederick Douglass Blvd
Fifth Avenue
Twelfth Av
St Clair Pl
Old Broadway
Tiemann Pl
Harlem
La Salle St
Hancock Pl
W 125th St (Martin Luther King Jr Blvd)
Morningside Heights
W 124th St
W 123rd St
W 122nd St
W 121st St
W 120th St
Mt Morris Pk W
Marcus Garvey Park
Reinhold Niebuhr Pl
Claremont Avenue
Riverside Drive
Riverside Park
Columbia University
College Walk
Morningside Drive
Morningside Avenue
Manhattan Avenue
Adam Clayton Powell Jr Blvd (Seventh Ave)
W 119th St
W 118th St
W 117th St
W 116th St
W 115th St
W 114th St
W 113th St
W 112th St
W 111th St
Morningside Park
Cathedral Pkwy
Central Park North
Columbus Avenue
Central Park
Harlem Meer
W 106th St

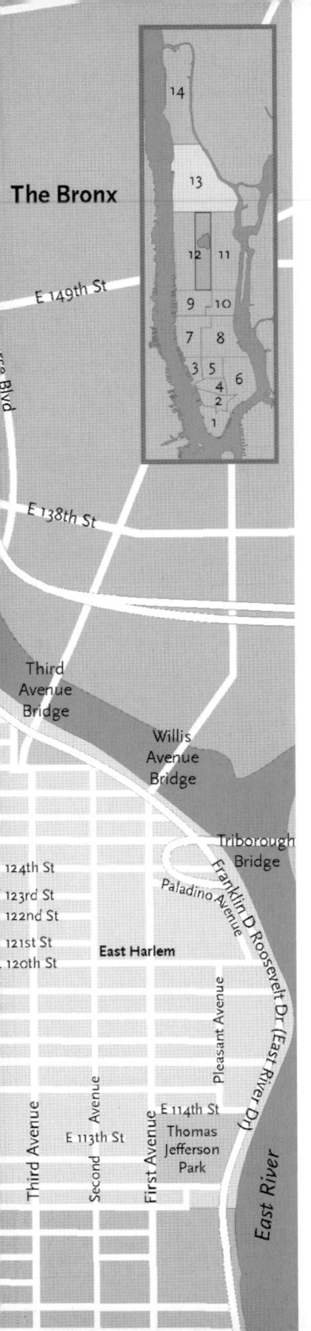

CHAPTER 13

MORNINGSIDE HEIGHTS

1 Hungarian Pastry Shop
2 St. John the Divine
3 Columbia University
4 Riverside Church
5 Sakura Park
6 General Grant National Memorial
7 Amiable Child Monument
8 Riverside Drive Viaduct

HARLEM

9 Lenox Lounge
10 The Studio Museum in Harlem
11 Sylvia's Soul Food
12 The Schomburg Center
13 Harlem Y.M.C.A.
14 Strivers' Row
15 Countee Cullen Library
16 Abyssinian Baptist Church
17 Mother A.M.E. Zion Church
18 St. Nicholas Park
19 Riverbank State Park

Morningside Heights & Harlem

MORNINGSIDE HEIGHTS

13.1 Hungarian Pastry Shop

1030 Amsterdam Avenue between West 110th and West 111th Street
212 866 4230

Slotted into the ground floor of an anonymous apartment building on Amsterdam Avenue just below 111th Street, the Hungarian Pastry Shop is one of the sweetest retreats in the city. Despite its generic name, and with no decor to speak of, it's been a bastion of the Columbia University neighborhood for at least a quarter of a century. You give your order at the front counter along with your first name, which a waitress then circulates about five minutes later. Usually she misreads her own handwriting, so whose order she has is always a matter of interpretation (Mel? Bill? Cal?). This is neatly appropriate for a place in which the table reading is as likely to be Derrida as *The New York Post*. But the real secret to the Hungarian Pastry Shop's success is the pots of mediocre coffee with which you can refill your initial overpriced order as frequently as you wish—for hours or, as seems the case of some perennial students, decades. Thus the place has probably fueled more Ph.D.'s than any institution in the hemisphere.

One fringe benefit of the Hungarian Pastry Shop is its view across the avenue to the gardens of the Cathedral of St. John the Divine and especially the so-called Peace Fountain. Hands down the ugliest public sculpture in New York, it rises massively from a placid marble pool to a bulging man-in-the-moon face from which a gigantic winged figure, who appears to be strangling a gazelle, emerges while huge bronze crab claws drip over the edge. Local rumor has it that the sculptor donated a million dollars to the cathedral—in the days when that was real money—in return for the permanent display of his well-intended statement of universal amity gone grotesquely awry. So be it; the thing is so awful you can't help but admire it as you pour a cup of coffee and return to your reading.

MELVIN JULES BUKIET
Author and literary critic

13.2 Cathedral Church of St. John the Divine

1892–1911, Heins & La Farge; 1911–1942, Cram & Ferguson
1047 Amsterdam Avenue at West 112th Street
212 316 7540; www.stjohndivine.org

On the hillside of Morningside Heights stands the Cathedral of St. John the Divine, unfinished more than a hundred years after the first stone foundations were laid in 1892. The Episcopal diocese purchased this lot north of 110th Street in the 1880s and began planning a cathedral that would rise above the city and be visible throughout the island of Manhattan. It was to be like Paris's Sacré-Coeur. That was before skyscrapers began to sprout on the city's grid. Today, the cathedral is largely hidden from view, unless you're right in front of it, but it's well worth a visit. Even incomplete, it's the largest church in America and one of the largest cathedrals in the world. Its main vault, standing one hundred and twenty-four feet high, is more than six hundred feet long and could hold two football fields in a row. Along the edge of this expanse, individual niches filled with sculptures, stained glass, and historical artifacts catch the eye.

After viewing the interior, walk around the outside to see the results of changing architectural tastes. The Episcopal diocese initially chose a Romanesque and Byzantine plan by Heins & La Farge, which was used for the sanctuary and choir. In 1911, however, the church, concerned with changing tastes, chose Ralph Adams Cram as its new architect and adopted a Gothic Revival design to complete the building. This shift is visible inside the building, but even more from the street along the north side, where you can see the rounded Romanesque choir next to Gothic flying buttresses.

To get the full experience of the cathedral, take advantage of the Vertical Tour, which is offered periodically. This guided walk takes you a hundred and twenty-four feet up stone spiral staircases onto the roof of the cathedral. As you ascend through the walls of the building, you get close-up views of gargoyles, and other ornamentation, that are barely visible from the floor below. At the "summit," there are spectacular views down to the city below. From there you get a sense of the geography that made the site so attractive to its planners.

THORIN TRITTER
Historian

The guidebooks will tell you that it is the largest Gothic cathedral in the world, that the Statue of Liberty could stand upright in the nave, that the figure of Christ in the rose window is six feet tall, but more telling for me is that at most times of the day you can't see the ceiling. It's that far away. The impression is that heaven has somehow been included in the congregation.

CYNTHIA ZARIN
Poet and writer

Believe it or not, one of the largest cathedrals in the world sits across from a funky Hungarian coffee shop at the edge of Harlem. Pass through St. John's Portals of Paradise under the gaze of Moses, John the Baptist, and thirty other limestone figures from the Old and New Testaments and feel the transformation take place as you enter sacred space. Though the cornerstone was set in 1892, like much of New York, the cathedral is still a construction site—its scaffolded stone towers are not yet finished. But the magnificent breadth of the room inside inspires a sense of utter completeness and can convince even the faithless to believe. The first time I walked the length of the vaulted nave to the great choir and looked up at the dome one hundred and seventy-seven feet above, I got weak in the knees. The Statue of Liberty could stand on her toes and still fit underneath. Built as a sanctuary for faiths of all nations, the cathedral has seen the Dalai Lama, as well as Sufi masters, Zen *roshis*, and rabbis, lead prayer services. This is the place to surrender to your higher power or to the simple need for refuge from the chaos of urban life.

RENEE SHAFRANSKY
Psychotherapist, writer, and film producer

13.3 Columbia University

1897, McKim, Mead & White
West 114th Street to West 120th Street between Broadway and Amsterdam Avenue; entrance at West 116th Street and Broadway
212 854 4900; www.columbia.edu
Columbia offers regularly scheduled tours of the campus and its buildings.

Buell Hall/Maison Française

1885, Ralph Townsend
Central campus, south of St. Paul's Chapel

Low Memorial Library

1897, McKim of McKim, Mead & White
Central campus, north of West 116th Street (College Walk)

St. Paul's Chapel

1907, Howells & Stokes
North campus, east of Low Library

Avery Hall

1912, McKim, Mead & White
North of St. Paul's Chapel

Alma Mater

1903, Daniel Chester

Central Campus, on the steps in front of Low Library

Columbia University is one of the oldest and largest institutions of higher education in America. Its Morningside Heights campus, designed by McKim, Mead & White, is one of the great urban spaces in New York and complements the university's prestige.

The history of the university's founding and expansion reflects the growth of the city. Chartered in 1754 as King's College, the fledgling institution quickly outgrew its original home on a site adjacent to Trinity Church. In 1760, it moved to a three-acre site near Park Place (then named College Place). By 1810, the city had begun to close in on the openness and greenery of that site: there were concerns about the noise from the city's nearby port, and the area was gaining notoriety for prostitution. Columbia College (patriotically rechristened after the Revolution) therefore acquired the failed Elgin Botanical Gardens, about twenty acres just north of 47th Street and fronting Fifth Avenue. As the city continued to expand northward, this landholding proved to be one of Columbia's most profitable investments, leased after 1929 to Rockefeller Center until it was sold in 1987.

In 1857, the trustees applied the proceeds of the sale of the College Place property to acquiring the grounds of the Deaf and Dumb Asylum located at 49th Street between Madison and Fourth (Park) Avenues. That institution's buildings were to serve as temporary quarters until a new campus could be built on the Botanical Garden site, just a block away, but the Civil War and volatile economy in its aftermath delayed such plans. After forty more years, the phenomenal growth of Manhattan above 42nd Street, especially the arrival of the railroad into Grand Central

and the northern push of speculative residences and commerce, made the conditions at 49th Street increasingly untenable. In addition, Columbia determined to expand along the model of a Germanic research university, as several other American institutions did during the ninteenth century. In 1891, the newly constituted Columbia University acquired the grounds of the Bloomingdale Insane Asylum in Morningside Heights (an irony generations of students and professors have relished). Construction began in 1897.
PETER J. HOLLIDAY
Historian of classical art and archaeology

One of the few great contributions of City Beautiful planning to New York City, the Columbia University campus is a permanent testimony to the impact of Chicago's ephemeral White City of 1893 (the World's Columbian Exhibition), from which master planner Charles Follen McKim was freshly graduated. At the same time, it is a place richly suggestive of the inherent tension between the Beaux Arts processional planning that captured the American civic imagination in the late ninteenth century and the nearly relentless grid of the Commissioner's Plan of 1811, which was laid out to the northern tip of the island even before building had reached the island's frontier.

When Columbia acquired the pastoral site of the old Bloomingdale Asylum (the quaint brick villa known today as Buell Hall/Maison Française just to the east of Low Library is the only remnant), McKim seized the opportunity to build on the four blocks uninterrupted by cross streets to compose in brick, limestone, and granite a vision of the American research university as a grand forum. Though he dreamed of an axial approach to its great central axis, and even a vista from the upper terrace of this academic sanctuary of the city to the south, neither the grid nor the city's vertical drive allowed that. Rather, we come obliquely upon the Pantheon-esque centerpiece of it all, Low Library

(1895–1897). Approached across a grand forecourt paved with deep-red bricks laid in a herringbone pattern to recall the floor of the Roman Forum, McKim's great outdoor room comes alive on warm fall or spring days, when the stairs become the bleachers for this civic stage. Students, faculty, and neighbors of all ages chat, distribute pamphlets, exchange footballs, or hurry upward to the grand plateau on which McKim arranged a backdrop of redbrick classroom buildings, accented by a trio of cupolas of the library, the student center, and the chapel. Be sure to go before 5 p.m., when the great bronze doors of Low Library close, for the interior, even without its grand central desk and concentric reading tables reminiscent of the old British Museum and the Library of Congress, is one of the most solemn Beaux Arts interiors in New York.

For decorative subtlety and even technological innovation, McKim's former employees, Howells & Stokes, outdid the master in St. Paul's Chapel (1903–1905). In their use of the recently patented thin-tile vaults of the Guastavino system (you saw some in the IRT subway as you arrived), they elevated this new technology to new aesthetic heights in the dome, vaults, galleries, and even stairways of this richly textured sanctuary. The small spiraling stair, visible by entering the right side door off the narthex porch of the chapel, is a veritable primer in how this medieval Spanish technique revolutionized American building circa 1900. Take a peek into Avery Library, one of the great repositories of architectural books anywhere in the world. And maybe before you leave school you'll discover Columbia's most famous secret—as hundreds of first-year students do each autumn—by gazing between the folds of the statue of Alma Mater, Daniel Chester French's great enthroned matron who presides over the whole scene.

BARRY BERGDOLL
Philip Johnson Chief Curator of Architecture and Design, The Museum of Modern Art

13.4 Riverside Church

1930, Allen & Collens and Henry C. Pelton
490 Riverside Drive between West 120th and West 122nd Streets
212 870 6700; www.theriversidechurchny.org

Laura Spelman Rockefeller Memorial Carillon

Unconcerned with the liability insurance that transformed the Empire State Building observation deck into a rat cage, the carillon at Riverside Church provides the best chance to ascend one of the city's spires and gaze out over the city. An ecclesiastical office building disguised as a cathedral, the tower offers a bank of elevators in place of the winding spiral stair.

SEBASTIAN HARDY
Urban planner

13

13.5 Sakura Park

1934, Olmsted Landscape Architecture Firm
West 122nd Street between Riverside Drive and Claremont Avenue
www.nycgovparks.org

Sakura Park, one of New York's prettiest and least-known parks, at first seems little more than an annex of Riverside Park, which it adjoins at the northern tip of Morningside Heights. But spend a few minutes here and you'll realize that it has a peaceful, melancholy charm all its own. Situated directly across Riverside Drive from Grant's Tomb, elevated slightly from the street, filled with benches, big trees, and a gazebo, it's a perfect place to rest your feet, eat your lunch, or simply contemplate the teeming city that lies beyond.

RACHEL WETZSTEON
The late Rachel Wetzsteon was a poet and the author of three collections of poems, including The Other Stars.

13.6 General Grant National Memorial (Grant's Tomb)

Riverside Drive at West 122nd Street

212 666 1640; www.nps.gov

General Grant National Memorial Bench

1973, Pedro Silva and Cityarts Workshop, with Phillip Danzig

These colorful, tile-covered benches stretch four hundred and fifty feet along both sides and the rear of the solemn mausoleum to the general and president, and his wife. They were completed in 1973 as a community folk art appreciation of Grant's role in preserving the nation in 1865. More than two thousand people volunteered to complete the benches.

PHILLIP DANZIG

The late Phillip Danzig was an architect and a muralist.

13.7 Amiable Child Monument

Riverside Drive and West 123rd Street

www.nycgovparks.org

On July 15, 1797, a small child fell to his death from the edge of the cliffs overlooking the Hudson River. Just north of Grant's Tomb, on the edge of Riverside Park, is a fenced enclosure surrounding a stone monument, "Erected to the Memory of an Amiable Child, St. Claire Pollock, Died 15 July 1797 in the Fifth Year of His Age."

GERALD WEALES

Author and Emeritus Professor of English, University of Pennsylvania

13.8 Riverside Drive Viaduct

1901, F. Stewart Williamson, engineer; rebuilt 1987

West 125th Street and the Hudson River

The viaduct at 125th Street at the Hudson River is a little-known but elegant metal bridge structure.

M. PAUL FRIEDBERG

Landscape architect

HARLEM

13.9 Lenox Lounge

288 Lenox Avenue (Malcolm X Blvd.) between West 124th and West 125th Streets

212 427 0253; www.lenoxlounge.com

The Cotton Club and Savoy are long gone, but this legendary lounge remains and has played host to Bird and Billie (Holiday), Miles Davis (with Malcolm X watching), and a thousand other jazz journeymen. This joint is living history and I get the chills just thinking about what went down here. The famous back room is where you can hear some young cats wail, while the hard, loud, long front bar is jammed with a rainbow coalition of locals mixed with up- and downtowners. The original Art Deco decor, complete with zebra-striped walls and padded leather ceiling, has been over-restored. I miss the sixty-year-old nicotine-blackened ceiling and the sconces falling off the walls. 13

FREDERIC SCHWARTZ
Architect

13.10 The Studio Museum in Harlem

144 West 125th Street between Lenox Avenue (Malcolm X Blvd.) and Adam Clayton Powell Jr. Blvd.

212 864 4500; www.studiomuseum.org

Closed Mondays, Tuesdays, and Wednesdays.

The least ivory-tower museum in town, the Studio Museum in Harlem has both serious historical exhibitions and contemporary artists at work in studio areas of the building. There is an outdoor space for art and a sense of interaction and porousness between the museum and the community. After visiting the Studio Museum, have lunch at Sylvia's.

REBECCA SMITH
Artist

13.11 Sylvia's Soul Food Restaurant

328 Lenox Avenue (Malcolm X Blvd.) between West 126th and West 127th Streets
☎ 212 996 0660; www.sylviassoulfood.com

In the heart of Harlem, Sylvia's (now seating and serving four hundred and fifty) has been a soul food institution since 1962. Sylvia and her husband, Herbert Wood, met in a beanfield when they were kids and they've been together ever since. Stick to the basics like the ribs, fried chicken, collard greens, and sweet-potato pie. Go late at night to bypass the tour buses or try the gospel brunch after Sunday services at the Abyssinian Baptist Church.
TRACEY HUMMER AND FREDERIC SCHWARTZ
Writer and Architect

13.16 Abyssinian Baptist Church

1923, Charles W. Bolton & Son
132 Odell Clark Place (West 138th Street) between Adam Clayton Powell Jr. Blvd. and Lenox Avenue (Malcolm X Blvd.). Visitors should use the entrance on the corner of West 138th Street and Adam Clayton Powell Jr. Blvd.
☎ 212 862 7474; www.abyssinian.org
Only open to the public for the 11 a.m. Worship Service on Sundays. Check the website for hours, as the service is sometimes closed to the public.

The ashlar neo-Gothic stone church became famous for its prominent ministers, notably Adam Clayton Powell Sr. and his son Adam Clayton Powell Jr., the first black congressman from New York City. Founded in 1808 by black worshippers who wanted independence from the First Baptist Church, the congregation took a name associated with ancient Ethiopia. The city's second-oldest black church took more than a

century to move north to Harlem, as did the city's downtown "Little Africa" population.
CHRISTOPHER PAUL MOORE
Historian, author, and research coordinator, New York Public Library's Schomburg Center for Research on Black Culture

Harlem Stroll

13.12 **Schomburg Center for Research in Black Culture, The New York Public Library**
1980, Bond Ryder Associates
515 Lenox Avenue (Malcolm X Blvd.) at West 135th Street
212 491 2200; www.nypl.org
Closed Sundays and Mondays.

13.13 **Harlem Y.M.C.A.**
1932, James C. Mackenzie Jr.
180 West 135th Street between Lenox Avenue (Malcolm X Blvd.) and Adam Clayton Powell Jr. Blvd.
212 912 2100; www.ymcanyc.org

13.14 **Strivers' Row**
West 138th and West 139th Streets between Frederick Douglass Blvd. and Adam Clayton Powell Jr. Blvd.

13.15 **Countee Cullen Branch, The New York Public Library**
1942, Louis Allen Abramson
104 West 136th Street between Adam Clayton Powell Jr. Blvd. and Lenox Avenue (Malcolm X Blvd.)
212 491 2070; www.nypl.org
Closed Sundays.

13.16 **Abyssinian Baptist Church**
1923, Charles W. Bolton & Son
132 Odell Clark Place (West 138th Street) between Adam Clayton Powell Jr. Blvd. and Lenox Avenue (Malcolm X Blvd.). Visitors should use the entrance on the corner of

West 138th Street and Adam Clayton Powell Jr. Blvd.
212 862 7474; www.abyssinian.org
Only open to the public for the 11 a.m. Worship Service on Sundays. Check the website for hours, as the service is sometimes closed to the public.

Near the geographic center of Harlem stands the New York Public Library's Schomburg Center, one of the world's great research facilities for studying African-American and African life and culture, and a mecca for the curious about Harlem and the fabled 1920s Harlem Renaissance. A modern three-story complex, it incorporates a landmark building as well as the Countee Cullen Library, the site of heiress A'Lelia Walker's mansion and literary salon known as the Dark Tower. One half-block west on 135th Street is the Harlem Y.M.C.A., temporary home of Langston Hughes and Claude McKay. Walk three blocks north on the west side of Seventh Avenue and you come to Strivers' Row, two streets of elegant turn-of-the-century Italianate houses designed by architect Stanford White. Half a block east, down 138th Street, is the historic Abyssinian Baptist Church.

If you are less adventurous, a few steps from the IRT Seventh Avenue express subway exit at 135th Street will put you inside the lobby of the Schomburg Center. Sign the visitor's register and, comfortably indoors, you can begin to satisfy an hour's curiosity or a lifetime's scholarly interest. For the sightseer, a tour is recommended before a leisurely visit to the several exhibition galleries. One can also attend a lecture, film screening (some are free), or performance in either of two theaters. Peek into the sculpture garden on your way to browse in the gift shop for that hard-to-find book. A walk through the large, sunlit lobby of the Langston Hughes Auditorium is essential. Its terrazzo and brass-strip floor, designed by Houston Conwill, illuminates the Langston Hughes poem "The Negro Speaks of Rivers." Beneath the center of the floor rests the poet's ashes.

Before you leave, stand at that spot in the center of Harlem and read the inscription: "My soul has grown deep like the rivers."

RAYMOND R. PATTERSON

The late Raymond R. Patterson was a poet and Professor Emeritus at City College of New York.

13.13 Harlem Y.M.C.A.

1932, *James C. Mackenzie Jr.*

180 West 135th Street between Lenox Avenue (Malcolm X Blvd.) and Adam Clayton Powell Jr. Blvd.

212 912 2100; www.ymcanyc.org

On this important thoroughfare stands a proud institution that has been a beacon for the community since the first Harlem Renaissance. Opened in 1933, the eleven-story neo-Georgian Harlem Y.M.C.A. received landmark status in 1999. As one of the country's major African-American Y.M.C.A.'s, its handsome halls and rooms, with their original tiles, wooden doors, and carved ceiling beams, have embraced countless children and adults, nurtured great talents, and sheltered many aspiring souls. Renowned writer Langston Hughes stayed in its residence; Paul Robeson, Harry Belafonte, Ossie Davis, and Ruby Dee, among others, graced its Little Theater program for more than forty years; major artist Aaron Davis painted a still-extant wall mural, *The Evolution of Negro Dance*, during the Great Depression; and revered baseball hero and one-time Y member Jackie Robinson lives on in the youth center named for him opposite the main Y.M.C.A. building.

13

Sharing the block with two other major community institutions—Harlem Hospital and the Schomburg Center for Research in Black Culture (see p. 309)—the Y.M.C.A. is a key player in the second Harlem Renaissance, now underway.

PAMELA BAYLESS

Writer and communications consultant

13.17 Mother African Methodist Episcopal Zion Church

1925, George W. Foster Jr.

140 West 137th Street between Adam Clayton Powell Jr. Blvd. and Lenox Avenue (Malcolm X Blvd.)

212 234 1545; www.amez.org

Open to the public for services only.

Organized in 1796 by black worshippers who withdrew from the John Street Methodist Church in lower Manhattan, the Mother A.M.E. Zion Church is the city's oldest African-American church and, as its name implies, the "mother" church of the international A.M.E. Zion denomination. Designed by George W. Foster Jr., one of the first black architects in the United States, the neo-Gothic stone church is the sixth edifice and location for the congregation, which started in a house neighboring the eighteenth-century African Burial Ground (see p. 43) and moved gradually up to Harlem in the 1900s.

CHRISTOPHER PAUL MOORE

Historian, author, and research coordinator, New York Public Library's Schomburg Center for Research on Black Culture

13.18 St. Nicholas Park

West 128th to West 141st Street between St. Nicholas Avenue and St. Nicholas Terrace

www.nycgovparks.org; www.stnicholaspark.org

Commemorating colonial New Amsterdam's patron Saint Nicholas, who through local writers Washington Irving and Clement Clarke Moore and local artist Thomas Nast became our beloved Santa Claus, the frontier-like park is my family's favorite Christmas holiday spot. Built in 1906 to the designs of landscape architect Samuel Parsons on a massive, rocky outcrop following the rugged and hilly topography of northern Manhattan, the park's development and the construction of the elevated rapid transit line made this section of Harlem a fashionable residential district at the turn of the century. In the park is "The Point of Rocks," where George Washington commanded and observed the Battle of Harlem Heights in 1776. During the seventeenth century, the steeple of Manhattan's first permanent church (built in 1642 and popularly called the St. Nicholas Church by the children of the Roosevelts, Stuyvesants, and my grandcestor Nicholas Manuel) could be seen from the point nine miles south in downtown Fort Amsterdam. New York City may not look like the North Pole, but it is the birthplace of Santa Claus!

CHRISTOPHER PAUL MOORE
Historian, author, and research coordinator, New York Public Library's Schomburg Center for Research on Black Culture

13.19 Riverbank State Park

1991, Richard Dattner & Associates
West 137th to West 145th Street, west of the Henry Hudson Parkway; entrance on West 145th Street
Park: 212 694 3600; Pool: 212 694 3666
www.nysparks.state.ny.us

My favorite pool in New York is the splendid fifty-meter pool at Riverbank, over the Hudson River at 145th Street in Harlem. This is part of an extraordinary recreational and cultural complex that is virtually unknown to most New Yorkers.

OLIVER SACKS
Neurologist and author

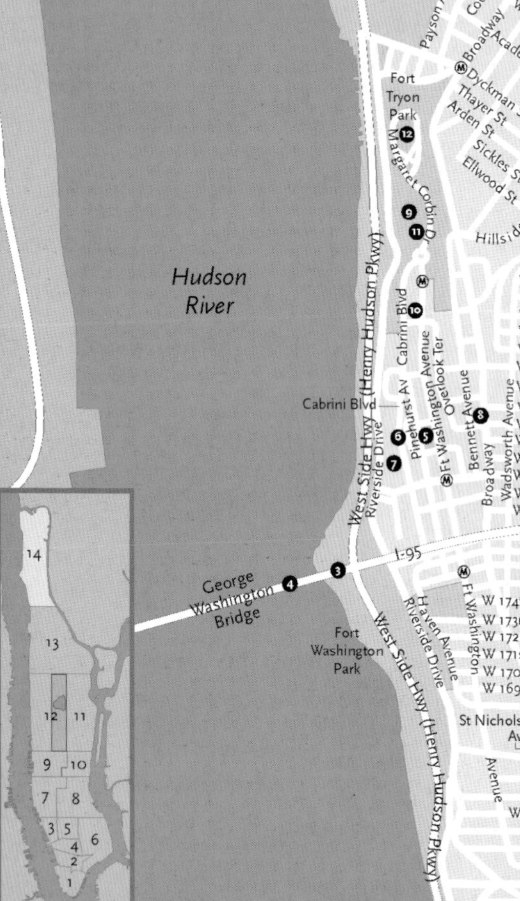
Henry Hudson Bridge
Spuyten Duyvil
West Side Hwy (Henry Hudson Pkwy)
W 218th St
Indian Rd
Inwood Hill Park
Inwood
Isham St
W 207th St
Payson Avenue
Cooper St
W 204th St
Broadway
Academy St
Tenth Avenue
Dyckman St
Fort Tryon Park
Thayer St
Arden St
Nagle Avenue
Margaret Corbin Dr
Sickles St
Ellwood St
High Bridge Park
Hillside Avenue
Hudson River
W 192nd St
Cabrini Blvd
W 190th St
W 189th St
W 188th St
W 187th St
Amsterdam Avenue
Ft Washington Avenue
Overlook Ter
W 186th St
W 185th St
W 184th St
W 183rd St
W 182nd St
W 181st St
W 180th St
W 179th St
Laurel Hill Ter
Pinehurst Av
Riverside Drive
Bennett Avenue
Wadsworth Avenue
St Nicholas Avenue
W 178th St
W 177th St
W 176th St
W 175th St
I-95
George Washington Bridge
Fort Washington Park
Haven Avenue
Riverside Drive
Ft Washington
W 174th St
W 173rd St
W 172nd St
W 171st St
W 170th St
W 169th St
Audubon Avenue
W 168th St
St Nichols Av
W 167th St
W 166th St
W 165th St
W 164th St
W 163rd St
W 162nd St
W 161st St
W 160th St
W 159th St
W 158th St
W 157th St
W 156th St
Audubon Ter
Edgecombe Avenue

CHAPTER 14

INWOOD, FORT GEORGE, WASHINGTON HEIGHTS & AUDUBON

1 Hispanic Society of America
2 Morris-Jumel Mansion
3 Jeffrey's Hook Lighthouse
4 George Washington Bridge
5 Bennett Park
6 Hudson View Gardens
7 Castle Village
8 Birthplace of Maria Callas
9 Fort Tryon Park
10 St. Frances Cabrini Shrine
11 New Leaf Restaurant
12 The Cloisters
13 Arts for Transit
14 Inwood Hill Park

Inwood, Fort George, Washington Heights & Audubon

14.1 Hispanic Society of America

1908, Charles Pratt Huntington
Audubon Terrace: Broadway between West 155th and West 156th Streets
212 926 2234; www.hispanicsociety.org
Closed Mondays.

The Hispanic Society has far and away the best museum and library in this country for the study of Spanish culture. The fact that the society is in one of the most culturally vibrant cities in the world, in a neighborhood that is almost entirely Spanish-speaking, and yet is largely unknown, simply makes it more intriguing. The grand Beaux Arts terrace that it occupies on Broadway between 155th and 156th Streets serves as a reminder of how swiftly this part of Manhattan evolved over the twentieth century.
WILLIAM AMBLER
Curator

The Hispanic Society of America was hugely popular at first. In 1909, when it opened a big show devoted to Valencian Impressionist Joaquín Sorolla, it obliged a total of one hundred and fifty thousand visitors by staying open until 11 p.m. At the time, *ARTnews* reported that the exhibit "won the most emphatic popular success ever known in the history of art in New York." Today, however, you might feel as though you're in a dark ducal home in a Spanish province, about fifty years ago.

The Hispanic Society sits on a recessed courtyard off Broadway between 155th and 156th Streets in a bustling, mostly Dominican neighborhood. It has changed very little since it was founded in 1904 by Archer Milton Huntington, who used the family fortune (shipbuilding and the Central Pacific Railroad) to acquire the best collection of Spanish art, books, and manuscripts in the United States.

He bought objects chronicling the panorama of Spanish history, from paleolithic stone tools to modern Catalan porcelain, rare Roman glass vessels and ivory combs, silken textiles woven in Moorish patterns, intricately illuminated medieval Bibles, and some of the best lusterware you will see anywhere. And he amassed paintings by masters including El Greco, Velázquez, and Zurbarán. Principal among the major works is Goya's portrait of his alleged mistress, the Duchess of Alba, who flaunts a ring with the artist's name on it.

Huntington also bought a parcel of farmland from the naturalist John James Audubon, with the intention of creating an acropolis on the Upper West Side. Known as the Audubon Terrace Historic District, it includes buildings for the American Numismatic Society, the American Academy of Arts and Letters, and one for George Gustave Heye, whose great collection of Native American art has since been transplanted downtown to the Smithsonian's National Museum of the American Indian (see p. 17). The inner court of the Hispanic Society, in the style of the Spanish Renaissance, looks like a palace and was, in fact, inspired by the Vélez Blanco Castle in the province of Almería. Sculptures of El Cid, Don Quixote, and Boabdil, the last Moorish king of Granada, by Huntington's wife, Anna Hyatt Huntington, adorn the outdoor space.

ROBIN CEMBALEST
Executive editor, ARTnews

This is a neglected museum with some fine Old Master paintings.

VICTORIA NEWHOUSE
Architectural historian and writer

14.2 Morris-Jumel Mansion

1765

65 Jumel Terrace between West 160th and 162nd Streets

212 923 8008; www.morrisjumel.org

Closed on Mondays and Tuesdays (except by appointment).

This house, on a rise overlooking Harlem Valley, was built in 1765 for Roger Morris, an English colonel. During the American Revolution it was used as General George Washington's headquarters. In 1810 it became the residence of Stephen and Eliza Jumel, who decorated it in the French Empire style. After the death of her husband, Eliza married former vice president Aaron Burr, the man who had shot Alexander Hamilton in a duel years before. Eliza had been a prostitute in her youth and had amassed a fortune that Burr managed to squander in bad investments. She sought a divorce from Burr in 1834, and he died two years later, on the day the divorce was granted. Eliza remained in the house until her death in 1865.

Today the house is open to the public as a museum, with period furniture in all the rooms. Entering the house is like stepping back into the nineteenth century. It is a true part of American history, with ties to President George Washington and Vice President Aaron Burr.

CELEDONIA JONES
Manhattan Borough Historian Emeritus

Women Who Soared the Heights

14.9 Fort Tryon Park

1935, Frederick Law Olmsted Jr.

West 192nd Street to Dyckman Street between Broadway and Riverside Drive

www.nycgovparks.org

14.10 **St. Frances Cabrini Shrine**
701 Fort Washington Avenue at West 190th Street
212 923 3536; www.mothercabrini.org

14.11 **New Leaf Restaurant and Bar**
1 Margaret Corbin Drive in Fort Tryon Park
212 568 5323; www.newleafrestaurant.com
Closed Mondays.

14.5 **Bennett Park**
West 183rd to West 185th Street between Fort Washington and Pinehurst Avenues
www.nycgovparks.org

The rock layer of Manhattan schist that forms the solid foundation for the city's famous skyscrapers runs the full length of the island and is highest at the northern end. Motorists on the George Washington Bridge and Henry Hudson Parkway will notice the sheer faces of cliffs in the section of upper Manhattan called Hudson Heights. Possibly inspired by its geological supremacy as the highest point in the city, Hudson Heights has long been home to women who soared to great heights themselves.

At the time of the American Revolution, upper Manhattan was the home of farmers who were mostly Tory sympathizers. Our boys lost big time at the battle of Fort Washington in 1776, fought in what is now Bennett Park. (The site is bordered by Hudson View Gardens, New York City's first cooperative apartments.)

The ramparts of the fort are outlined in granite blocks, and include the site of the highest natural point in Manhattan (two hundred and sixty-eight feet above sea level). A plaque on Fort Washington Avenue relates the details of the battle, but not the story that a turncoat informed the British of the placement of patriot guns. George

Washington watched the capture of twenty-eight hundred troops from the New Jersey side of the Hudson. The captured patriots were marched to lower Manhattan and placed in the notorious prison ships in the harbor downtown.

Among the wounded from the Battle of Fort Washington was Margaret "Captain Molly" Corbin, a camp follower who had accompanied her husband, John, who served in the patriot army as a matross, loading and swabbing the cannon. When John was killed, Molly took his place. Left for dead after suffering severe wounds to her arm and face, Molly was found and transported by the patriots to Philadelphia. She survived, but never fully recovered from her wounds. In 1779, she was made part of the Invalid Corps—soldiers who had been disabled fighting for freedom—and received a lifetime half-pension for the wounds she suffered. But her lifestyle did not inspire D.A.R. types to promote her as a figure of feminine patriotism as they did her more genteel Revolutionary sister, Molly Hays McCauley (Molly Pitcher), with whom she often is confused. It appears that our Molly was a hard-drinking girl.

Molly Corbin, first heroine of the American Revolution, is buried in West Point, just up the Hudson River, but she is commemorated by various sites in upper Manhattan. Going uptown a few blocks, you'll come to a traffic circle before the park entrance—Margaret Corbin Plaza. The spot from which her statue was stolen years ago by some enterprising New Yorkers now has a carved wooden sign announcing the entrance to Fort Tryon Park.

Fort Tryon Park is named after the last English civil governor of New York—a bit of a kick in the face for our guys and Molly. But pro-British feelings were at a high in 1935, when park renovations were completed and Rockefeller gave the land to the city. A plaque along the paved road near the site of the battle attests to Molly Corbin's contribution to the Revolution.

Just south of Margaret Corbin Plaza is the St. Frances Cabrini Shrine. The shrine, adjacent to Mother Cabrini High School, houses the relics of the saint known commonly as Mother Cabrini. In the chapel is a large mosaic relating the story of Mother Cabrini's life and works. She was born in Italy on July 15, 1850, and originally wished to become a missionary in China, choosing the name Frances Xavier for the martyred saint. After visiting Rome to request permission to travel to China, she was instructed by Pope Leo XIII, "Not to the East, but to the West." Mother Cabrini was sent to America. Here she cared for the immigrants flooding into New York who had neither social services nor access to the sacraments. She established schools, hospitals, orphanages, and nursing homes throughout the city. Mother Cabrini became an American citizen in 1909 and was canonized as "Mother of the American Immigrant" in 1946—the first American saint.

Mother Cabrini's relics are housed in a crystal coffin directly under the altar. It is a bit startling to see the relics of this pint-sized nun close up. Mother Cabrini is wearing the black habit of the nuns of her order, the Missionary Sisters of the Sacred Heart of Jesus. The chapel is crammed full of votive offerings and plaques thanking the saint for her intercession in granting miracles, and mementos from her life are displayed in the glass cases lining the gift shop. There are photos, medals, articles of clothing, and even the springs from her dentures. The nuns can be persuaded to open the cases to allow the faithful direct access to the saint's ribbons.

Saint Cabrini's feast is November 13. Every year the chapel celebrates with eight masses in five languages. An annual birthday celebration on July 15 includes masses in

English, Spanish, and Creole, as well as a children's carnival to which all Hudson Heights children are invited.

St. Frances Cabrini Shrine is located on a cliff overlooking the Hudson River at a site chosen by Mother Cabrini herself. As she drove her buggy to what was then a remote corner of New York City, she stopped there to rest her horses and enjoy the view. Much like those who visit here today, Mother Cabrini found great peace of mind in contemplating the magnificent view over the Hudson River and the Palisades. She purchased the property and opened Sacred Heart Orphan Asylum, a boarding school for girls. Now known as Mother Cabrini High School, the school continues to educate young Catholic women and was named a Blue Ribbon School by President Clinton in the year 2000, a hundred years after its founding.

World War II brought such an influx of German Jews to Hudson Heights that it became known as "Frankfurt on the Hudson." Today it is one of Manhattan's nicest residential neighborhoods, attracting families with small children as well as sizable Polish and Russian immigrant populations. It is not unusual to visit the famous Heather Garden of Fort Tryon Park and find young mothers who speak Spanish, Russian, or Polish seated beside older ladies chatting in German and Yiddish. Each may have a tale of courage to relate.

Visitors to Hudson Heights should be on the lookout for families of yellow hawks, which can occasionally be seen resting after their return from hunting in the thick woods of Fort Tryon Park. Human visitors looking for a place to rest and a bite to eat should head for New Leaf Restaurant in the Heather Garden, or bring a picnic and sit at the chess tables in Bennett Park. Here, you can enjoy the views and contemplate the scene where Molly Corbin made history as America's first heroine of the Revolution.

KIM DRAMER

Art historian

14.3 Jeffrey's Hook Lighthouse

1880

West 178th Street and the Hudson River under the east tower of the George Washington Bridge

Tours only, spring through fall: ☎ 212 304 2365; www.nycgovparks.org

The cast-iron Little Red Lighthouse was originally the North Hook Beacon from 1880 to 1917 in Sandy Hook, New Jersey. In 1921, ten years before the George Washington Bridge was built, it was moved to this spot, known at the time as Jeffrey's Hook. After the erection of the bridge, the lighthouse's beacon was no longer required, but it was saved from auction by letters from young readers who loved the classic children's book *The Little Red Lighthouse and the Great Gray Bridge.*

JAMES BOORSTEIN
Architectural conservator and artist

14.4 George Washington Bridge

1931, O.H. Ammann (engineer) & Cass Gilbert (architect)

West 178th Street and Fort Washington Avenue (Manhattan) to Fort Lee (New Jersey)

www.panynj.gov

Wear your sneakers, walking shoes, or hiking boots. Whatever your walking pleasure, New York has myriad unique places—parks, gardens, bridges, and boardwalks in which, on which, and over which to walk. And well within an hour of the city you can hike through wilderness and sand dunes or even climb stone faces.

One of the most exciting city walks is crossing the George Washington Bridge into New Jersey. From the bridge's north walk you can see upstream to the mountains along the Hudson River and watch the river's swift tidal current rush below your feet. Behind you are cars, buses, and trucks,

and beyond them, the city's towers, but for a few moments in mid-span, you feel as free as the seagulls above you.
ESTELLE GILSON
Writer, journalist, and translator

If your time in New York has not humbled you, then a trip to the base of the George Washington Bridge might. Rising six hundred and four feet above the water, the most influential twentieth-century suspension bridge was completed in 1931; the lower level was added thirty years later, making it the world's only fourteen-lane suspension bridge. Le Corbusier famously described it as "the most beautiful bridge in the world."

To understand why, try examining its underbelly. There is a perfect point, directly under the roadway, where the lines of the span and the towers converge and everything falls—abstractly, serenely—into place.

When you get there, notice the two granite abutments that project well beyond the metal structure, just a few feet from the water. These were designed as the pedestals for the granite cladding designed by Cass Gilbert. The stone covering was abandoned, however, during the Depression, leaving the bridge's intended skeleton exposed. The commissioners and the public came to appreciate the Modernist view of the bridge's elegant structure, and over the years, it achieved iconic status. Beginning in 2001, the steel towers were illuminated for special occasions.

Before you leave, take some time to enjoy the Hudson River views. To the south, Manhattan arcs toward the east, allowing a view of the tall Riverside Church tower, seemingly nestled beside the Statue of Liberty and the skyscrapers of downtown. To the north are Manhattan's northern tip, the great Palisades, and the majestic, lazy Hudson, all looking amazingly rural.
JAMES BOORSTEIN
Architectural conservator and artist

Hudson Heights Stroll

14.6 **Hudson View Gardens**
1925, George F. Pelham
116 Pinehurst Avenue between West 183rd
and West 185th Streets
212 923 7800; www.hudsonviewgardens.com

14.8 **Birthplace of Maria Callas**
689 West 184th Street between Broadway and Bennett Avenue

14.7 **Castle Village**
1939, George F. Pelham II
120-200 Cabrini Boulevard between West 181st
and West 186th Streets
www.castlevillage.com

14.9 **Fort Tryon Park**
1935, Frederick Law Olmsted Jr.
West 192nd Street to Dyckman Street between Broadway
and Riverside Drive
www.nycgovparks.org

Upper Fort Washington Avenue begins at the George Washington Bridge in Manhattan. As you proceed north, you'll see Hudson View Gardens, a Tudor-style co-op apartment complex built in the 1920s. One street over is Castle Village, another co-op built over the Hudson in the 1930s. Beginning at 184th Street, several 1930s Art Deco-style apartment buildings remain. The brick Romanesque building at No. 689, now a co-op, was once a hospital where it's said that Maria Callas was born. Fort Washington Avenue ends at Fort Tryon Park, one of the city's most beautiful, with gorgeous views of the Hudson and the George Washington Bridge. The Cloisters, which houses part of the Metropolitan Museum's medieval collection, is located there.

ALFRED CORN
Author and educator

14.12 The Cloisters, The Metropolitan Museum of Art

1939, Allen, Collens & Willis
In Fort Tryon Park
99 Margaret Corbin Drive
212 923 3700; www.metmuseum.org
Closed Mondays.

The Cloisters, an extraordinary branch of the Metropolitan Museum at Fort Tryon Park, is a time machine that takes us back to medieval days. It is rich in its collection of tapestries, windows, statues, and icons from before the Renaissance, and the music playing softly throughout is authentic and reverent.

HUGH MARTIN
The late Hugh Martin was a songwriter. He wrote the score for Meet Me in St. Louis, in which Judy Garland sings "The Trolley Song" and "Have Yourself a Merry Little Christmas."

Unicorn Tapestries

c. 1500
Unicorn Tapestries Room

The Cloisters houses the celebrated Unicorn Tapestries, a series of late medieval tapestries depicting The Hunt of the Unicorn. The medieval legend, an allegory of both human love and the Incarnation of Christ, relates that only a virgin can tame the swift and powerful unicorn. An ivory tusk from a narwhal, once thought to be that of a unicorn, stands in one corner of the tapestry room.

KIM DRAMER
Art historian

The Cloisters' Gardens

1938, Margaret Freeman and James J. Rorimer

In the spring and summer visit the outdoor, early-fouteenth-century-style herb garden, located in the Bonnefont Cloister. The enchanting smells of two hundred and fifty species of flowers, plants, and herbs include those used for medicinal

purposes, for painting illuminated manuscripts, for poison, and for cooking.
CHRISTINE MOOG
Graphic designer

There are three different gardens: the Trie Cloister and the Bonnefont Cloister Herb Garden are located on the lower level; the Cuxa Cloister is located near the entrance on the upper level.

Three cloisters in the building have gardens planted according to horticultural information gathered from medieval art and literature. This place is relatively tourist-free and there are magnificent views of the Hudson from the terraces. All this, along with the smell of the flowers and herbs, makes you feel as if you're in an old palazzo in Tuscany, even though the building itself is constructed from various buildings from France.
KATHARINE RISTICH
Editor, Theheart.org and Femina.com

14.13 Arts for Transit: *At the Start... At Long Last...*

1999, Sheila Levrant de Bretteville
www.mta.info

Traveling north to Fort Tryon Park or the Cloisters at the last (or first) stop on the A train in Inwood, one passes through Sheila Levrant de Bretteville's multifaceted oral history project at 207th Street and Broadway. *At the Start... At Long Last...* includes on the walls of the mezzanines scores of reminiscences about the neighborhood by community members past and present, representing several waves of immigration. The words and notes of the jazz classic "Take the A Train" are etched into the railings, and long, leggy mosaic Caribbean festival dancers descend or ascend the elevator with you from the street to the station.
JOYCE KOZLOFF
Artist

14.14 Inwood Hill Park

Entrance on West 215th Street and Indian Road
www.nycgovparks.org

Take the A train to 207th Street and walk a few blocks west to Inwood Hill Park. The park, bounded on the west by the Hudson River, on the north by the Harlem River and on the south by Dyckman Street, occupies the northernmost tip of Manhattan Island. From the entrance on Seaman Avenue, wide paths wind along the edge of acres of ballfields. The fields descend to a broad tidal marsh tucked into a cove of the Harlem River. Covered by mud and reeds at low tide, and shallow water at high tide, the marsh attracts legions of birds. On the south side of the open fields are dense woods and soaring ridges of stone, and at the opening of a narrow valley between two ridges is a small boulder bearing a bronze plaque that reads: *Shorakkopoch.*

According to legend, on this site of the principal Manhattan Indian village, Peter Minuit in 1626 purchased Manhattan Island for trinkets and beads worth about sixty guilders. This boulder also marks the spot where a tulip tree (*Liriodendron tulipifera*) grew to a height of a hundred and sixty-five feet and a girth of twenty feet. It was until its death in 1933, at the age of two hundred and eighty years, the last living link to the Reckgawawanc Indians who lived here.

Beyond the boulder, paths snake through thick woods up the face of the western ridge. The trails pass alongside tall cliffs and through groves of ancient, towering tulip-poplar trees, perhaps the last vestige of primeval forest on the island. At the summit of the ridge, the foliage opens to reveal panoramic views of the Hudson. There are expansive vistas across to the New Jersey Palisades, south to the George Washington Bridge, and many miles upriver to the Tappan Zee. The serenity of the spot is only slightly undercut by the sounds of traffic on the West Side Highway far below.

Peter Minuit's meeting with Native Americans at their village may be apocryphal. Historians have proposed other locations for the exchange, or suggested that an official purchase never took place. Native people had no conception of the private ownership of land, so even if the "purchase" occurred, it had little meaning for them. Still, there is a palpable sense of history here. It is easy to imagine Indians living in this valley. Fish and small game would have been abundant in the tidal marsh, and patches of corn or squash would have grown nicely in the low fields. A scout could run quickly up the western ridge, and from its peak observe anyone approaching from the Hudson. The proximity of two rivers made the village easily accessible, yet the high ridge hid and protected the valley behind it. Stone caves in the cliffs provided convenient shelter, as confirmed by Indian artifacts discovered there and removed in 1909.

The undisturbed landscape of Inwood Hill Park and the presence of a Native American past join to convey an impression of what Manhattan was like before being reshaped by Europeans.

DAVID L. REESE
Director, Gunster Hall, Virginia

Inwood Hill Park is virgin forest, not chopped down since the days of the Dutch.

PETE SEEGER
Songwriter

INDEX OF CONTRIBUTORS

MARGOT ADLER is an NPR correspondent based in NPR's New York bureau. Her reports can be heard regularly on *All Things Considered*, *Morning Edition*, and *Weekend Edition*. She is the author of *Drawing Down the Moon*. pp. 118, 247, 264, 265, 267, 273

DAN ALGRANT is a filmmaker. His credits include *Anything for Jazz*, *Naked in New York*, and *People I Know*. p. 211

WILLIAM AMBLER is a curator. p. 316

DENNIS ASHBAUGH is an artist living in New York City whose work is in the collections of most major art museums. He is a Guggenheim Fellow and a surfer. p. 201

PAMELA BAYLESS is a writer and communications consultant. She is the author of *The YMCA at 150*. p. 309, 311

CLARE BELL is program manager at the Roy Lichtenstein Foundation. She is the author of *Hirschfeld's New York* and co-author of *Jim Dine: Walking Memory*. p. 271

BARRY BERGDOLL is the Philip Johnson Chief Curator of Architecture and Design at the Museum of Modern Art in New York. He is a professor of art history at Columbia University. He specializes in the architectural history of nineteenth- and early twentieth-century France and Germany. pp. 69, 164, 270, 303

Architect FREDERICK BIEHLE is a professor at Pratt Institute, where he is the academic coordinator of the Pratt Rome Program. He is a partner at viaArchitecture, a multidisciplinary design firm. p. 24

LUCIENNE S. BLOCH is the author of *On the Great-Circle Route* and *Finders Keepers*. She has received fellowships from the New York Foundation for the Arts and Yaddo. p. 220

CLARISSA BLOCK is a fashion stylist and children's jewelry designer. p. 46

SANDRA BLOODWORTH is an artist and the director of the Metropolitan Transportation Authority Arts for Transit program. She is the co-author, with William Ayres, of *Along the Way: MTA Arts for Transit*. p. 207

JAMES BODNAR is an architect in private practice in New York City. p. 67

JAMES BOORSTEIN is the president of Traditional Line Architectural Restoration, specialists in interior woodwork restoration and conservation for private residences and institutions. The firm's projects include moving and reassembling a seventeenth-century farmhouse inside the Brooklyn Museum, restoring period rooms in the American Wing of the Metropolitan Museum. pp. 323, 324

LANA BORTOLOT is a culture writer and editor based in New York City. pp. 47, 131, 163, 176

A native New Yorker, ALEXANDER R. BRASH is chair of the Habitat

Committee in the EPA's Harbor Estuary Program, a member of the Harbor Roundtable and Nature Network, and a council member of the Linnaean Society of New York. He has received the Wildlife Management Trust's prestigious Presidential Award and the New York State Department of Environmental Conservation Commissioner's Award, among others. pp. 17, 261

The Honorable JAMES J. BRUCIA is a justice, now retired, of the New York State Supreme Court. pp. 43, 152

The late MARGARET BRUCIA was a schoolteacher in Roslyn Heights, New York. p. 152

MARGARET A. BRUCIA is a Latin teacher. pp. 118, 203

JOHN BRYANT received a grant from the National Endowment for the Humanities to launch Melville Electronic Library, a digital "critical archive" of the works of Herman Melville. He is the author of *Melville and Repose* and *The Fluid Text*, and the editor of *Leviathan: A Journal of Melville Studies*. He is a professor of English at Hofstra University. p. 15

MARIO BUATTA, also known as the "Prince of Chintz," is one of America's foremost decorators. His high-profile clients include Henry Ford II, Malcolm Forbes, and Barbara Walters. p. 279

MELVIN JULES BUKIET is a novelist and literary critic. He is the author of six books of fiction, including *Strange Fire*, *Signs and Wonders*, and *A Faker's Dozen*. p. 298

The late PETER BURCHARD was an author, designer, and illustrator. His book *One Gallant Rush* was a major historical source for the motion picture *Glory*, which won three Academy Awards. He also wrote several children's books about slavery, abolitionism, and the American Civil War. He was a Guggenheim Fellow. p. 96, 100

CHRISTOPHER CAHILL is the author of *Perfection*. He has edited the essays of Thomas Flanagan under the title *There You Are: Writings on Irish and American Literature and History* as well as an anthology of Irish popular poetry, *Gather Round Me*. He is the executive director of The American Irish Historical Society and editor of its journal, *The Recorder*. p. 130

GEORGE CAMPBELL JR. recently retired as president of the Cooper Union for the Advancement of Science and Art. A physicist, he is a director of Con Edison, Inc., and Barnes & Noble, Inc., and a trustee of Rensselaer Polytechnic Institute. A recipient of the 1993 George Arents Pioneer Medal in Physics, he is a Fellow of the American Association for the Advancement of Science and the New York Academy of Sciences. p. 97

SARAH CAPLAN is a graphic designer and author of the Pratique shopping guides to SoHo, Nolita, the Meatpacking District, and the West Village. She is also the designer of paper dresses made of Tyvek, which

THERESA CRAIG is the author of *Edith Wharton: A House Full of Rooms—Architecture, Interiors and Gardens*. She has taught literature at City University of New York and humanities at the New School University. pp. 29, 170

MICHAEL CUNNINGHAM is the author of the novels *A Home at the End of the World*, *Flesh and Blood*, *Specimen Days*, and *The Hours*, which was awarded a Pen/Faulkner Award and a Pulitzer Prize. p. 83

The late PHILLIP DANZIG was a muralist and an architect. He worked with the Cityarts Workshop project to design and implement *Rolling Bench*, a mosaic tile bench around Grant's Tomb in upper Manhattan. p. 306

GLORIA DEÁK is a scholar of American art and cultural affairs. She is the author of many books about American cultural history, including *Picturing America* and *Picturing New York*. p. 79

LISA DENNISON is an executive at Sotheby's auction house. She was formerly the deputy director and chief curator at the Solomon R. Guggenheim Museum. p. 243

LORRAINE B. DIEHL is the author of *The Late, Great Pennsylvania Station*; *Subways: The Tracks That Built New York City*; and *The Automat: The History, Recipes, and Allure of Horn & Hardart's Masterpiece*. She has contributed to *New York* magazine, *The New York Times*, *Travel & Leisure*, *American Heritage*, and the *New York Daily News*. p. 270

The painter SIMON DINNERSTEIN has had numerous one-man exhibitions, and two monographs of his work have been published. He is the recipient of the Rome Prize from the American Academy in Rome and a Fulbright grant. p. 217

KIM DRAMER is a specialist in the art and archaeology of early China. She is the author of numerous books on China for the young adult audience, and lectures extensively on Chinese culture. She is an assistant professor in humanities and social sciences at the Cooper Union. pp. 318, 326

LAURIE DUCHOVNY is a teacher and a writer. She has taught at Saint Ann's School, a private school in Brooklyn, for many years. p. 120

ALEXANDER DUFF is a restaurateur in Miami and New York whose endeavors have included A Fish Called Avalon, Rebar, Pacific Time, Pacific East, Groovejet, Gigi Bistro, and Top of the Strand. p. 188

KATE HARTNICK ELLIOTT is president and founder of Hartnick Consulting, a marketing strategy, communications, and executive search firm in New York City. On the weekend, she is an avid urban explorer. pp. 115, 291

LOUISA ERMELINO's novels celebrate the power of women, her Italian American ancestry, and her New York City neighborhood. She is the author of *Joey Dee Gets Wise*, *The Black Madonna*, and *The Sisters Mallone*. She is chief of reporters at *InStyle* magazine. p. 63

MATTHEW FIELD has edited more than fifty books on magic and is the video reviewer for *Genii*, the international conjurer's magazine. He is the editor of the *Magic Circular* magazine. p. 119

JANE FISHER is a consultant in publishing and direct marketing whose career has included stints at such companies as Oxford University Press, Macmillan, Condé Nast, and Scholastic. pp. 38, 45, 177

DAVID FISHMAN is an architectural historian at Robert A. M. Stern Architects. He is co-author, with Robert A. M. Stern and Thomas Mellins, of *New York 1880* and *New York 1960*, and co-author, with Robert A. M. Stern and Jacob Tilove, of *New York 2000*. pp. 201, 204

Since 1989, CHRISTOPHER FORBES has been vice chairman of Forbes, Inc., which publishes *Forbes Magazine* and Forbes.com. He is the chairman of the American Friends of the Louvre, and he sits on the boards of the Friends of New Jersey State Museum, the New York Academy of Art, and the Prince Wales Foundation. In 2003, he was appointed a Chevalier of the Legion of Honor by the French Government. p. 76

BRUCE S. FOWLE co-founded FXFOWLE Architects in 1978. His work has been widely published and includes numerous award-winning projects. He is a member of the American Institute of Architects' College of Fellows and Academician of the National Academy of Design. In 2010, he received the Harry B. Rutkins Award for Service to the AIA New York Chapter. He is a founder of the New York chapter of Architects, Designers, and Planners for Social Responsibility. p. 179

ALEX FRENCH is a writer and journalist. His work has appeared in numerous publications, including *GQ*, *New York* magazine, the *Los Angeles Times Magazine*. p. 53

M. PAUL FRIEDBERG is a landscape architect, planner, product designer, and author. Principal in charge of design at M. Paul Friedman & Partners since founding the firm in 1958, he is best known for his work in urban landscape, including urban playgrounds, plazas, malls, and parks. He received the ASLA Design Medal, the highest honor of the American Society of Landscape Architects, and the AIA Medal in recognition of his influence on the architectural profession. He is Professor Emeritus at City College New York. p. 306

The late MARGOT GAYLE was an eminent preservationist, and co-founder, in 1966, of the Victorian Society in America. She was also the founder of the Friends of Cast Iron Architecture and is credited with raising public awareness nationwide of the significance of iron-fronted buildings of the Victorian era. Her preservation efforts extended from the 1960s when she successfully campaigned to save the Jefferson Market Courthouse in Greenwich Village, to a drive in the 1990s to restore the Yorkville sidewalk clock on Third Avenue near 85th Street.

Among her books are *Cast-Iron Architecture in America: The Significance of James Bogardus* and *Cast-Iron Architecture in New York*. p. 247

LEE GELBER, a born and bred New Yorker, is an urban historian and tour guide. He gives architecture walking tours, as well as tours of neighborhoods such as the Lower East Side, Harlem, and the Financial District. He was dubbed the "Dean of Guides" by *The New York Times*. p. 192, 294

ESTELLE GILSON is a writer, journalist, and translator. She is the translator of works by Umberto Saba, Massimo Bontempelli, and Giacomo Debenedetti, and (from Hebrew) of poet Gabriel Preil. She is the recipient of numerous awards for journalism and translation, including the PEN Renato Poggioli Translation Award. p. 323

KENNETH SEEMAN GINIGER is a publisher, an editor, and the author of ten books. p. 168

SCOTT GLASS is a founding principal of Guerin Glass Architects, a full-service firm with a focus on architecture, interior design, and planning. Previously, he was a founder of BDDW, Inc., a design and manufacturing firm. p. 222

MARYELLEN GORDON is the director of the Magazine/Digital Program at the Summer Publishing Institute at New York University. She is the founder of Stable of Content, consultants to lifestyle and fashion brands, helping to create an editorial vision for their websites and published content. Previously, she was the deputy editor at *Glamour* magazine. p. 23

ALEXANDER GORLIN is principal and founder of Alexander Gorlin Architects in New York City. The firm has won numerous awards, most notably AIA Design Awards for the Ruskin Place town house, House in the Rocky Mountains, North Shore Hebrew Academy, and the Southampton House. p. 158

JOHN GUARE was awarded the Gold Medal in Drama by the American Academy of Arts and Letters for his Obie-, New York Drama Critics' Circle–, and Tony-winning plays, including *House of Blue Leaves*, *Six Degrees of Separation*, and *A Few Stout Individuals*. He teaches playwriting at the Yale School of Drama. pp. 85, 135, 213, 259

AGNES GUND is President Emerita of the Museum of Modern Art and chairman of its International Council. She is currently chairman of the Mayor's Cultural Affairs Advisory Commission of New York City. In 1977, she founded the Studio in a School Association in response to budget cuts that virtually eliminated arts classes from New York City public schools. A philanthropist and collector of modern and contemporary art, she has served on the boards of numerous arts organizations, including the Barnes Foundation and the Menil Collection, and currently serves on the boards of Chess in the Schools, Contemporary Art Center, P.S. 1, the Frick Collection, and Socrates Sculpture Park, among others. p. 216

JUDITH MARA GUTMAN is a writer, lecturer, and academic. She is the author of seven books, including a biography. She is a member of PEN and its Freedom-to-Write committee, and the Authors' Guild. p. 26

Born in New York City and raised by two architects, SEBASTIAN HARDY has been exploring New York City without supervision since he was old enough to unlock the front door. pp. 111, 127, 305

ANGELA HEDERMAN is editor and publisher at The Little Bookroom. pp. 56, 181

STEVEN HELLER is an art director, author, and the co-founder and co-chair of the MFA Design Department and co-founder of the MFA Design Criticism Department at the School of Visual Arts in New York. He is the author, co-author, or editor of over a hundred books on graphic design, illustration, and political art, and a columnist for *The New York Times Book Review*. He was an art director at *The New York Times* for thirty-three years. pp. 93, 175

DAVID J. HELLERSTEIN is the director of Medical Communications at the Columbia University Department of Psychiatry and associate professor of Clinical Psychiatry at the Columbia University College of Physicians and Surgeons. He has also received national recognition for his literary writing, and has been awarded the Pushcart Prize and several MacDowell Colony Fellowships. His books include *Battles of Life and Death*, *Loving Touches*, and the memoir *Family of Doctors*. His journalism has been published in magazines including *Harper's* and *The New York Times Magazine*. A Distinguished Fellow of the American Psychiatric Association, he has served as President of the New York County District Branch of the American Psychiatric Association. p. 186

SCOTT HESS is a screenwriter, an award-winning writer/performer, and author. He is a regular contributor to several national magazines, as well as the gay/lesbian section editor of Harper Collins' *Access Guide New York City*. p. 84

SAM HOFFMAN has produced, directed, and assistant–directed movies such as *The Royal Tenenbaums*, *School of Rock*, *Dead Man Walking*, *Groundhog Day*, and *Curse of the Jade Scorpion*. He is the founder, with Eric Speigelman and Tim Williams, of the website Old Jews Telling Jokes. p. 142

PETER J. HOLLIDAY is a professor of the history of art and classical archaeology at California State University, Long Beach. He has written extensively on Greek and Roman art. pp. 225, 275, 301

RACHAEL HOROVITZ's feature-film producing credits include *About Schmidt*, *State and Main*, and *Next Stop*, and she was the executive producer of HBO's *Grey Gardens*. She recently returned to independent producing after a decade as a senior production executive at Revolution Studios and New Line Cinema. She co-founded, with Joe Hall, the Cinema School, a public high school in the Bronx. p. 90

MARIE HOWE is a poet. Her books include *The Kingdom of Ordinary Time*, *The Good Thief*, and *What the Living Do* and her poems have appeared in literary journals and magazines including *Poetry*, *The New Yorker*, *The Atlantic*, *Ploughshares*, and *Harvard Review*. She is on the writing faculty at Sarah Lawrence College and New York University. She is the recipient of a Guggenheim Fellowship and a National Endowment for the Arts Fellowship. p. 55

TINA HOWE is a playwright whose work includes *Painting Churches*, *Pride's Crossing*, and *Coastal Disturbances*. Her honors include two Pulitzer Prizes for Drama, a Tony Award for Best Play, an Obie Award for Distinguished Playwriting, an American Academy of Arts and Letters Award in Literature, and the William Inge Award for Distinguished Achievement in the American Theatre. p. 259

TRACEY HUMMER is a New York–based writer and editor covering architecture, art, and design. She is a former managing editor of *Artforum* and contributing editor of *Art in America*. pp. 25, 44, 95, 126, 129, 174, 188, 189, 211, 253, 308

JOHANNA HURWITZ is the award-winning author of seventy popular children's books. She lectures to students, teachers, parents, and librarians from Mississippi to Mozambique. p. 134

COLTA IVES is the founder of Colta Ives Landscape design, with studios in New York City and the Berkshires in Massachusetts. She is the author of prize-winning books and articles on the arts, a frequent lecturer, and former adjunct professor at Columbia and New York University. She is Curator Emerita at the Metropolitan Museum of Art. p. 186

THOMAS JAYNE is head of Thomas Jayne Studio, Inc. Along with his private commissions he has consulted on the preservation and decoration of interiors at the Winterthur Museum and Country Estate and the Shelburne Museum. His projects have been featured in *The New York Times*, *Town & Country*, *House Beautiful*, and *Vogue*. p. 170

JOHN JILER is a playwright. He received both the Richard Rodgers Award and the Kleban Award for Most Promising Librettist for his musical *Avenue X*, and the Weissberger Prize from New Dramatists for his play *Sour Springs*. His literary works include *Sleeping with the Mayor* and *Dark Wind*. His current project is a one-man show, *Explicit Vows* (Playwrights Horizons\The Flea Theatre). p. 188

FENTON JOHNSON is the author of two novels, *Crossing the River* and *Scissors, Paper, Rock*; a memoir, *Geography of the Heart*; and *Keeping Faith: A Skeptic's Journey among Christian and Buddhist Monks*. He has contributed stories and cover essays to *Harper's*, *The New York Times Magazine*, and many literary quarterlies. He has received fellowships from the Guggenheim Foundation and the National Endowment for the Arts. He is on the faculty of the creative writing program at the University of Arizona. p. 242

The late PHILIP JOHNSON came to prominence in the 1930s as the first director of the Department of Architecture at the Museum of Modern Art. He had a long and influential career as an architect, curator, and critic. He was awarded the American Institute of Architects Gold Medal and received the first Pritzker Prize in 1979. p. 200

CELEDONIA JONES is Manhattan Borough Historian Emeritus. In 1998, he was recognized as one of New York City's Centennial Historians. p. 318

FIONA KAHN is managing editor of City Secrets and co-founder of Fang Duff Kahn Publishers. p. 175

LAWRENCE KAHN is a Professor Emeritus of Pediatrics at Washington University in St. Louis. Currently, one of his main activities is leading a group from the Lifelong Learning Institute in reading and interpreting all of Shakespeare's plays. He takes great pleasure in the practical application of his son's City Secrets guides. p. 243

ROBERT KAHN, editor of the City Secrets series, is founding principal of the award-winning firm, Robert Kahn Architect, based in New York City. A recipient of the Rome Prize in Architecture from the American Academy in Rome, he has received numerous awards from the NY chapter of the American Institute of Architects. He has taught at Columbia University, Ohio State University, and Yale University, where he held a Davenport Chair Professorship. He is co-founder, with his wife Fiona Kahn, of Fang Duff Kahn Publishers. pp. 37, 68, 71, 156, 161, 213

PAUL KANE is a professor of English and co-associate chair of English at Vassar College. He has published four collections of poems. He has been poetry editor of *Antipodes* since 1987 and has served as artistic director of the annual Mildura Writers Festival. He was a Fulbright scholar to Australia in 1984–1985. Other awards include fellowships from the National Endowment for the Humanities and the John Simon Guggenheim Memorial Foundation. p. 134

DAVID BAR KATZ is a writer and director in every medium other than comic books, though he hopes to break into them soon. p. 105

ROBERT KAUFELT is the proprietor of Murray's Cheese Shop, one of Greenwich Village's oldest continuously running businesses. He writes and teaches about food and lives in Greenwich Village with his wife, Patricia, an artist. p. 54

EDMUND KEELEY is a novelist, translator, critic, and the author of thirty-two books. He is a prize-winning novelist and a noted expert on Greek poets and on post-Second World War Greek history. A former president of the PEN American Center, he received the Rome Prize from the American Academy in Rome, the Academy Award in Literature from the American Academy of Arts and Letters, and the Ralph Manheim Medal for Translation. In 2001, he was awarded with Commander of the Order of the Phoenix by the Greek government. He is the Charles Barnwell Straut English Professor Emeritus at Princeton University. p. 56

BETTY KEIM is an editor, writer, and musicologist. She is the founder of Keim Publishing, which provides editorial, production, and design services to publishers, nonprofit organizations, and other companies. She has written scripts for documentary films on American architecture. p. 205

BINNIE KIRSHENBAUM is the author of two story collections and six novels, the most recent of which is *The Scenic Route*. She is the chair of the M.F.A. program at Columbia University. p. 146

HOWARD KISSEL, who blogs as the Cultural Tourist for the *Huffington Post*, has written about the arts in New York for four decades. He was the chief theater critic of the *New York Daily News* for twenty years. Before that he was the arts editor of *Women's Wear Daily* and *W*. He is the only person to have been the chairman of both the New York Film Critics Circle and the New York Drama Critics Circle. He is the author of several books, including *The Abominable Showman*, a biography of producer David Merrick, and *The Art of Acting*. He has also written for *The Wall Street Journal*, *Vogue*, *Playbill*, and *Interview*. p. 290

EDWARD I. KOCH served in the United States House of Representatives from 1969 to 1977 and three terms as the mayor of New York from 1978 to 1989. He was born and raised in the Bronx. p. 224

BILL KOMOSKI is a painter and native New Yorker. He teaches at the School of Visual Arts. p. 132

JOYCE KOZLOFF is an artist. She lives in New York City. pp. 144, 274, 327

GAIL KRIEGEL is a playwright, librettist, and composer. Her plays include *On the Home Front* and *Sweetie*.The film *Fragments*, adapted from her play and for which she wrote the screenplay, won top awards at five film festivals. She was a visiting artist at the American Academy in Rome and is the recipient of a Rockefeller Foundation Fellowship. pp. 28, 30

EVELYN and PETER KRAUS are the owners of Ursus Books and Prints, specializing in art books, rare books of all kinds, and decorative master prints. p. 111

ALISA LAGAMMA is an art historian and a curator in the Department of the Arts of Africa, Oceania, and the Americas at the Metropolitan Museum of Art. p. 232

ANNE LANDSMAN is the author of *Rowing Lessons*, for which she won the Sunday Times Fiction Prize, and

The Devil's Chimney, which was nominated for the PEN/Hemingway Award and the Janet Heidinger Kafka Prize, among others. She has been awarded fellowships from the Sundance Institute, MacDowell Colony, and Yaddo. p. 249

RICHARD LAVENSTEIN is a principal at Bond Street Architecture & Design. p. 76

JANE DANIELS LEAR, a food and travel writer based in New York City, is the former senior articles editor at *Gourmet* magazine. A contributor to *The Gourmet Cookbook: More than 1000 Recipes* and *Gourmet Today: More than 1000 All-New Recipes for the Contemporary Kitchen*, she also co-wrote (with chef Floyd Cardoz) *One Spice, Two Spice: American Food, Indian Flavors*. pp. 122, 248

DANY LEVY is the founder and editor in chief of *Daily Candy*, a daily e-mail newsletter dedicated to fashion, trends, and deals of the day. pp. 109, 112

HILARY LEWIS is an urban planner and architectural historian. She is the co-author of *Philip Johnson: The Architect in His Own Words* and author of *THINK New York: A Ground Zero Diary*. p. 204

LAURA LINNEY is an actress of film, television, and theater, as well as a native New Yorker. She has won three Emmy Awards, two Golden Globes, and has been nominated three times for an Academy Award and for a Tony Award for Best Actress in a play. She received a Golden Globe award for her role in *The Big C*. p. 253

LAURIE LISLE is a journalist, biographer, essayist, and lecturer. Her books include *Portrait of an Artist: A Biography of Georgia O'Keeffe*, *Louise Nevelson*, *Without Child*, and *Westover: Giving Girls a Place of Their Own*. p. 135

ROBERT LIVESEY is director of the Knowlton School of Architecture at Ohio State University. pp. 13, 202

IAIN LOW is a professor of architecture at the University of Cape Town. As a practitioner he was Project Architect for the World Bank/GoL, where he designed schools for the Training for Self Reliance Project throughout Lesotho, and he designed an award-winning reinstallation of Iziko SA Museum's San Rock Art in Cape Town. He is editor of the *Digest of South African Architecture* and the *Digest of African Architecture*. He was Fulbright scholar at the University of Pennsylvania and visiting scholar at the American Academy in Rome. p. 73

GLENN LOWRY is the director of the Museum of Modern Art. Previously, he was curator of Near Eastern Art at the Smithsonian Institution's Arthur M. Sackler Gallery and the Freer Gallery of Art. He is a Fellow of the American Academy of Arts and Sciences. In 2004, the French government honored him with the title of Officier dans l'Ordre des Arts et des Lettres. p. 236

CHARLOTTE MANDEL is the author of six books of poetry, including *Sight Lines*, *The Marriages of Jacob*, and *The Life of Mary*. She is the recipient of the Geraldine R.

Dodge Foundation Fellowship at Yaddo. She teaches poetry writing at Barnard College Center for Research on Women. p. 198

MARIA MANHATTAN is a painter, illustrator, graphic artist, and native New Yorker. Her work has been exhibited at Galerie Valerie, the New York Historical Society, the Bronx Museum of the Arts, and the Whitney Museum of American Art. She has taught at the New School and the School of Visual Arts. p. 77

BRICE MARDEN is a painter. In 2006, the Museum of Modern Art presented a retrospective exhibition of his work, and he has been the subject of one-person exhibitions at the Solomon R. Guggenheim Museum in New York; the Stedelijk Museum in Amsterdam; Documenta IX in Kassel; and the Serpentine Gallery and Tate Gallery in London. In 1988, Marden became a member of the American Academy of Arts and Letters and, in 2000, Brown University awarded him an honorary degree of Doctor of Fine Arts. p. 218

HELEN MARDEN is a painter who has had numerous exhibitions. She lives in New York. p. 154

CHARLES MARSDEN-SMEDLEY is a designer whose practice specializes in museum and exhibition design. p. 12

A native of Birmingham, Alabama, the late HUGH MARTIN started his career is New York as a vocal arranger. He wrote, with Ralph Blane, the score for *Meet Me in St. Louis*, in which Judy Garland sings "The Trolley Song" and "Have Yourself a Merry Little Christmas." Together, Hugh Martin and Ralph Blane received four Tony Award nominations, and two Academy Award nominations for Best Song. pp. 172, 217, 326

JOSEPH MASHECK is an art historian and former editor in chief of *Artforum*. He has taught at Hofstra Univeristy, Harvard University, and Columbia University, where he was also a member of the Society of Fellows in the Humanities. He is the author of *Marcel Duchamp in Perspective*, *Building-Art: Modern Architecture under Cultural Construction*, and *Modernities: Art-Matters in the Present*. He is a Fellow of the Royal Society of Arts. pp. 24, 148, 200, 206

MICHAEL MASSING is the author of *The Fix*, a critical study of the U.S. war on drugs, and a contributing editor of the *Columbia Journalism Review*. He frequently writes for the *New York Review of Books*, and has written for *The New York Times*, *The New Yorker*, and *Atlantic Monthly*. He is the recipient of a MacArthur Fellowship. pp. 288, 289

TERRY MAYER is a bellologist. She designs miniature bells as jewelry and is a collector of international bells. She lectures on bells and has been president of the Metropolitan New York Chapter of the American Bell Association. She is a native New Yorker. p. 191

The late LAURIE MCLENDON was the owner of Shi in Noho, where she sold one-of-a-kind objects and housewares—each of which reflected her unique aesthetic. She was also the owner of Papivore, a paper store geared to customized invitations. p. 215

RICHARD MEIER's international practice has encompassed major civic commissions in the United States and Europe, and he has received the highest honors in the field including the Pritzker Prize for Architecture. Among his well-known projects are the acclaimed Getty Center in Los Angeles, the Barcelona Museum of Contemporary Art, and the City Hall, Central Library in The Hague, the Ara Pacis Museum in Rome, and the Arp Museum in Rolandseck. p. 199

JAYNE MERKEL is an architectural historian and critic who contributes regularly to *Architectural Design* in London. A former editor of *Oculus*, the monthly magazine of the AIA New York Chapter, she has written for *Architectural Record*, *Art in America*, *Artforum*, *Connoisseur*, *Design Book Review*, and served for eleven years as architecture critic of the *Cincinnati Enquirer*. She has taught at various colleges and curated numerous museum exhibitions. p. 140

DANNY MEYER is the CEO of Union Square Hospitality Group, which includes New York establishments such as Union Square Cafe, Gramercy Tavern, Eleven Madison Park, Blue Smoke, the Modern, and Maialino. Meyer is the author of the best-selling book *Setting the Table*, and co-author (with chef Michael Romano) of the *Union Square Cafe Cookbook*. He is an active national leader in the fight against hunger, serving on the board of Share Our Strength. p. 145

YURI MILOSLAVSKY is a writer, literary scholar, and journalist. He is a Russian Writers Union member, PEN member, and an Honorary Fellow of Writing at the University of Iowa. He has published five books of fiction, as well as many cultural and political essays. p. 248

MICHAEL MISCIONE is the Manhattan Borough Historian and a native New Yorker. pp. 121, 272

CAROL MOLESWORTH is the co-writer of *Manhattan User's Guide*, *New York's 350 Best Places to Celebrate the Holiday Season*, and *New York Holiday Guide*. pp. 133, 159

CHRISTINE MOOG is a graphic designer based in New York. She has taught at the Parsons School of Design, Yale University, City College of New York, and Ontario College of Art and Design. pp. 64, 326

RICHARD E. MOONEY is retired from the editorial board of *The New York Times*, where he wrote on city affairs—economic, cultural, and political. pp. 214, 241

CHRISTOPHER PAUL MOORE is a historian and research coordinator for special projects and exhibitions for the New York Public Library's Schomburg Center for Research in Black Culture. He is author and co-author of several works including *The Black New Yorkers* and *Slavery In New York*. He wrote and co-produced the History Channel's award-winning series *The African Burial Ground: An American Discovery*. He is commissioner of the NYC Landmarks Preservation Commission and the New York City Archival Review Board. In 2008, he received the U.S. Congressional Black Caucus's Veterans' Braintrust Award. He founded Teaching America, a historic walking-tour program for educators and students. He is a twelfth-generation descendant of Manhattan's first African, Dutch, and Native American community. pp. 20, 43, 308, 312

GREGORY MOSHER is a director and producer of nearly two hundred stage productions and has received every major American theater award, including two Tony Awards and a Drama Desk Special Award. He was the director of Lincoln Center Theater from 1985 to 1992 and created the Arts Initiative at Columbia University in 2004. He is also a film and television director, producer, and writer, as well as an adjunct professor at the School of the Arts at Columbia University. pp. 62, 169, 274

ANTONI MUNTADAS is a multidisciplinary media artist. His work has been exhibited widely, including at the Museum of Modern Art, the Venice Biennale, Documenta VI, and Documenta X. He was a Research Fellow at the Center for Advanced Visual Studies at MIT from 1977 to 1984, and is currently visiting professor at the MIT Visual Arts Program. p. 162

GERALDINE NAGER-GRIFFIN is a senior vice president at Sotheby's New York. p. 252

VICTORIA NEWHOUSE is an architectural historian. She is the author of *Towards a New Museum and Art* and *Art and the Power of Placement*, two studies of museums and their relationships with collectors, trustees, artists, and the public. She lectures internationally on museums and architecture, and has published on the subject in *The New York Times*, *Architectural Record*, and *ARTNews*. p. 317

KATHRYN NOCERINO is a writer. Her fiction appears in *Growing up Ethnic in America* and *Identity Lessons*. Her books of poetry include *Death of the Plankton Bar and Grill*, *Candles in the Daylight*, and *Wax Lips*. p. 281

STARR OCKENGA is a garden photographer, writer, and lecturer. Her books include *Eden on Their Minds: American Gardeners with Bold Visions* and *Earth on Her Hands: The American Woman in Her Garden*, which received an American Horticultural Society Book Award. Her work has appeared in numerous national publications, including *Horticulture* and *Country Home*. She has been granted fellowships from the National Endowment for the Arts and the Massachusetts Artists Foundation. p. 150

GEORGIA O'NEAL and her husband own the Tree and Leaf Farm, a sustainable vegetable farm in Unionville, Virginia. She is a native New Yorker. pp. 94, 292

AL ORENSANZ is a sociologist, semiologist, and the director of the Angel Orensanz Foundation in New York. He is the author of five books on sociology and the semiology of urban communities. He received the Award of British Council from Beijing University. p. 104

NADINE ORENSTEIN is a curator in the Prints and Drawings Department at the Metropolitan Museum of Art. pp. 215, 288

JANET B. PASCAL is a writer and a production editor at Viking Children's Books. She is the author of *Arthur Conan Doyle: Beyond Baker Street*, *Jacob Riis: Reporter and Reformer*, and *Who Was Abraham Lincoln?* She has been exploring the nooks and crannies of New York for the past twenty years. pp. 46, 86, 98, 127, 129, 232

The late RAYMOND R. PATTERSON was a poet and Professor Emeritus at the City College of New York. He founded the college's annual Langston Hughes Festival. p. 309

ANDREW S. PAUL has been general counsel of a large hedge fund for many years. Accordingly, he says, he rarely sits with his back to the door and never near an open window. p. 83

JOHN PENOTTI is the founding partner of GreeneStreet Films, an independent film, television, and digital-content production company based in New York and Los Angeles. GreeneStreet has produced numerous films including the five-time Academy Award nominee *In The Bedroom*, *Piñero*, *Swimfan*, *Uptown Girls*, *A Prairie Home Companion*, and the documentary *Once in a Lifetime: The Extraordinary Story of the New York Cosmos*. p. 110

PETER PENNOYER is principal of Peter Pennoyer Architects. Many of the firm's institutional and commercial projects have involved historic buildings. He has served as a trustee of the New York Architectural Foundation, the Municipal Art Society, and the Institute of Classical Architecture. p. 20

CAITLIN PETRE is a PhD student in the Sociology Department at New York University, where she studies how the migration of news to the Internet is changing journalistic ethics and practices. Her writing has appeared in *Newsday* and *Newsweek*. p. 149

JEAN PARKER PHIFER is an architect who specializes in planning, restoration, and sustainable design projects for cultural institutions. She has designed or restored numerous distinguished buildings, monuments, public spaces and landscapes, primarily in New York State. She is an adjunct associate professor of environmental design at New York University and a Fellow of the American Institute of Architects. She served as architect member and president of the Art Commission of the City of New York, now the Public Design Commission, from 1998 to 2003. She is the author of *Public Art New York*. pp. 242, 263

Before moving to San Francisco, LISA B. PODOS was the director of public programs at the Bard Graduate Center for Studies in the Decorative Arts, Design and Culture. p. 244

SAM POSEY is a race-car driver, an artist, and a designer. He has competed in the Indianapolis 500, the United States Grand Prix, and the 24 Hours of Le Mans, where he set the lap record with a Ferrari that had a top speed of 248 m.p.h. p. 260

GERALD POSNER is an investigative reporter and the author of seven books on subjects ranging from major political assassinations to Nazi war criminals to Triads and the heroin trade. He has written for *The New York Times*, *The New Yorker*, *Vanity Fair*, *Newsweek*, and the *London Telegraph*. p. 78

FRANK PUGLIESE is a playwright, screenwriter, and director. His plays include *The King of Connecticut*, *The Summer Winds*, *Hope Is the Thing with Feathers*, and *Aven'U Boys*, which won an Obie Award. As one of the Naked Angels' first artistic directors, Frank helped develop the Issue Project, Tuesdays @9, and Angels in Progress. Frank is a member of Naked Angels and Drama Department, and is the co-founder of both the Writer's Group and the Screenwriter's Collective. He is also a consultant for the Cherry Lane/Alternative Mentor program for young playwrights. He teaches screenwriting and playwriting at Columbia University. p. 153

ANNA QUINDLEN is an author, journalist, and opinions columnist whose *New York Times* column, "Public and Private," won the Pulitzer Prize for Commentary in 1992. She has written five best-selling novels, including *Blessings*, *Black and Blue*, *One True Thing*, and *Object Lessons*, three of which have been made into movies. p. 21

MICHAEL RATCLIFFE is a former literary editor and chief book critic of *The Times* in London, and a former theater critic and literary editor of *The Observer*. He has written on opera in Britain, on European travel for *The New York Times*, and led specialist cultural tours to Prague, Vienna, Provence, and Berlin. pp. 177, 240

JEAN RATHER is a painter. p. 216

PETER REED is the senior deputy director for curatorial affairs at the

collections of neurological case histories, including *The Man Who Mistook His Wife for a Hat*, *Musicophilia*, and *The Mind's Eye*. *Awakenings*, his book about a group of patients who survived the great encephalitis lethargica epidemic of the early twentieth century, inspired the Academy Award–nominated feature film starring Robert De Niro and Robin Williams. He is a frequent contributor to *The New Yorker* and the *New York Review of Books*, and a Fellow of the American Academy of Arts and Letters and the American Academy of Arts and Sciences. p. 313

The late ARTHUR SAINER was a playwright, teacher, and critic. His plays were honored with awards from the Ford and Rockefeller Foundations, and the National Foundation for Jewish Culture. His books include *Zero Dances*, a biography of Zero Mostel, and *The New Radical Theatre Notebook*. p. 312

BARNET SCHECTER is a historian and the author of *George Washington's America*, *The Devil's Own Work*, and *The Battle for New York*. He was an advisor for the New-York Historical Society's exhibit *Lincoln and New York*, and a contributor to the companion volume. A contributing editor of the three-volume *Encyclopedia of the American Revolution* and *Landmarks of the American Revolution*, he is also a contributor to the *Encyclopedia of New York City*. He is a Fellow of the New York Academy of History. p. 280

MARTHA SCHULMAN, a native New Yorker, is a writer and teacher whose short stories have appeared in *Gulfstream* and *The Seattle Review*. She is a Writing Associate and Writing Fellow at the Cooper Union Center for Writing. pp. 57, 113, 289

MICHAEL SCHWARTING is an architect, urban designer, and professor. He is a professor of architecture, and director of the graduate program in Urban and Regional Design at New York Institute of Technology, where he has also served as chair at the Central Islip Campus. He has taught at Columbia University, the Cooper Union, University of Pennsylvania, Yale University, and Cornell University. He received a Rome Prize Fellowship from the American Academy in Rome, for which he is a Trustee Emeritus. p. 40

FREDERIC SCHWARTZ is an award-winning architect and planner with particular expertise in affordable, sustainable housing. He was recently selected by the citizens of New Orleans and the New Orleans City Planning Commission to replan one-third of the city for forty percent of its post-Katrina population. As winner of an international competition, he designed the Staten Island Ferry Terminal in Manhattan. He is a Fellow of the American Academy in Rome, and was selected by the Architecture League of New York for both the Young Architect's Award and the Emerging Voice in Architecture Award. He has taught at Princeton, Columbia, Harvard,

Yale, and University of Pennsylvania, and has lectured extensively throughout the world. pp. 14, 25, 27, 44, 65, 95, 126, 174, 188, 189, 211, 253, 307, 308

For seventy years, PETE SEEGER has been singing and leading songs at schools, camps, colleges, unions, and peace rallies. pp. 31, 115, 329

RENÉE SHAFRANSKY is a psychotherapist, writer, and award-winning independent film producer. She has written screenplays for Columbia, Tri-Star, Universal, and Disney studios, as well as teleplays for HBO and PBS. A former freelance journalist and film critic for the *Village Voice*, her articles have appeared in *Condé Nast Traveler*, *Harper's Bazaar*, and *American Film* magazine, as well as other publications. She has a therapy practice in New York City and Sag Harbor, NY. p. 300

SAMUEL SHEM is a psychiatrist and the author of *House of God* and *Mount Misery*, as well as the play *Bill W. and Dr. Bob*. He is a professor of psychiatry at Harvard Medical School. p. 149

ALIX KATES SHULMAN is a writer of fiction, memoirs, and essays. Her books include *Memoirs of an Ex-Prom Queen* and *Drinking the Rain*. She has taught writing and literature at New York University, the New School, and Yale University. She was a visiting artist at the American Academy in Rome, and is a Fellow of the Rockefeller Foundation Center in Bellagio, Italy, and the National Endowment for the Arts. She is listed in *Feminists Who Changed America, 1963–1975*. p. 56

JOAN SILBER is the author of the novels *The Size of the World*, *Household Words*, *In the City*, and *Lucky Us*, and of the short-story collection, *In My Other Life*. Her fiction has appeared in *The New Yorker*, *Ploughshares*, and the *Voice Literary Supplement*. She is the recipient of a National Endowment for the Arts Fellowship, a Guggenheim Fellowship, and a PEN Hemingway Foundation Award. pp. 72, 95

AMY SILLMAN is a painter. She has had numerous shows, and her paintings are in the permanent collections of the Museum of Modern Art, the Art Institute of Chicago, and the Whitney Museum of American Art, among others. She has received fellowships from the Guggenheim Foundation, Tiffany Foundation, and National Endowment for the Arts. p. 234

NATHAN SILVER is an architect, critic, educator, and the author of books on architecture and design. He is the recipient of the Brunner Prize scholarship and a Guggenheim Foundation Fellowship. His book, *Lost New York*, was nominated for the National Book Award. He was the architecture critic of the *New Statesman* for eight years. p. 136

STEPHANIE SILVERMAN is an architect and graphic designer. p. 114

DEBORAH SKELLY has held executive positions at Paramount and Sony Studios and is a former motion picture agent in the New York office of the William Morris Agency. p. 210

REBECCA SMITH is an artist. She has had numerous shows worldwide. p. 307

RICHARD SNOW is the author of several books, including two historical novels and a volume of poetry. He has also consulted for historical motion pictures, among them *Glory*, and documentaries, including the Burns brothers' *The Civil War* and Ken Burns's World War II documentary. He wrote the screenplay for Ric Burns's PBS *American Experience* feature on Coney Island. He was the editor in chief of *American Heritage* magazine for many years. pp. 169, 187

ANDY SPADE co-founded the designer brand Kate Spade New York with his wife, Kate Spade. He then launched Jack Spade, a line of accessories for men, which was nominated for the Perry Ellis Award for New Accessories Talent by the Council of Fashion Designers of America. In 2008, he cofounded, with Anthony Sperduti, Partners & Spade, a small store in Noho that serves as a showcase for art, objects, and unusual projects. p. 65

KATE SPADE is co-founder and namesake of the designer brand Kate Spade New York. She has won numerous awards throughout her career, including two from the Council of Fashion Designers of America. She is the author of three books: *Manners*, *Occasions*, and *Style*. p. 224

ELISSA STEIN is a graphic designer, illustrator, and writer of offbeat and often quirky books. In addition to writing, she runs her own graphic design business. Her books include *Flow: The Cultural Story of Menstruation*, *Don't Just Stand There*, *Awfully Wedded*, and *City Walks with Kids: New York*. p. 81

Actor ERIC STOLTZ has appeared in a number of films, including *Pulp Fiction*, *Kicking and Screaming*, *The Waterdance*, and *Mask*, for which he was nominated for a Gold-en Globe Award for Best Supporting Actor. He has also had a successful theater career, receiving a nomination for a Tony Award for his performance in the Broadway revival of Thornton Wilder's *Our Town*. pp. 13, 52, 72, 118, 126, 158, 210

GEORGE C. STONEY's career spans more than seventy years as a filmmaker, educator, and social activist. And at the age of ninety-four, he continues to make films of social relevance. He is Emeritus Professor in the Tisch School of the Art's undergraduate film division at the Kanbar Institute of Film & Television. p. 84

SARAH STONICH is the author of a memoir, *Shelter*, and two novels, *The Ice Chorus* and *These Granite Islands*, which was short-listed for France's prestigious Grand Prix de lectrices d'Elle. She has been awarded a number of grants, including a Minnesota State Arts Board Fellowship. p. 222

MARK STRAND is the author of numerous collections of poetry, including *Man and Camel*, *The Continuous Life*, and *Blizzard of One*, which won the Pulitzer Prize. His many honors include the Gold Medal for Poetry from the American Academy of Arts and Letters, and a Rockefeller Foundation award, as well as fellowships from the Academy of American Poets and the MacArthur Foundation. He has served as Poet Laureate of the United States and is a former chancellor of the Academy of American Poets. pp. 70, 173

ALEXANDRA STYRON is the author of the novel *All the Finest Girls* and of the memoir *Reading My Father*. She has written for, among other publications, *The New York Times*, *The New Yorker*, *Real Simple*, and *Interview*. p. 141

CHARLES SUISMAN launched *Manhattan User's Guide* in 1992, creating the first city newsletter. He has written several guidebooks to New York, including *The New York Times Guide to Hotels in New York City*, and co-wrote *Manhattan User's Guide* and *The New York Holiday Guide*. pp. 133, 159

LIONEL TIGER is the Darwin Professor of Anthropology at Rutgers University and co–research director of the Harry Frank Guggenheim Foundation. He is a consultant to the U.S. Department of Defense on the future of biotechnology. Among his books are *Men in Groups*, *The Pursuit of Pleasure*, and *The Decline of Males*. He is a regular contributor to *Psychology Today* and *The New York Times*. p. 132

KAREN MOODY TOMPKINS is an artist whose work has been included in numerous exhibitions, and can be found in museum and corporate collections. pp. 268, 294

THORIN TRITTER is a research fellow in the School of Advanced Study at the University of London, working in New York on a project about the history of book publishing in North America. Previously, he was the program coordinator at the Gilder Lehrman Institute of American History and was a lecturer in the History Department and Program in American Studies at Princeton University. In addition to his academic work, he has worked as a tour guide for Big Onion Walking Tours for many years. pp. 39, 279, 299

SUSAN TUNICK is an artist working in ceramic, and has written extensively about architectural ceramics. She is the president of the Friends of Terra Cotta, a national preservation organization devoted to protecting historic and architec-tural ceramics. pp. 69, 157

KATHLEEN DEMARCO VAN CLEVE is a novelist, screenwriter, film producer, and teacher. She co-wrote, with John Leguizamo, the screenplay for *Fugly*, and produced *Joe the King*, *Piñero*, and *Undefeated*.

Her other novels are *Cranberry Queen*, *The Difference Between You and Me*, and *Drizzle*. She has been a consultant for NYU's Tisch School of the Arts M.F.A. dramatic writing program, as well as for Tisch's undergraduate dramatic writing candidates. She is a senior lecturer in Cinema Studies at the University of Pennsylvania. pp. 16, 37, 38, 52, 68, 294

JANE TUCKER VASILIOU has held various positions at Wall Street firms, including five years as vice president of Institutional Corporate Bonds at Paine Webber Jackson and Curtis. Currently she is with Vasiliou & Co., Inc., an investment management firm. She is on the board of trustees of the Graduate Center Foundation, City University of New York. p. 278

ANITA VELEZ-MITCHELL is a poet, short-story writer, essayist, actress, and dancer. She has received four Ibero-American Writers Awards. p. 250

THOMAS VON ESSEN was appointed the thirtieth FDNY Commissioner of the City of New York in 1996, and served in that position until 2001, nearly four months after the September 11, 2001, attacks. In 2002 he was made an Honorary Commander of the Order of the British Empire. p. 293

BASIL WALTER is the founding partner of Basil Walter Architects (BWA), an international architecture and design firm with offices in New York City and Beijing, China. Recent projects include the preservation and reinvention of the former IRT Powerhouse and the re-design of the Monkey Bar restaurant, both in New York. He is the architecture and design advisor for *Vanity Fair*. p. 182

GERALD WEALES is an Emeritus Professor of English at the University of Pennsylvania. A former drama critic for *The Reporter* and *Commonweal*, he is the author of many books on theater and film, as well as a novel and several children's books. p. 306

The late GEORGE WEISSMAN was a former president of Philip Morris Companies, board chairman of the Lincoln Center for the Performing Arts, founding board member of Jazz at Lincoln Center, a trustee of the Whitney Museum, and a director of the New York Chamber of Commerce and Industry. Baruch College's Weissman School of Arts and Sciences is named after him and his wife. p. 274

MARJORIE WELISH is a poet, artist, and art critic. She is the author of *Signifying Art: Essays on Art after 1960* and *The Annotated "Here" and Selected Poems*, which was a finalist for the Lenore Marshall Prize from the Academy of American Poets. Her writing on art has appeared in *Art in America*, *Art International*, *ARTNews*, *Bomb*, and *Salmagundi*. She has received grants and fellowships from the Gottlieb Foundation, the Djerassi Foundation, the International Studio

Program, and the Mac-Dowell Colony. She teaches art and literary criticism and art history at Pratt Institute. p. 73

FRED WESSEL is an artist and Professor Emeritus at the Hartford Art School, University of Hartford. He co-directs the program Workshops in Italy, bringing small groups of artists and art-lovers to Tuscany and Umbria to paint and study the Italian Renaissance. His work is included in many private and public collections including the Museum of Modern Art, the Brooklyn Museum, the Philadelphia Museum of Art, and the Library of Congress. p. 239

The late RACHEL WETZSTEON is the author of three collections of poems, including *Sakura Park*, *Home and Away*, and *The Other Stars*, which was selected by John Hollander for the 1993 National Poetry Series. She received an Ingram Merrill grant and the Witter Bynner Prize for Poetry from the American Academy of Arts and Letters. She taught at William Paterson University and the Unterberg Poetry Center of the 92nd Street Y. She served as poetry editor for the *New Republic*. p. 305

GORDON J. WHITING is a managing director of Angelo, Gordon & Co. He founded and leads the AG Net Lease Realty Group. Prior to joining Angelo, he was an executive director and deputy director of acquisitions with W. P. Carey & Co. p. 147

KASSY WILSON is the exhibitions coordinator at the Museum of The City of New York. p. 264

ELIZABETH WINTHROP is the author of more than fifty works of fiction for all ages. Her children's books include *The Castle in the Attic*, *Counting on Grace*, and *Dumpy La Rue*. She has also written novels for adults, including *In My Mother's House* and *Island Justice*, as well as short stories and poetry. p. 254

SUSAN WYLAND, a magazine consultant, is the former editor of *Martha Stewart Living* magazine, the former vice president and editorial director of Disney's Family.com, and the founding editor of *Real Simple* magazine. p. 147

CYNTHIA ZARIN is a poet. She is the author of four books of poetry and several books for children. She has taught at Yale University and is the recipient of National Endowment of the Arts and Guggenheim fellowships. p. 300

JAMES ZUG is an award-winning historian, journalist, and the author of six books. A former book-review columnist for *Outside*, he has reviewed books for the *Daily Beast*, *New York Times Book Review*, and *Philadelphia Inquirer*. p. 78

Robert Kahn, creator and editor of the City Secrets series, is founding principal of Robert Kahn Architect, based in New York City. A recipient of the Rome Prize in Architecture from the American Academy in Rome, he has received numerous awards from the New York chapter of the American Institute of Architects. His work has been featured in *The New York Times Magazine*, *The New York Times*, and *Architectural Digest*, among other publications. He has taught design at Ohio State University, Columbia University, and Yale University, where he held a Davenport Chair Professorship.

A portion of the proceeds of the sale of this book will be donated to the Municipal Art Society of New York and The New York Times Neediest Cases Fund.

The Municipal Art Society of New York is a private not-for-profit membership organization whose mission is to promote a more livable city. Since 1893, the society has worked to enrich the culture, neighborhoods, and physical design of New York City. The Municipal Arts Society advocates for excellence in urban planning, contemporary architecture, historic preservation, and public art. (www.mas.org)

The New York Times Neediest Cases Fund was founded in 1912 by Adolph S. Ochs, then publisher of *The New York Times*. Each year, the Foundation administers a fundraising campaign during the holiday season, with daily stories describing the hardships of many of the city's neediest children, disabled, and elderly. The campaign draws contributions from thousands of readers, totaling about $6 million each year. Assistance by the fund is rendered through seven large multi-service agencies that serve New Yorkers of all denominations in the metropolitan area. Over the years the Fund has raised $250 million. (www.nytco.com)

A

B

C

D

E

F

G

H

I

J

K

L

M

N

O

R

S

T

U

V

W

Y

Z

I am deeply grateful to all the contributors who have so generously and eloquently shared their insights, expertise, and love of New York. It has been a privilege and an honor to receive each one of your essays.

NOTES

NOTES

NOTES

NOTES

NOTES

NOTES

NOTES

PRAISE FOR CITY SECRETS

CITY SECRETS ROME

"After using *City Secrets Rome*, you'll never want to go back to the standard guidebook." —*GQ*

CITY SECRETS LONDON

"Niles and Frasier Crane would love this book... crammed with tips... Full marks for letting words do the work."
—*The Observer* (London)

"The next time I go to London, this book goes with me."
—*San Francisco Chronicle*

CITY SECRETS FLORENCE, VENICE & THE TOWNS OF ITALY

"Architect Robert Kahn's *City Secrets Florence, Venice & the Towns of Italy* is full of interesting finds, even for those who know Italy well." —*Town & Country*

"They are the hot guide... Wonderful keepsakes."
—*Savvy Traveler*, Public Radio International

CITY SECRETS MOVIES

"Surprising and revealing, *City Secrets Movies* is the instant response to the lament 'There's nothing to watch.'"
—*Town & Country*

CITY SECRETS BOOKS

"So much concise and persuasive passion by such smart and interesting people about so many intriguing and unfamiliar works! My next several years are hereby, um, booked." —Kurt Andersen, NPR radio host